75

Sonic Time Machines

The book series RECURSIONS: THEORIES OF MEDIA, MATERIALITY, AND CULTURAL TECHNIQUES provides a platform for cuttingedge research in the field of media culture studies with a particular focus on the cultural impact of media technology and the materialities of communication. The series aims to be an internationally significant and exciting opening into emerging ideas in media theory ranging from media materialism and hardware-oriented studies to ecology, the post-human, the study of cultural techniques, and recent contributions to media archaeology. The series revolves around key themes:
– The material underpinning of media theory
– New advances in media archaeology and media philosophy
– Studies in cultural techniques

These themes resonate with some of the most interesting debates in international media studies, where non-representational thought, the technicity of knowledge formations and new materialities expressed through biological and technological developments are changing the vocabularies of cultural theory. The series is also interested in the mediatic conditions of such theoretical ideas and developing them as media theory.

Editorial Board
– Jussi Parikka (University of Southampton)
– Anna Tuschling (Ruhr-Universitat Bochum)
– Geoffrey Winthrop-Young (University of British Columbia)

Sonic Time Machines

Explicit Sound, Sirenic Voices, and Implicit Sonicity

Wolfgang Ernst

Amsterdam University Press

For the book cover, the author articulated SONIC TIME MACHINES for electric recording, and from that sound file, a wave form oscillogram and a spectrogram have been produced which serve as a background diagram for the typographical title, to suggest the passages inbetween 'analog' and 'digital' sonicity in a not just metaphorical, but rather self-expressive way.

Cover design: Suzan Beijer
Lay-out: Crius Group, Hulshout
Printed and bound by CPI Group (UK) Ltd, Croydon, CR0 4YY

Amsterdam University Press English-language titles are distributed in the US and Canada by the University of Chicago Press.

ISBN	978 90 8964 949 2
e-ISBN	978 90 4852 847 9
NUR	674

Content

Part I Definitions of Sonicity and the Sonic Time Machine

Part II Cultural Soundings and Their Engineering

Part III Techno-Sonicity and Its Beeing-In-Time

Preface

This book investigates the manifold existence of sonic articulations *in* and *as* time: its explicit tempor(e)alities in the techno-cultural context and its implicit dynamics as object of knowledge.[1] Phenomena ranging from resonance to signalling in recording and transmission technologies can be conceptualized in their temporal essence as inherent *sonicity,* even if their engineering (such as coding or compression) do not always directly relate to cultures of listening and the audible. The method of research applied here is media archaeology, which closely investigates artifacts *and* 'listens' to the time-critical and chronopoetic conditions (ancient Greek *arché*) of their operativity. Sonic terminology turns out to be most appropriate for describing such technical temporalities for which historical discourse is no longer sufficient.[2] When sonic communication is not reduced to acoustics in the narrow sense, but understood as signal events (be it continuous 'analog' wave forms, be it discrete 'digital' impulses), even vibrational events in optical physics can be identified in their processual sonicity. Differentiating between the acoustic, the sonic, and the musical, the aim of this investigation is to apply such notions for a better understanding of the deep epistemological dimensions of media temporalities.

The following arguments result from an ongoing research focus on the affinity and privileged alliance between technological media and musical sound, based on the assumption that their common denominator is temporal processuality.[3] Such investigations on sonic media tempor(e)alities and sonicity in its physical, cultural, and technological sense have been inspired by the unique academic umbrella of otherwise separated disciplines, the Institute of Musicology and Media Studies at Humboldt University, Berlin. I am grateful to my colleagues Peter Wicke and his assistant Jens-Gerrit Papenburg for the initial impulse to explore *Das Sonische* and ongoing discussions on the subject.[4] Special thanks go to Jussi Parikka for many reasons; it was he who originally suggested composing this monograph in English. Further gratitude goes to Jan-Claas van Treeck for a critical reading of my manuscript, to an anonymous reviewer for concise suggestions, and to Liam Cole Young for helping me to polish my English. All stylistic and argumentative idiosyncrasies, of course, remain my responsibility.

Printed texts necessarily exclude sound matter – even if, in a deeper sense, there is implicit sonicity in diagrams and graphs that are derived from sound sources. Media-archaeological purism in this book resists the temptation to use substitute imagery. The question to what degree a sonagram (spectrum analysis) or sonogram (ultrasound-based visualization) keeps an indexical relation to the measured event would lead to a debate worthy of a new book in itself.[5]

Foreword: Wolfgang Ernst's Media-archaeological soundings

Liam Cole Young[1]

In Sean Michaels's 2014 novel *Us Conductors,* a fictionalized Lev Sergeyevich Termen describes his most famous invention:

> My theremin is a musical instrument, an instrument of the air. Its two antennas rise up from a closed wooden box. The pitch antenna is tall and black, noble. The closer your right hand gets, the higher the theremin's tone. The second antenna controls volume. It is bent, looped, gold and horizontal. The closer you bring your left hand, the softer the instrument's song. The farther away, the louder it becomes. But always you are standing with your hands in the air, like a conductor. That is the secret of the theremin, after all: your body is a conductor.[2]

Us Conductors explores a time when sound and music were less rigidly understood than they are today. Musicians of the early twentieth century, both serious and casual, imagined devices like the theremin – which generates a signal audible to human ears by integrating two electric oscillator frequencies – as the future of their craft. We catch a glimpse of a possible-future not achieved, in which the new, strange sounds of the electric *avant garde* would fundamentally transform the Western acoustic canon.

> The sound of the theremin is simply pure electric current. It is the hymn of lightning as it hides in its cloud. The song never strains or falters; it persists, stays, keeps, lasts, lingers. It will never abandon you.
> In that regard, it is better than any of us.[3]

Termen plays only a small part in Wolfgang Ernst's *Sonic Time Machines,* but the Soviet inventor and German media theorist are very much in-tune. They share an experimental approach to sound and expansive understanding of its relationship to human physiology and culture. Michaels' fictitious Termen believes that implicit in the temporal oscillations of electric current is the potential for a peculiar kind of poetry. He understands how sonic media like his theremin disrupt conventional understandings of music, sound, noise, and time. Such are the stakes for Ernst, and in *Sonic Time Machines* he channels some of Termen's experimental zeal. Ernst forges new conceptual and methodological orientations for analyzing sonic articulations not as conventional 'sound' or 'music', but rather in terms of *sonicity*. His media-archaeological inquiry into this concept excavates hidden epistemological and temporal aspects of chrono-poetic sonic media like the oscilloscope, monochord, gramophone, even the Sirens of Homer's *Odyssey*. He proposes the neologism 'sonicity' to account for articulations made by such media, which, though they elude human perception, are constitutive of what Marshall McLuhan and Edmund Carpenter understood as the 'acoustic space' of modernity.[4] The book is a challenging and provocative attempt to expand the horizon of media research beyond socio-cultural and historical interpretive paradigms that have traditionally dominated the field. To help contextualize Ernst's contribution, the following remarks draw on both *Sonic Time Machines* and the 2013 edited volume *Digital Memory and the Archive* (Ernst's first major work in English).[5] I outline three pillars of the approach: its media-archaeological method, emphasis on 'time-criticality', and commitment to modular, non-narrative modes of relaying information.

Media Archaeology
Ernst's at times controversial intellectual project has taken shape in recent years under the rubric of media archaeology.[6] Though trained in History and Classics, he turned toward media after becoming convinced that the theoretical, methodological, and narrative frameworks of these disciplines (and the traditional humanities generally) were not capable of offering a comprehensive picture of historical change and dynamism. To address such limitations, Ernst has drawn on the work of media theorist Friedrich Kittler in developing a radically materialist approach to studying history, memory, and culture through a series of books, a prolific lecture circuit, and initiatives such as the Berlin Media-archaeological *Fundus* (a laboratory at Humboldt University devoted to the study and operationalization of 'dead' media). *Digital Memory and the Archive* compiles essays written over the last fifteen years in a broad overview of this research program. *Sonic Time Machines* is a logical follow-up that develops theoretical ideas from the previous work through a series of media-archaeological case studies specific to the relation between sound and time. The book thus expands media archaeology's mandate and sharpens its focus (previously, discussions tended to be heavy on theory and light on empirical analysis). Whereas the essays of the earlier book elaborated a time-critical research agenda by opening up operative media and rethinking their archival dimensions, in *Sonic Time Machines,* Ernst develops a more expansive exploration of time-criticality

by casting it into the sonic realm. What is revealed is nothing less than an updated 'acoustic space' (or, better: sonic space) in which the beings of the world (human and non-human) dwell together in sound-as-time. Together, *Digital Memory and the Archive* and *Sonic Time Machines* position 'Ernstian' media archaeology as what he calls a 'transatlantic bridge' between developments in continental and German media analyses and those in North America such as software and platform studies,[7] logistical media studies,[8] media forensics,[9] and sound studies.[10]

Following Foucault's emphasis on historical and epistemological ruptures and McLuhan's non-content based understanding of media, Ernst's media archaeology is an 'epistemological reverse-engineering'[11] that 'makes us aware of discontinuities in media cultures as opposed to the reconciling narratives of cultural history.'[12] Media archaeology displaces the human subject from its traditional role as the centre of historical and technological change, seeking instead to unearth the 'nondiscursive infrastructure and (hidden) programs of media'[13] that structure what and how humans think and do. According to Ernst (and here he follows Kittler closely) the contours of these infrastructures are shaped by the media-technical conditions of possibility that obtain in any given historical moment; these are, namely, the means by which data are processed, stored, and transmitted. While thinkers like McLuhan and Virilio demonstrated the extent to which medial conditions structure perception, Ernst goes a step further in arguing that they also delineate cultural data such as history and memory – because media measure, process, and thus structure time, they are the true archivists of pasts both human and non-human. The archive itself becomes a historical subject. In his introduction to *Digital Memory and the Archive,* Jussi Parikka summarizes this point:

> even before a historian or a media archaeologist steps in to tell stories about history, past media cultures, and lost ideas, there is a prior level on which the past has been recorded. The documents of the past are such concrete instances of pasts present but even more so of the way in which technical media records time and acts as a time machine between current times and the past.[14]

Sonic Time Machines conceives of technical devices of observation, measuring, and recording like the gramophone and oscilloscope (among others) as such archivists of 'sonic knowledge and nonhuman agencies of listening' (p. 45). While Sound Studies would emphasize the cultural, historical, and institutional vectors that shape sound media, Ernst takes a more oblique, 'sonicistic' angle – hence his opening gambit: *this is not sound studies* (a cheeky, Kittleresque provocation that will no doubt elicit a strong response, for there are many planes on which sonicity and sound studies coexist). The knowledge he is after is tied to physical reality rather than language or text. Only by going 'under the hood' of sonic media forms and their attendant cultural techniques can such knowledge be accessed. We develop ears to hear the sonic past and understand its epistemological contours by absorbing the vibrations and resonances of media in operation.

This epistemological quest takes us through familiar territory – De Martinville's *phonautographe,* Edison's and Berliner's phonographs and gramophones, Parry and Lord's oral poetry – but also takes surprising turns toward discussions of, for example, John Logie Baird's phonovision technology and Bill Viola's video art. Readers will take particular delight in an extended description (pp. 49-57) of a field experiment that attempted to recreate the sonic environment where Homer's Sirens apparently made their famous call (as described in *The Odyssey*). The research team from Humboldt University, Berlin actually travelled to the Li Galli islands (off Italy's Amalfi coast) with their microphones and loudspeakers to conduct experiments with sound. The goal was to test the extent to which knowledge about the location of this event handed down in the occidental tradition was not solely (or even primarily) a product of cultural memory and storytelling as conventionally understood (whether as oral or written tradition). Rather, they tested the hypothesis that the essential microtemporal vibrations of this acoustic environment determined it as the only place in which the sonic event of the Siren call could possibly occur. The specificity of its description in Homer's *Odyssey* would not therefore be a product of slippery cultural memory or geographical knowledge, but precise mathematics. Such passages demonstrate the media-archaeological commitment to respecting material conditions of sonic possibility absolutely.

Time-critical
Media archaeology generally, and *Sonic Time Machines* specifically, outline a privileged relation between media and time (in a tantalizingly short passage on p. 59, Ernst suggests that Aristotle discovered the category of 'medium' – the 'in-between', *to metaxy* – through research on perception involving acoustic delay). Ernst is interested in the way categories and practices of memory and history emerge as a corollary of the ways that media technologies process and store time. Foregrounding this relation allows him to argue persuasively that media studies must be 'time-critical'. Technical media (typified by Kittler's famous Gramophone-Film-Typewriter

trifecta[15]) inaugurate time-critical media studies because they record the 'flow' of human and machine time and enable time-axis manipulation: gramophone technology enables the delayed playback of recorded voices now deceased, cinematography allows for manipulation of the way images unfold in time (by reversibility, speed up and slow down, etc.).[16] Digital media offers another rupture: the temporal flow of techno-cultural data streams comes to be comprised of discrete, operative units and processes that escape human perception. 'It is only with the digital computer that the symbolic regime *dia*lectically returns, this time in a genuinely dynamic mode (which differentiates implementation of software from the traditional Gutenberg galaxy): algorithmic time and operative diagrams.'[17] Digital times are processual and discrete, rather than static and continuous; they are operational rather than narrative, re-inscribing the symbolic as binary 1s and 0s in place of alphanumeric letters.

Sonic media are privileged because of what Ernst sees as an 'entanglement' between the time and frequency domains. 'Technical sound is not just acoustic pressure on the ear or deriving aesthetic pleasure from musical sensation but addresses the human sense of temporality in unforeseen ways' (p. 87). *Sonic Time Machines* investigates these entanglements through the wide-ranging concept of sonicity. 'The epistemic insight of sonicity is found across the whole spectrum between mythology and media archaeology, between the human voice and electronically produced frequencies' (p. 52). The concept is most alive, however, when cast in the *milieux* of electronic and digital media. 'Electronically-generated high frequency oscillations' – radio, electromagnetic, etc. – come under the media-archaeological gaze to be understood in their operative temporality. Ultrasound, for instance, is a process by which imperceptible sonic articulations are rendered accessible to human senses as visual data by a process of transduction and pixelization. Radar's visualization of sonic data is a similar mode of processing. While technical media like the gramophone store sound for replay, electronic media store implicit sonicity as information. 'Any electronic instrument electromagnetically transubstantiates [...] the essence of sound from mechanical vibration into an essentially different, but physically analog form of existence – from explicit sound to implicit sonicity' (p. 75). Physical inscriptions enter the symbolic regime of computation and become implicit sonic data that can be re-called and re-formed rather than re-played (as with a record groove). The digital moment of transmission is a product of *processing* rather than storage-playback.[18] The real-time processuality of digital recall mirrors the essential temporality of sonic articulations from the physical realm (which are the vibrations of microtemporal waves in and as space). Sonicity captures this relation: when digitized, temporal articulations of the real become implicit information of the symbolic, available for digital re-call via computational algorhythmics (a term Ernst adopts from Shintaro Miyazaki[19]). Sonic data become part of the digital archive, a 'dynarchive' (p. 116) that is continuously in flux and in-formation.

Ernst's media archaeology is neither socio-historical, nor bare psycho-acoustic analysis. It is epistemologically tuned to uncover knowledge and techniques embedded and encoded in the media devices that relay sonic articulations. 'Media-archaeological research can never definitively reconstruct what has been said (or sung), but rather explores and defines the conditions of possibility regarding what *could have* been enunciated' (p. 57). The temporal dimension is primary among these conditions. In the moment of performance, the singer of tales (one of whom, Hamdo, we meet in later pages) channels a flow of time utterly foreign to the modern listener. Elsewhere, Ernst writes 'The moment a singer of epics sings into a current recording device, two different regimes clash as human performativity is confronted with technological algorithmical operations.'[20] This is a short-circuiting of time *à la* Walter Benjamin. Operational media, in their very functioning, bring forth the temporal aspects of the epistemological conditions under which they were created. As a result, our own temporalities can be more clearly absorbed and understood (for Ernst, understanding is linked to affect). 'When coupled to technical media interfaces, humans are placed in temporal situations that differ from culturally-specific experiences of previous times' (p. 108). A Pythagorean monochord is not simply an instrument for creating audible frequencies that we understand, culturally, as music. It is the material manifestation of an entire way of knowing particular to the Greeks: music as an expression of the beauty inherent in mathematics – culture and technics, *poiesis* and *technê,* as two sides of a single coin. When we play its strings and are affected by its temporal vibrations, the monochord becomes a sonic time machine into this way of knowing.

Instruments like the monochord channel alternate tempor(e)alities (to use another of Ernst's neologisms), but our ability to understand them as such arises only after the spectrum of sound is expanded to incorporate frequencies that lay beyond the threshold of human perception. 'Sound' and 'music' describe things we can hear; 'sonicity' gives us a concept to grapple with things we cannot. Before such waves are rendered audible (or visible) to humans, they reverberate through, and are in fact constitutive of, physical reality. 'Sonicities' delineate the modern sonic environment, McLuhan's 'acoustic space', which 'does not simply refer to sound and music but designates a specific temporal form that [McLuhan] correlates with electronic media sphere of itself – the sphere of resonances' (p. 108). Acoustic space is actually temporal because sonic waves are finite expressions of time. Because McLuhan's term does not account for articulations that escape human perception, Ernst pushes beyond 'acoustic space' to develop a concept that accounts for how microtemporal vibrations are constitutive of the very space of being itself: sonicity.

Modular Style

Ernst pushes (media) historiography from mythology and semiotics to mathematics and computation – from telling stories to counting units. In *Digital Memory and the Archive,* he reminds us that for centuries telling actually *was* counting, and that the tendency toward narrative is only a relatively recent development in human memory systems.[21] Other historical modes of transmitting cultural information (such as the epic and the chronicle) functioned for thousands of years as non-narrative forms of *telling as counting.* These would enumerate, accumulate, and describe events, offering a 'glimpse of a way of processing cultural experience that does not need stories.'[22] The resonant time of sonicity similarly contrasts historical time. 'The specificity of [...] sonic articulation cannot be captured and subsumed by the logocentrism of traditional narrative historiography. Acoustic space is of a different temporal nature: not linear, but synchronous, simultaneously from every direction at once – *echo land'* (p. 59). The point is not that narrative modes of telling have no value, but that they are no longer adequate for describing the sonicity of electric and digital modernity. Operational infrastructures of computing that now process, store, and transmit data about the past lay bare the limitations of narrative and inaugurate its crisis:

> Media archaeology deals with this crisis in the narrative memory of culture. Digital narrative, on a media-archaeological (not interface) level, is linked to discrete mathematics [...] A computing culture, from a media-archaeological view, deals not with narrative memory but with calculating memory – counting rather than recounting, the archaeological versus the historical mode.[23]

Since time-critical media studies must break with narrative historiography, Ernst experiments with form and content in developing a non-narrative mode of relaying information that is, at times, closer to counting than recounting. This modular, staccato style is difficult. It produces unconventional texts

that unfold more via affirmation and aphorism than analytic argumenta-
tion. The style is at times exhilarating, at others frustrating. Ideas fly at the
reader at a breakneck pace. Certain sentences seem incongruous. Multiple
readings are not simply rewarded but required. Ernst continues a stylistic
lineage that can be traced back to Harold Adams Innis through Marshall
McLuhan and Friedrich Kittler. Ernst is closer to Innis than McLuhan or
Kittler (he does not delight in language to the same extent as McLuhan,
or in provocation as Kittler). What Alexander John Watson wrote of Innis
we might use to describe Ernst: 'We should not be surprised [...] that Innis,
in trying to break through the limitations of the worldview of his time,
was experimenting with the oral presentation and material production of
the ideas he was formulating.'[24] Such experiments are not always perfect.
Staccato can be sublime one moment, grating the next. The style is, however,
both stimulating and generative, a cool medium that demands much of
the reader (not the least of which is reflection on their own preconcep-
tions about the production and circulation of ideas). The form of *Sonic
Time Machines* also channels the peculiar media poetics excavated by its
archaeological method. Ernst writes:

> while it is true that "inside the computers themselves everything becomes
> a number: quantity without [...] sound, or voice", it is only by coupling
> the binary world of the symbolic machine with physical impulses and
> time-discrete clocking that mathematics becomes rhythmically operative
> (biased) and thus implicitly belongs to the chronosphere of the poetic
> (p. 109).

Latent sonicities are articulated in the convergence of digital computation's material elements – mathematics as cultural technique, number
as symbolic system, mechanical components as infrastructure, etc. Ernst
writes of early digital computers that sounded like rhythm machines, of
the machine-to-machine sonicity of the Modem, and the reverberations of
electromagnetic instruments like the theremin. The strange modulations
of *Sonic Time Machines* as a text reflect the temporal poetics of these and
many other examples discussed throughout.

The media-archaeological ideal is that an accurate picture of the world
only arises via the knowledge and poetics disclosed by true, non-human
archivists of present and past: media objects, operations, and sonic articulations. The imperative to uncover (dis-cover) such knowledge is a
continuation of the Heideggerian project of revealing the hidden contours
of modernity.[25]

For Ernst, as it was for Heidegger, the truth of being is time. 'Sonic media address humans at the existential level of affective sensation, being, which is essentially temporal' (p. 107). Media are the infrastructures that comprise the worldliness of the world. The temporal drone of electromagnetic sound is the drone of being itself.

Part I
Definitions of Sonicity and the Sonic Time Machine

1. Introduction: On 'sonicity'

'Sonicity': Arguments for a modest neologism

Inquiries into *sonicity* should not be confused with Sound Studies. Acoustic sound is the section of the bandwidth of waves and vibrations mechanically transmitted through a physical medium that is audible to humans. Acoustic sound compares to the deceptive top of an iceberg visible above water, whereas electronically generated high frequency oscillations are of a different nature.[1] These 'waves', which are familiar from radio transmission, correspond to the part of the electromagnetic spectrum that animals immediately perceive as 'light'. Sound in its generalized sense as temporal enunciation refers to continuous ('analog') and discrete ('digital') vibrational and frequential dynamics of all kinds. These range from the most precise (electro-)physical micro-mo(ve)ment related to the human affect of temporal perception, up to culturally emphatic modulations[2] – similar to the so-called Projection Theatre in Revolutionary Russia of the 1920s, which grounded body movements in the epistemology of soundings: 'The sound is not heard, but formed. Practice: independent Translation of muscular sensation into a body: A O U I E.'[3]

Sonicity is where time and technology meet. Technosonic time-mechanisms and their charming power to seduce the human sense of time deserve a study of their own. If time is neither reduced to an internal state of subjective consciousness nor to an external physical *a priori* but conceived as a complex layering of the imminent, of presence and of past(s)[4], rich forms of temporal articulation can be identified in a chrono-tonal sense.

This study does not refer to time machines in the sense of H.G. Wells's mechanical device for time travelling;[5] sonic tempor(e)alities are everything but metaphoric. They can rather be expressed in terms known from the epistemology of the electromagnetic field.[6]

Even the emphatic concept of cultural time – which in narrative writing is organized in the name of history – is affected by the sonic approach:

> To understand the ways that media inscribe themselves on our bodies, we need a philosophy of history that recognizes the production of a "new already". [...] Before the phonograph, no sound had the option but to be fugitive. A historical rupture in the nature of sound arises that, in turn, rewrites its entire history.[7]

But maybe this irritation is more fundamental: not just a historical rupture, but a rupture of the dominance of historical discourse over the phenomenology of emphatic time as such. The generation of vocal or even musical 'presence' deriving from a source that is cognitively known to be absent, as induced by the phonograph, does not simply ask for a rewriting of media historiography, but requires different ways of writing temporal figurations as such. Such a project calls for the kind of archaeography that has been performed for decades by the oscilloscope's visualization of sonic wave forms.

Sound and music let us experience transient time. It is this processuality that the sonosphere shares with high-electronic media. Just as musical culture tries to save sound itself from ephemeral temporality (favouring invariance), signal recording media for the first time in cultural history mastered the time axis, thus enabling arbitrary manipulation and repeatability. Phonographic recording is not historiography but signal storage.[8] Any such graphic trace of an acoustic event cannot be considered sound. The *implicit* sonicity of an acoustic event depends on a temporalizing medium like the record player to make it *explicit* through time-sequential unfolding, just like cinema needs the projector to restore movement to otherwise discrete chrono-photographical film frames.[9] Recording does not take place in or as historical time, but is a time operation itself. This makes it a privileged form of investigating tempor(e)alities.

Sonicity as a neologism is meant to be kept apart from acoustic *sound* and primarily refers to inaudible events in the vibrational (analog) and rhythmic (digital) fields.[10] *Sonicity* is intended to sound awry so that it is differentiated from sound, a culturally familiar term that is academically somewhat restricted to musicology. Sonicity names oscillatory events and their mathematically reverse equivalent: the frequency domain as an epistemological object.[11]

Musical theory in the occidental tradition continued the Pythagorean epistemology of harmonic calculations. Sound is thus not perceived as the sonic event in itself but becomes a phenomenon of mathematics in the widest sense of the symbolic regime. But actual sound is implemented mathematics *in performance*, integrating space, time, and matter. Early experiments with 'drawn sound' led to a remarkable chain of conclusions that anticipate the concept of sonicity:

Graphical representations of the sound wave could be analysed and represented as a Fourier series of periodic functions (sine waves). Consequently, the sound wave could be re-synthesized back with the same set of sine

waves. [...] As with electrons [...] the number of which defines the quality
of the atom, so do sine waves define the quality of the sound – its timbre.
The conclusion: why not initiate a new science – synthetic acoustics?[12]

With the relatively primitive circuitry of an oscillator-driven series of
flashing LEDs as an operative diagram, one can simulate the swinging
of electrons around an atomic kernel that radiates in pulses. The visual
transition of discrete pulse trains into an impression of continuous waves
is implicitly sonic. This is not just a metaphor but an essential emanation
of electronics itself. The technical impulse diagram reveals the coming-
into-existence of this electro-rhythmic sequentiality. Two elementary
qualities of sonic articulation (electrified rhythm in impulses and continuous waveforms) do not belong to different worlds but can be revealed as
interrelated phenomena. Longitudinal waves make the molecules of air or
water swing in the direction of the propagation, while the periodic waves
themselves can be mathematically counted in symbolical frequencies in
reverse. The interlacing of matter and number in sound takes place on the
most elementary level.

In its non-human embodiment within electronics, a special subclass
of sonicity is *sonics*. This is meant to name sound that does not originate
from physically resonant bodies but from electro-technical and techno-
mathematical processes. These become audible at all only by explicit
sonification. Otherwise, *sonics* exists in electronic latency like songs and
voices recorded on magnetic tape prior to playback. Speech recorded on
magnetic tape is not just 'electrified voices'[13] but a re-definition of the voice
itself. At first glance, a familiar motive known from cultural analysis reappears with the 'humanized' voice. This motive is hidden in thick layers of
the techno-aesthetic apparatus: that most media technologies still circulate
around the human in the anthropocentric mode. In contrast, revolutionary Russian experiments in technological sound intentionally aimed at
de-humanizing the voice.

The term 'sonicity' does not primarily refer to the apparent phenomenological quality of sound, but rather to its essential temporal nature,
which is its subliminal message behind the apparent musical content.[14]
Nicole Oresme's late medieval *Tractatus de configurationibus qualitatum
et motuum* defines the 'sonus' in its physical materiality as a function of
the time axis[15] and thus comes close to the present definition of sonicity as
epistemic articulation. The etymology of *sonus* ranges from the concrete
physical materiality of sound up to its epistemological definition[16] for which
the retro-neologism *sonitas* might be allowed.

Techno-cultural dimensions of sonicity

In a sublime rather than noisy intervention, the concept of sonicity questions the supremacy of the visual in occidental aesthetics and knowledge. The impact of sound and aural operations, especially in their non-musical variants, has long been under theorized. A major feature of the relationship between visibility and audibility is that they have markedly different temporalities. Western cultures have been predominantly visually oriented in their ways of information processing – an effect of the reading, writing, and printing culture that privileges transmission and absorption of information via the optical channel of communication.[17] It was not until recently that an 'auditory turn' was declared in the humanities and aesthetic practice. The past neglect of the acoustic dimension originates in visually-oriented media studies, which as an academic discipline stems either from philology's privileging of the eye as information absorbing channel (i.e. reading), or from film and TV studies. In order to focus on the practices, aesthetics, technologies, and concepts of sound, noise, and silence,[18] it makes sense first to differentiate between *music* as a heavily semanticized cultural art and the *sonic* – which, while culturally conditioned, is also a function of psycho-physiological perception. We must also, then, factor in the materiality of (electro-)acoustics as (techno-)physical event.

In the symbolic order of musical notation, so-called structural listening can take place in the mind through intelligent score reading without the physical presence of an external sound source. As once conceived by Theodor W. Adorno, 'the silent, imaginative reading of music could render actual playing as superfluous as speaking is made by reading of written material.'[19] But it *matters* that sonicity takes place as a physical vibrational event that is distinct from mere symbolization. It is academic commonplace now to claim that the socio-cultures of hearing and the sonospheres of listening have been extended by the impact of technical media in modernity.[20] A true media archaeology of listening is not limited to acoustic phenomena but also takes listening in its hermeneutic and even epistemological sense as *understanding*. Sonicity (understood here in its neologistic sense) differs from a simply physical notion of sound (*Klang*) because of its strict dependence on physical or technical embodiments and algorithmic implementations. In audio recording, the forms of electronics make a difference.

By considering technologically induced delays and manipulations of the sonic time axis, media archaeology furthermore questions the 'sound' of tradition. Questioning the historicity of musical articulation leads to a discussion of affects related to time-invariant presence that result from the technological reproduction of sound – archiving presence and re-presencing the archive.[21] Active media archaeology remembers past sonospheres by technical means. Listening to the archive in such ways not only produces unexpected audio recordings and other revelations of the sonic past but also new forms of articulation (sonification) for recordings themselves. Listening to modernity, conceived as sound from the archive, does not simply expand source material available for research into for cultural history, but leads to a different modelling of cultural time in terms of resonance. The message of the media of modernity is 'acoustic space' (McLuhan). A privileged alliance between sound events and operative media reveals the moment that their common denominator is detected: both come into being only when being in time.

Implicit sonicity: 'Acoustic space' (McLuhan)

Since the emergence of phonetic writing, knowledge has been primarily connected to an act of seeing; 'idea' and the 'visual' stem from the same etymological root *vid*.[22] Ancient Greek *gignóskein* (the creation of an object by the very act of recognition) can be traced back to seeing and the eye. But with the telephone, gramophone, and analog radio a non-visual and post-literate acoustic space took off. Marshall McLuhan defined the immediacy of electricity as the definitive difference from the Gutenberg world of scriptural and printed information:

> Visual man is the most extreme case of abstractionism because he has separated his visual faculty from the other senses [...]. [...] today it is threatened, not by any single factors such as television or radio, but by the electric speed of information movement in general. Electric speed is approximately the speed of light, and this constitutes an information environment that has basically an acoustic structure.[23]

We are therefore, McLuhan declared at the climax of analogue electronic media culture, back in acoustic space. *Acoustic* space is understood here not in its physical sense but as the epistemological existence of sound.[24] When McLuhan made his crucial discovery about the intrinsically acoustic structure of electronic mediascapes, he implicitly co-defined *sonicity*. Whereas physical sound establishes a mechanical, haptic, and tactile coupling between the material source and the human receiver through a vibrating medium (be it hard matter, water, or air), a sonic articulation, once transduced by an electronic device into variations of electric voltage, has an intermediary spatio-temporal *in between* existence. Within an electronic system, sound exists implicitly. While a media-archaeological device of early electro-acoustic instruments, the Mellotron, reproduced sound by single tone 'samples' recorded on magnetic tape stripes attached to each key, primordial 'electro-acoustic spaces aren't simply a genre of music [...] – they are interfaces with the machine [...].'[25] Human perception is not affectively absorbed by musically semantic content anymore, but by the medium's very technological message – by assimilation to the medium itself. 'Anyone who wishes to receive a message embedded in a medium must first have internalized the medium [...].'[26]

McLuhan's notion of an implicit acoustic structure media-archaeologically refers to an epistemological ground, not to the acoustic figures ears can hear. This groundbreaking took place with the collapse of Euclidic space into Riemann geometries and culminates around 1900 with the quantum physical wave / particle dualism.[27] This has led to the 'superstring' theory of contemporary physics, which borrows from operative sounding to name vibrational dynamics as universal ground – the Pythagorean monochord.[28] The equation of world and number in terms of musical harmonies turns musical instruments into analog computers of a kind that model laws of temporal order in the physical world. This insight comes into being either by historical transmission of cultural knowledge or by original knowledge generated from within the sonic techniques themselves. This resonates with the epistemology of music in Indian culture. Additive Western music builds up synthetically, with its base being silence, whereas subtractive Indian music actually begins from sound.

> All the notes and possible notes to be played are present before the main musicians even start playing, stated by the presence and counting of the tambura. A tambura is a drone instrument [...] that, due to the particular construction of its bridge, amplifies the overtone or harmonic series of the individual notes in each tuned string. It is [...] continually present throughout.[29]

This extends to the concept of non-struck sound like the theoretical fiction of vibrational forces called 'ether'.[30] Sonicity refers to, on the one hand, sonic knowledge that is implicit within instruments of sound analysis and synthesis,[31] and, on the other, graphically or mathematically derived sound.[32]

Once the tuning of such string instruments is extended beyond musical (harmonic) aesthetics to sonic techno/logies (in two senses, as an electronic measuring apparatus and a mathematical modelling of the temporal dynamics of the vibrating string),[33] integer numbers representing well-ordered harmonic relations between tones dissolve into infinitesimal sub-graduations. At that point, musical theory (which since Pythagoras has been pushed to its limits by well-tempered tuning) has to be replaced by the epistemology of sonicity.[34]

The essence of McLuhan's term 'acoustic *space*' is that oscillating *time* functions in the same way that the spatial interval turns out as a negative sound: silence.[35] In an epistemological sense, *sonicity* is not primarily about or limited to the audible, but is a mode of revealing modalities of temporal processuality – just as technology is 'a way of revealing' essential features (*archai*) of handling the world.[36] To some extent, hearing is a memory, but in ways radically different from static storage and the archive. Reverberative sonic memory challenges the symbolic order of the archive. Thereby the philosophy of history itself is provided with a question mark. In *The Presence of the Past* (1988), Rupert Sheldrake proposes a theory of evolution that is not based on historical development any more but on electromagnetic resonance.

Phonovision and the sonic nature of the electronic image

Henri Bergson in *Matière et Mémoire* (1896) formulated an idea of dynamic matter as 'image'; this is meant not in an iconological but a sonicistic sense, as vibrating waves and frequencies.[37] Ironically, it is not acoustic sensation, but human eyes that come closest to a radio detector of sonicity in their ability to perceive non-mechanical, ultra-high frequency electromagnetic waves called 'light' and 'colours'.

Information coming at the speed of light simultaneously from all directions (different from asynchronous communication in online worlds) recalls the structure of the act of *hearing*. Recalling McLuhan, the *message* or effect of electric information is acoustic – even when it is perceived as an electronic image. In fact, the sonic ground of the electronic image is 'hidden' in the media-archaeological and Heideggerian sense of ancient Greek *aletheia*: 'It is acoustic. It resonates. But this is a hidden ground, because superficially people think they're looking at a visual program. And they're not. They're not looking at all – they're absorbed, involved in a resonating experience.'[38] Such immersion is into a *sonic* (rather than *acoustic*) sphere.

A synthaesthetic transfer and an audio-visual metonymy take place when the time-critical video image is discovered in its 'vibrational acoustic character.'[39] This is not a theoretical, epistemological or philosophical supposition but a media-archaeological truth: 'Technologically, video has evolved out of sound (the electromagnetic). Its close association with cinema is misleading since film and its grandparent, the photographic process, are members of a completely different branch of the genealogical tree (the mechanical / chemical).[40] The inherent sonicity of the video image is reminiscent of the deep media-archaeological link between the television signal and telephonic voice transmission. The transmission of sonic articulations over distance served as technical *a priori* of television; this implicit techno-structural affinity became manifest in the development of the Picturephone by the Bell Laboratories.[41]

There are technological settings in a laboratory that serve as the apparatus from which knowledge emanates.[42] In reverse, from a media-archaeological point of view, there is knowledge materialized, embedded, and implemented within operative media themselves that deserves to be extracted and derived by explicit academic inquiry and verbalization.[43] This can be illustrated with the so-called Phonic Wheel (*Phonisches Rad*) as an individual element in the otherwise optically oriented early electro-mechanical image transmission Nipkow system.[44] This electromagnetic 'phonetic' wheel inside the apparatus is meant to synchronize the image lines between transmitter and receiver – a kind of *tuning* by *resonance*. The sonic is implicit, with no sound to be heard, as chrono-technical sound knowledge (sonicity). Visible tuning takes place with the stroboscopic disc (attached to the Nipkow disc), which is on the front side ('interface') visible to the user and parallel to the actual television image. The message of this medium process is *timing*.

John Logie Baird's *Phonovision* technology, developed in 1927/28 for his electro-mechanical television system, allowed for the recording of low-resolution images (12.5 frames of 30 lines per second) on gramophone records. Amplified and connected to a loudspeaker, the time-varying electric signals – transformed from light impulses by a photocell – were within the human audible realm and could indeed be transmitted line by line via medium wave radio.[45] That induced the idea of *quasi*-phonographic recording; video recording *avant la lettre* transformed electric images into sonic temporality. In Baird's *Phonovision* recordings, audio is the original vision signal.[46] Different from the cinematographic image, the classical electronic TV image is closer to sound due to its one-line scanning. The auditive is thus *immanent* to the electronic image in a sonicistic sense.

Human perception when confronted with electronic images from cathode ray tubes is affected in its subliminal temporality, a parameter that is otherwise located within the auditory system. In reverse, the electric 'reading' of graphic inscriptions on celluloid and their transformation into electric signals by the photo cell allowed for sound to accompany discrete photographic image series in movies.[47]

The earliest known recording from a television program is the revue *Looking In*, performed by the Paramount Astoria Girls on the BBC Baird television system in April 1933, recorded on aluminium disc by an enthusiastic amateur using the Baird Phonovision system.[48] Processed and restored by digital filtering, the cue to clarity seems to be movement itself. Any photographic reproduction of one of the 30-line television broadcast stills in a book as illustration gives a wrong impression of what was actually perceived. Here, the time-critical argument comes in, since printed records (be they texts or images) miss a crucial element: *passing* time. The human brain builds up a dynamic model of what eyes might actually discretely look at. This process is remarkably close to the cognitive synthesis of musical melody recognition against acoustic perception, as analyzed by Hermann von Helmholtz:

> A single frame of the Paramount Astoria Girls may be crudely recognizable, but when seen as a moving dynamic television image, the girls come to life before our eyes. [...] it has much more to do with what we perceive than what is there in pixels, lines and frames. What we are experiencing is not the detail that the eye sees, but the recognition of movement that the brain sees.[49]

Similar to Jean-Luc Godard's notion of the *son-image,* Bill Viola explicitly identified the sonicity of the electronic image.[50] The video camera, as a transducer into electrical impulses of varying light input, 'bears a closer original relation to the microphone than to the film camera.'[51] Viola comes close to McLuhan's notion of *acoustic space* as describing the chrono-epistemological background of electronic communication. The signal regeneration of television or computer images on a CRT monitor is a form of *implicit* sonification, since the electromagnetic waves emanating from such transduction can easily be detected by an aptly tuned radio receiver.[52] Such a sound turns into (algo)rhythm when it comes to eavesdropping on digital images[53] somewhat akin to the electro-chemical transduction of light in human eyes when communicated in pulse trains to the brain. Sometimes technology *resonates* with human perceptual modalities in a privileged way.

The Berlin Dada artist Raoul Hausmann oscillated between synaesthetic metaphor and technological precision with his construction of a light-to-sound converting *Optophon.*[54] But apart from trivial archaeological metaphors, the epistemic level of sonicity is reached only by uncovering its implicit dynamics. In 1932, Boris Yankovsky from the Moscow Graphic Sound group refrained from optophonic metaphors since he was not simply a sound-imagining artist but also an acoustician. He founded his own Syntonfilm Laboratory in Moscow based on media-operative insights into the genuinely time-critical nature of sound waveforms. These he conceived as temporal transitions contained in the dynamic sound spectrum 'instead of monotonous colouring of stationary sounding fixed geometric figures (wave shapes)'[55] – even if he admitted that the nature of this phenomenon was not yet completely clear to him. Sonicity remains implicit. 'The premises leading to the expansion of these phenomena – life inside the sound spectrum – give us the nature of the musical instruments themselves [...].'[56] Such observations are close to contemporary Physical Modelling. The mathematical approach (Fourier analysis) and 'graphic sound' of a different kind – namely sonagrams as the diagrammatic expression of dynamic development of the sound spectrum in time – uncover the epistemic layer of sonicity in sound itself. According to Jean-Babtiste Fourier's *Analysis of Heat*, any periodic expression can be decomposed into its single sine waves, which – in reverse – can be computationally addressed as frequency, i.e. numbers. Sound is thereby understood as addition of tones. In implicit sonicity, kymatics and mathematics converge: '*Plusiers questions de mécanique présentent des résultats analogues, tels que l'isochronisme des oscillations, la rèsonnance multiple des corps sonores.*'[57] The sonicistic approach is not restricted to audible sound; electronic images are techno-mathematically analysed and digitized for compressed transmission in the same way.

Not for human ears: Ultrasound and radar
On a more fundamental level, a decisive feature of culture is its wilful creation of unnatural sounds. On the one hand, such sounds are bound to traditional arbitrary articulations like speech or singing and are typically generated by the human body and/or musical instruments. Tonal and impulse-like articulations generated by electronics are not simply an escalation of traditional sound, but testify to an epistemic rupture – from sound to the sonic, as Stockhausen insists.[58] These different, electron-based sounds embrace a much greater spectrum than what human ears can acoustically perceive. The very term ultrasound is still anthropocentric – defined by the upper limit of frequencies that provoke an acoustic sensation within *human* hearing. For sound beyond this acoustic threshold to be perceived by humans, it takes deceptive sonic transpositions or signal transductions such as the *imaging* of ultrasound. In such cases, what looks like a visual event in fact turns out to be a function of time-based sounding. Visual information is being unearthed by means of ultrasound. In order to generate such *imaging*, well known in medical diagnosis, the run time of acoustic

waves (echo delays, Doppler effects) is used to create electric signals that (after electronic amplification) can either be transposed down again to hearable sound or (aided by signal processing) be transformed into optical patterns. There is no organic co-existence of the binaural auditive and the visual regime in the perceivable world, but rather an alternating exclusion.[59]

At that point, ultrasound images, as known from clinical monitoring of the human organism, become an allegory of dynamic mediality itself. Ultrasound by definition transcends the realm of sound that can be recognized by the human ear (between 16 Hz and 20 kHz); it is rather part of what Marshall McLuhan named 'acoustic space': electronically mediated communication. Electro-technically-generated ultrasound waves belong to the world of aggressive mechanical oscillations, while at the same time are coupled to electromagnetic waves. In medical sonography, organic tissue fractures and returns high frequencies as echo to the sender, which can then be transformed into electric currents and encoded as numeric values by analog-to-digital transformers. This process results in a matrix that can be represented as a diagnostic image, a visual interface recognizable to humans. The medical gaze that has been analyzed as a discursive formation by Foucault thus turns out to be a function of the sonic. A sensitive apparatus algorithmically attributes the received resonant sonic signals to digital picture elements ('pixels'). The basic method behind this process is Fourier analysis, which identifies any kind of periodic signals as being composed of individual sine and cosine waves – a musical analysis that reveals the time-based essence of what finally looks like an electronic image. Ultrasound imagery reveals otherwise invisible structures using inaudible sound pulses – a technical answer to Martin Heidegger's understanding of ancient Greek *aletheia* ('non-hiddenness'). And at the most basic level of thermal oscillation within crystals, the energy packets are appropriately called *phonons*.

Media archaeology is not just a human mode of understanding technology, it is also a form of technical perception in which the technological device itself turns into a listening organ. The concept of sonicity is suspended from the privileged anthropocentric perspective in favour of its capacity for exploratory and open access to implicit sonospheres. Technical media provide a mode of listening (*hören*) prior to cognitive understanding (*verstehen*). In radar terminology, Round Trip Time names the travel time of the signal; in US naval jargon, *to ping* directly means to send a sonar impulse.[60] The vocabulary of sonar returns with implicit sonicity in the use of *ping* to describe a program that tests the time required to address an IP over the internet. In order to explore the physical properties of the ionosphere, i.e. the *stratum* used for signal transmission in electromagnetic waves, 'the technique of sounding the atmosphere using radio waves is [...] remarkably powerful.'[61] The very terms *sounding* and *radio* are not meant in the mass media sense of listening to musical or vocal broadcast content. They instead refer to 'radio' in its techno-physical sense – the message of the medium (immediate radio) that discloses itself to the human ear most expressively in shortwave AM.

Transforming the sonic event into the mathematics of sonicity

Aristotle's kinetic theory of time does not assume its transcendental existence but explains it as a quantity derived from measuring motion, i.e. discrete cinematography. Time emerges from observing and counting motion. This corresponds with the mathematization of continuous sound in numerical terms of frequency analysis. The sampling and quantizing of acoustic signals analytically transforms the time signal into frequency information (Fourier Transform), which is the condition for technical re-synthesis. Bill Viola in 1990 pointed out 'the current shift from analogue's sequential waves to digital's recombinant codes' in technology.[62] Coded sound that is mathematical sonicity emerged from within the electro-acoustic synthesizer.[63] Erkki Kurenniemi describes his development of an electronic music studio in Helsinki in the 1970s with combined voltage and digital control: 'Digital signals were used as triggers or gate signals, and also as square-wave sound,' while the recording and editing of the final musical pieces still happened on analog full track audio tape.[64]

There is a countable dimension within each tone. Pitch is nothing but a cognitive metaphor for frequencies; each tone itself is a periodic time event. Karlheinz Stockhausen, in his 1956 essay '... wie die Zeit vergeht', described the chromatic tempo scale starting from the observation that 'pitch may be understood as the microtime equivalent of rhythm.'[65] Rhythm follows the same proportions as harmonies, only below the hearing threshold – a transformation of static geometrical relations into time events as sonic media diagrammatics. Already Ivan Wyschnegradsky concentrated on the musical tone from the acoustic point of view as a primarily rhythmic phenomenon, a sequence of impulses. This interpretation not only results in a panson(or)ic temporality of space but in a mathematization of the sonic event itself.[66]

The fact that 'Western music builds things up'[67] synthetically (culminating in the electro-acoustic synthesizer) is a direct result of the procedure of *analysis* that decomposes complex articulations into its elements. This started with the phonetic alphabet symbolizing speech in antiquity and

escalated with mathematical Fourier analysis, which decomposes sound
into harmonically ordered sine waves – a sonic variance of logocentrism
(with *logos* in ancient Greek naming numerical relations as well).[68] Current
digitalization once more results in a radical transformation in the ontology
of the sound record – from the physical signal to a matrix (chart, list) of its
numerical values.

Beyond electronic 'acoustic space'?

Walter J. Ong emphasized that, in a culture dominated by the symbolic
order of perspective, 'vision comes to a human being from one direction at
a time.'[69] In contrast, when we hear, we 'gather sound simultaneously from
every direction at once: "You can immerse yourself in hearing, in sound".'[70]
Telephone and analog radio marked the technologization of post-literate
sonic space (understood here as an epistemological form of cultural existence). Electricity's immediacy marks its time-critical difference from the
symbolic world of scriptural and printed information. The epistemology
of *acoustic space* corresponds with the ultimate modernist media spatio-
tempor(e)alty. Notwithstanding his confusing electricity with electronics, McLuhan made a crucial discovery about the intrinsically 'acoustic'
structure of electronic mediascapes. In a letter to P.F. Strawson, author of
Individuals. An Essay in Descriptive Metaphysics (1959), McLuhan quotes
from that work: 'Sounds, of course, have temporal relations to each other
[...] but they have no intrinsic spatial characters.'[71] Sonic tempor(e)alities
belong to an epistemology of McLuhan's 'acoustic space' – a sonosphere of
electromagnetic waves that is currently being replaced by a digital immediacy of records. The result of this replacement is a geometrization of time,
a spatiality which in mathematical terms is the topology of the internet.[72]

To what degree is the internet 'sonic'?

'At the speed of light, information is simultaneous from all directions and
this is the structure of the act of *hearing*, i.e. the *message* or effect of electric
information is acoustic.'[73] McLuhan's point holds even when information
is perceived as an electronic image. This diagnosis, made in the age of live
signal broadcast media, is still true for communication in online worlds,
with a notable difference: the nature of signal transmission has dramatically
changed from live transmission to ultra-short intermediary data storage
in transmission. Furthermore, this archiving of presence introduces a
traumatic irritation of the metaphysical notion of presence as such.

Today, what McLuhan's understood as 'acoustic space' – electricity-
induced synchronicity – is replaced in internet communication culture

by radically asynchronous, non-linear, discrete temporalities. Instead of a homogeneous 'noosphere' (in the sense of Teilhard de Chardin), there are discontinuous rhythms; beats rather than waves. The familiar 'flow' of time is being replaced by calculated, 'clocked', mathematical time. The internet as the 'world' of today is based on *lógos* more than ever – on ultra-technical ratios, mathematical intelligence, operative algorithms and alphanumeric code. But this is a temporalized, dynamic *lógos* performed by postings and repeated status updates. This techno-logical mechanism is rooted in rhythms and delays, short-time storage and dynamic processing and is thus sonic by its very nature. The term *sonic* here refers to a specific coupling of acoustic tempor(e)alities with the practice of digital – that is, algorithmic – manipulation. In the world we currently experience as presence, there is an implosion of the transcendental reference 'time' into a chrono-poetic multiplicity of times and timings, such as clocking and data synchronization within computers.[74] The 'Time-To-Live' in internet data packet transmission determines the success of communication in virtual, calculated space in a radically time-critical way.[75] Sonicistic tempor(e)alities unfold even in the 'social web' with its data flows and rhythms: '[...] various techniques and technologies of time management [...] is what characterizes the specificity of reproducing existing worlds in network culture.'[76]

2.   Beeing as '*Stimmung*'

Sonification of time

There are two ways that sound is carried through time: musical memory as symbolically notated in scores (the archive) and sonic memory preserved in signal-based recording media (starting with the Edison phonograph). Digital sound processing technologies refer both to the symbolic ('digital') and physically real ('analog') regimes. But while the phonographic signal keeps an indexical relation to the waveform as acoustic event, encoded data allows for all kinds of time axis manipulation that disrupts its 'temporal indexicality'[1] in favour of the mathematical archive.

Sonic eventuality is not simply time-based. In a more radical reading it leads humans to experience time as such. When effectively (i.e. physically) implemented in instruments, human voices, or operative media, music is in itself already, *a priori,* a sonification of time – its sonic *Versinnlichung* as affect. In a more advanced interpretation, sound is even a soni*fiction* of time in the strict Latin sense as it *generates* temporality.[2]

Functional sonification (defined as the scientific or artistic use of non-speech audio to convey information or more specifically as 'the transformation of data relations into perceived relations in an acoustic signal for the purposes of facilitating communication or interpretation'[3]) is different from 'epistemological' sonification (sonicity). The latter is the 'acoustic' in McLuhan's *implicit* audio sense, an auditory mode taken as epistemological term – just like the Pythagorean tradition that conceives sound as the internal phenomenon of numbers.[4]

The present music field – be it experimental popular music or *avant garde* compositions – is characterized by an aesthetic multiplicity that extends human perception to the limits of infra- and ultra sound.[5] This pushing of sonic limits is itself an effect of the almost infinite flexibility of digital technologies, especially in the area of micro-temporal manipulations. Thus, it makes sense to extend the term 'sonic' to non-acoustic time-based events as well; that is to say, to all kind of vibrations and their mathematical reversal: frequencies. Mark Hansen channels media artists like Bill Viola when he remarks that the 'cinema-digital-video hybrid technique exposes the viewer to minute shifts in affective tonality well beyond what is visible to natural perception.'[6] Let us take this *tonality* literally: There is a sound in electronic media, with the sonic not taken in its physical (acoustic, audible) but in its epistemological sense: being an expression of tempor(e)alities. The privileged relation between sound and technological media is grounded in their analogous time-basedness and chrono-poietical time-basing. New media articulate themselves in well-ordered, even rhythmical times (be it electro-technical or algorithmic), which is their music.[7] Well-ordered musical harmonics that were related to social order by Damon of Athens in antiquity now return much more effectively in the sub-social regime of micro computing.

Since most terms to describe such technological temporality have been borrowed by engineers from musical terminology, it is justifiable to coin this time-critical aspect of operative media as *implicitly sonic* (*sonisch*, which in German sounds like a neologism; not to be confused with *klanglich* simply meaning 'sonic'). The privileged relation between the sonosphere and electronic media arises from their common denominator: the temporal axis. When the simultaneous structure of acoustic space is compared to the electromagnetic field, the real *message* of electronic signal communication is sonic time. While the cognitive modelling of emphatic cultural time as history is a function of the linearity of historiographic writing, 'acoustic space is capable of simultaneity, superimposition, and nonlinearity.'[8] Such times call for Fourier analysis of complex signals that would otherwise be conceived as *historical* events. Even geological layers of mountains, the product of deep natural time, can be sonically interpreted by Fourier analysis as wave forms.[9] The sonic alternative to textually and geometrically organized visual space results in a non-historic concept of cultural time; its figure is resonance, which 'allows things to respond to each other in a nonlinear fashion [...] overcoming the linear grids implied by text.'[10] Suddenly, a sense of the past is activated, not as history but as a time-varying response to and bringing-into-being ('tuning') of latent potentialities that are folded within the laws of nature itself.[11] After all, resonance executes a sonic (rather than symbolic) information transfer, a different kind of tradition. When two resonating systems causally interact, 'the simulating system begins to oscillate in a manner that provides information on the simulated system,' even after their subsequent separation.[12] For McLuhan, resonant communication is the alternative mode compared to the linear channel-based communication theory developed by Claude Shannon.[13]

If such phenomena reveal implicit sonicity, their technical terms in electronics turn the metaphor into a real sound event. The time-critical interplay between potential energy and actual movement – which is characteristic of the interplay between electric induction and capacity in transmission lines and within the electromagnetic field – has been termed *electric resonance* (German '*Schwingkreis*'). This term recalls both the swinging mechanical pendulum and the vibrating string. When this phenomenologically results in voices and music from loudspeakers attached to radios, it becomes literally sound again. In order to emphasize how widespread the mass media application of the media-epistemic principle (*arché*) of electric resonance has become, Julian Blanchard mentions how 'we turn the dials of our radio receivers and 'tune in' on the station.'[14] We use such language even though digital addressing of radio channels long ago replaced *tuning* with non-linear numerical frequencies; the other side of the Janus-like face of the relation between music and mathematics returns.[15] 'In order for one person to understand what another person says, he must be 'in tune' with him. [...] such intrapersonal synchrony is far more fine grained than that of any *corps de ballet*.'[16] This gives a sonic meaning to the common insight that 'all communication is a function of social context.'[17]

Being 'tuned'
Involuntary memory is triggered when humans listen to ephemeral recorded sound; 'a trace of a virtual past affects "in itself".'[18] Here, we are dealing with pre-cognitive temporal affects, with the past as 'contracted' in the present (Henri Bergson). This process is different from voluntary historical memory that arises from intentional research of recorded sound, and introduces a demarcating line between present and past. This difference reveals a deep epistemological issue. If the experience of being is not a static one (ontologic), but rather processual (being-in-time), then the definition of existence as *'Durchstimmung'* (Heidegger) recalls sonic resonance. The German word *'Stimmung'* relates both to the voice (*'die Stimme'*) and to the tuning (*'das Stimmen'*) of an instrument – constituting sonic media temporality. 'Being' is defined by Heidegger as the experience of finality as such.[19] This corresponds with the *transitive* essence of the articulated sound; any harmony mechanically created on a string instrument will fade out. Only by feedback-driven oscillations in the electronic circuit of synthesizers can such sounds be stabilized and, as long there is current, infinitely recreated as sinus waves.[20]

Beeing **'tuned' (Heidegger)**
Sound is transient and thereby a matter of time in its most physical sense. The reduction of the enunciative function of sound to its stationary core (which is addressable by frequency numbers) technically misses the worldliness – that is, temporality – of natural signals. The transients of sound (its beginning and ending) have to be simulated, which pushes mathematical analysis to its limits *in* and *of* time. German *verklingen* expresses the dying-out of sonic events ('unsounding'). Musical articulation always had to

take place in time, as a temporal unfolding. Even John Cage's composition for piano *4'33* is chronologically defined as four minutes and thirty-three seconds of silence; its first public performance consisted of David Tudor at the piano counting time without playing any tone.[21] In a McLuhanite sense the acoustic channel itself becomes the message. Musical *timing* was either expressed by automatisms (like the non-auditory planetary 'spheric' music, diagrammatically defined by Plato in opposition to a static, geometrical notion of *kosmos*) or by human musicians on instruments for human ears. Re-call depended on bodily re-enactment, as expressed by the saxophone player Eric Dolphy: 'Once it's in the air it's gone, you can never recapture it again.'[22]

Martin Heidegger's use of terms from the sonosphere does not refer to explicit acoustics (as physical sound event) or to music as conceptual art form in culture, but rather to the implicit, epistemological meaning of sound as vibrating space. Heidegger at the end of the 1930s defined human existence in resonance with ontological being.[23] Heidegger 'understood' (German: *vernahm*) the *implicitly sonic* nature of such vibrations – not in an acoustic sense, nor as an auditory listening experience. He turned to sonic vocabulary as an alternate way of expressing the microtemporal structure of the 'event' of being.[24]

The sound of Beeing: 'Drone'
Being-in-time, defined by Heidegger around 1933 as 'tuning' (*Stimmung* and *Bestimmtsein*) recalls the eventness of 'drone' sound – an ahistoric, almost time-invariant self-repetition of vibrations themselves, an ecstasy of time.[25] 'Musically speaking, the physics of a broadcast is a type of drone. The video image perpetually repeats itself without rest at the same set of frequencies.'[26] Once perceived as an epistemic event, the drone as sustained vibration with only minimal frequency variations represents a significant shift of conventional thought patterns in Western culture. Such sound is based on positive feedback. In its purest sense of short wave reception, radio is a drone device[27] that makes audible the electromagnetic wave reflections in the ionosphere. Drone suspends the arrow of time; sustained sound freezes sonic time into veritable *acoustic space*.

3. Sonic re-presencing

Delayed presence: Micro-tuning of space

Time machines are frequently associated with movie-like time travelling such as in H.G. Wells's novel. But it is rather sound and music that allow for the most flexible and dynamic time travelling: a kind of uchronia rather than utopia. Musical performance is a time machine that allows for time axis manipulation on the time-critical micro level, such as with electro-acoustic delay lines or electromagnetic tape delay in early electronic music studios. These enabled phase shifting and superposition of sound events.

From the microsonic field of samples up to the macrosonic domain of musical composition, sound can be sculpted in time.[1] Jacob Kirkegaard's audio-visual installation *AION* acoustically unfolded the abandoned space inside the forbidden zone of the collapsed nuclear plant of Chernobyl in Ukraine.[2] In each of the abandoned rooms, Kirkegaard made a recording of ten minutes that he played back into the same room, recording the playback and repeating these steps up to ten times. As the layers got denser, each room slowly began to unfold *a drone* with various overtones.[3] Kirkegaard's sonic time layering explicitly refers back to Alvin Lucier's installation *I am sitting in a Room* (1969) where the technical set-up created a tempor(e)ality of its own. A microphone positioned in a room catches Lucier's articulations played from magnetic tape together with the noise as generated in the room and feeds it into a tape recorder. When the recording is amplified and played back into the same room to be recorded again, the time-delayed sound loops result in increasing acoustic entropy. This setting transforms sound into a chrono-poetic event,[4] with the real chrono-poet being the tape recorder itself.

In architecture, this corresponds with reverberative time (the audio signal delay known as 'echo'). Even the digital manipulation of audio-visual echoes generated in architectural or bodily space keep an indexical relation to their origin; this is what lets human understanding 'feel like an enigmatic causality' (Ksenija Čerče). In the case of ancient and medieval churches, 'there is no mention of *intentionally* creating reverberation for its theological relevance';[5] long reverberation as created in huge cathedrals does not as such correspond with the Pythagorean epistemology of harmony, which is based on integer numbers that are infinitesimally broken by acoustic delay time. Such cathedrals are rather involuntary memories of past soundscapes: time machines.

Space can be explored by time-critical sound operations; the engineering of room acoustics by measuring operations such as pulse-response (developed by Walter Sabine around 1900) has even been extended to auralization as re-enactment of the sonic past.[6] Architecture is not just an empty vessel to be filled by arbitrary acoustics; sound is rather actively processed by the architecturally defined space itself. This concept of using the building as an instrument is inspired by Alvin Lucier's sonic explorations of architectural spaces. But it takes the memory capacity of an electronic device to provide ephemeral sound articulation with a recurrent index of temporal depth, to allow infinite repetition, as realized in Ksenija Čerče's sound/video environment *rec # 21* in the former Judgement Tower at Maribor, Slovenia (summer 2011). An initial acoustic articulation is first expressed in a closed room and its phenomena are recorded. Then the recording is played back into the room, re-recording it. This new recording is then played back and re-recorded again many times.[7] In exploring a closed architectural space by means of acoustic pulses, signals are folded upon themselves. The second signal is a replica of earlier information delivered within a temporal interval. Spatial extension thus turns out to be the medium of temporal delay; at the same time, space itself becomes a function of temporal measuring. For her installation in the Maribor Judgement Tower, Čerče subsequently repeated a sound sample 21 times in order for its acoustics to shape what she calls 'the sound image.'[8] What at first glance looks like a visual projection turns out to be of a sonic, tempor(e)al nature, revealing the asymmetries of audio-visual media, which time-critically fall apart.[9]

The hearing apparatus is much more sensitive to micro-time-critical processes than the eye. While the flickering of an electric bulb (50 times/sec.) does not register in the after-image of the eye (the cinematographical effect), the rising of acoustic pitch from 50 to 100 oscillations/sec. are very well perceived. The apparently smooth, subliminal perceptual integration of sound and vision by the audience in movies is an irritating rupture, since the voices do not come from the visually projected bodies themselves. Audio and vision belong to separate spatiotemporal worlds; bringing them together is not possible without doing violence to their tempor(e)alities.[10]

Sonic delay and media time
The so-called delay time between signal transmission (caused by the inertia of channel matter) and run time (alias 'dead time') is the temporal interval between a system input and its response at the output. This transport time refers to micro-mobility on the media-archaeologically accessible ground level of electronic circuitry. The time it takes for sonic signals to transmit from one point to another adds dead time to a loop. Infinitesimally short (almost punctual intervals) and more extended flow velocity 'can translate

into a meaningful delay."[11] This form of a temporal *in between* is central to the notion of media itself. Time in communication is a *medium* in Claude Shannon's functional definition of channels of transmission.

Such a temporality of acoustic signal transmission is functionally known from early electronic computing as a means for intermediary sonic storage of data. This so-called *acoustic delay line* is based on tubes filled with mercury, a kind of circulating micro-archive or dynamic memory in suspense:

> Because the pulses travelled at the speed of sound, they were not only sorted in space but in time, too. The distance from one crystal to the other and the time that the wave took to traverse this distance provided the basic beat. In addition a clock drove the line so that symbols could be positioned within the flow of time.[12]

Unrecognized by the viewing audience, in mass media culture ultra-sonic delay lines have been common in analog colour television reception (the Phase Alternating Lines system PAL, close to Séquentiel Couleur à Mémoire SÉCAM). The appropriate synchronization of the RGB electronic colour beams requires an acoustic runtime of 64 µs. But the slow run time of acoustic waves even leads to the reversal of the cause-effect relation of combat noise in the age of technological warfare. Time seems reversed. When, in the Second World War, a German A4-rocket hit near London, the acoustic articulation of its near-coming lagged behind the destructive event itself. The acoustic signal no longer is a warning but a sonic epitaph.

4.   The sonic computer

Sonic computing time

Music in itself is a symbolic order of time, but when it is effectively – that is, physically – implemented in operative media, a sonification of time itself takes place, a temporal affect as sonic sensation. Ancient Greek poetic articulation was already 'musical' (*mousiké*) in that temporal sense of 'computing'. Speech itself was not primarily alphabet, but time-based, a kind of variable clocking: 'In contrast to modern times, Greek rhythm measured syllables not according to their significance in the word, but simply to their acoustic length or shortness.'[1]

In early computing (especially for program process controlling), the auditory display of data cycling units was used. This was because algorithmic patterns unfolding in time are accessible to the ear in higher temporal resolution than occurs with visual representation. Alan Turing pointed out that the mercury-based acoustic delay line – an efficient device for intermediary storage of data in the electronic high speed computer – required clocking in order to allow a sufficient synchronization of memory with the processing unit. The imperative to treat computing time as discrete conditions the rhythmic bias of digital computation.[2] Computer memory thereby embodies a sonic time machine in its manifest (sonic delay) and implicit (algorithmic) sense.

The privileged affinity between music, human brain and machine

The 'musical' interlacing of time and machine was essential for George Antheil's *Ballet Mécanique*, performed in Paris and New York in 1926/27. The performance involved automatic pianos that used punched cards and aeroplane engines. *Ballet Mécanique* was a genuine composition with and by time as matter:

> Antheil [...] made silences and repetition (of rhythm and by creating loops in compositions) key elements [...]. Time itself, he said, had to work like music. For him, the most important feature of futurist music was not the microtone, but time. Antheil considered his *Ballet Mécanique* as an example of a new forth dimension of music, the first 'time-form'. For him, time was the sole canvas of music and not a by-product of tonality and tone. [...] According to Antheil, [...] *Ballet Mécanique* was the first work to ever have been composed out of and for machines, neither tonal nor atonal, just made of time and sound [...].[3]

Temporal [4] – patterns belong to the field of periodic oscillations.[5] In repeated action, time does not pass but is transformed into pure frequency as an a-temporal form of processing. Time is the channel for the transfer of sonic data, as opposed to the frequency matrix, which is invariant towards transformation on the temporal axis t.

New media phenomenology combines recent neuro-scientific research about brain temporalities[6] with the Husserlian definition of an augmented experience of presence (pro- and retention). This couples human-affective and media-specific temporalities[7] (which re-calls McLuhan's theorem of acoustic space opened by the age of electrified media). The privileged relation between the sonosphere and electronic media results from the temporal axis, which is their common denominator.[8]

Computing (musical) time

The real time machine that is at work in the digital processing of sound is hidden from human consciousness and listening. This is most evident with 'sampling', which is the transformation of a time-based audio signal into frequency measures on a time-discrete basis. Here, the digital takes place: with digitalization of time-based signals, time itself implodes into operative mathematics. Time-discrete sampling of the temporal acoustic flow is a practice in digital data processing. In reverse, the early digital computers themselves sounded like rhythm machines, and their sonification revealed this function to the engineers. The acoustic Modem (Modulator-Demodulator) coupled computer signals to the telephone itself, allowing for the first network-based transfer of data. This was not sonification for human ears but implicit sonicity for machine-to-machine communication.[9] The dominant way the twentieth century experienced sound as a mass medium is known as radio. However, behind its apparently continuous electromagnetic waves, the rhythm of oscillators beats, created by resonant circuits – a time machine. Shintaro Miyazaki's neologistic blending of musical 'rhythm' and mathematical 'algorithms' to describe operative computer codes is fully justified.[10]

Media archaeology of hearing vs. cultural analysis of listening

Sonic perception with media-archaeological ears is functionally related to sound technologies that go beyond the classic Pythagorean mode of listening. The latter hears *logos* as integer number ratios in musical harmonics and has a logocentristic focus on cosmic order. In early modern times, Johannes Kepler in his *Harmonia mundi* still conceptually privileged the rationality of cultivated sound, i.e. musical hearing. If the communicational approach to sound focuses on listening as cultural interpretation (in opposition to the acoustic study of sound propagation and hearing independent of social context[11]), the media-archaeological understanding assumes an interlaced option. It concentrates on neither the socio-historical, nor the bare psychoacoustic level but on the epistemological dimension that is embedded in sonic articulation. As a result, the study of the sonic signal event can refrain from immediate cultural contextualization without being reduced to mere physical acoustics.

In order to arrive at non-Pythagorean sound,[12] the notion of media archaeology has to first be taken literally by focusing on the technical devices of observation, measuring, and recording. These are shown to be active archaeologists of sonic knowledge and nonhuman agencies of listening – contextual in the technological sense. The emergence in recent years of so-called 'cultures of listening' and techniques of sonification is itself a media-technological effect. Mechanical speakers as sonifiers have played a crucial role in scientific knowledge generation such as electro-physiology. After the invention of the telephone, it was the vacuum tube-based amplifier that enabled loudspeakers to sonify previously non-audible phenomena, such as small electric currents in human nerves.[13]

Research into the physiology of hearing is exemplary here. The insertion of microelectrodes into the auditory nerve of cats for recording signal events created a cybernetic human-machine coupling. When J.C.R. Licklider undertook his auditory analysis of the essentials of what constitutes 'hearing' in humans and animals, he explicitly asked: 'Is there, built into the auditory nervous system, a mechanism [...] that supplements the cochlear frequency analysis?'[14]

His use of terms stems from electronic sound engineering and mathematics rather than from traditional physiology or musicology. Licklider's discursive choice disembodies the anthropocentrism of sound analysis.

Part II
Cultural Soundings and Their Engineering

5. Resonance of siren songs: Experimenting cultural sonicity

Excursion: Media Archaeology of 'Sirenic' sound

Any media archaeology of past acoustics has to confront a dilemma: how can a sonic event that is supposed to have happened long before the age of gramophonic recording be verified? The Siren singing in Homer's *Odyssey* (XII, 184-191) has long been interpreted as a mere poetic invention. To test and reconstruct acoustic events such as Homer's Siren songs by media-archaeological means is not only an academic provocation to philological methodologies, but also leads to different understandings of cultural tempor(e)alities.

Since antiquity (as reported by Strabo the geographer), the Li Galli islands at the Amalfi coast in South Italy are supposed to have been the place where Odysseus heard the infamous voices of the Sirens. Is there something like a physically given grounding in the 'real' of signal processing that kept cultural memory insisting on that place? Acoustic environments in natural landscape have temporal endurance because their sonic effects can be recreated, more or less invariantly, across different time periods. Sonic memory can not be arbitrarily shifted to just any place; however it still remains unclear what Odysseus could hear. Were there specific acoustic phenomena in that region? Did he hear real sounds or was the sound sensation just an auditory hallucination? And finally, if there were voices, what is the appropriate understanding of their sonic message?

For 2500 years, tradition – like a cultural phonograph – claims to have known exactly the place where the Sirens sang. Such an insistent memory is itself indicative of acoustic evidence. But it requires special devices and methods to decode such engravings of acoustic memory: media-archaeological gramophony and an archaeology of sound. A media-archaeological research expedition by members of Humboldt University Berlin, assisted by the Centre for Media Arts and Technology Karlsruhe, in early April 2004, conducted experiments with sound propagation at the Li Galli Islands. These experiments used both human organs and technical apparatuses. Both synthetic signals (sine tones, white noise) and natural voices (chanted intervals of vowels previously recorded on tape) were tested *via* loudspeaker. Two trained human voices (opera singers) also sang *glissandi* on the spot. The signals were recorded along a line supposedly taken by Odysseus to approach the Siren Island. Analysis of the recordings revealed an acoustic

effect that tentatively explains the nature of the myth: the specific position of two rock formations opposed to the large curved island results in a
deformation of vocal signals emitted by amplification and changes in the
timbre of these signals.

If the precision of this location in cultural memory has a foundation in
the acoustic real, it can be identified by an experi/mental approach that
establishes frequency spectography using a set of measuring points and
loudspeaker positions. The measurements performed by the bio-acoustician
Karl-Heinz Frommolt and the media archaeologist of musicology Martin
Carlé led them to conclude that the specific geographical constellation of
the island acts as an acoustic amplifier that corresponds with archaic Greek
diaphonic musical tuning in a way that might explain why Homer explicitly
has *two* Sirens singing.[1] The Sirens play more than just a metaphorical role
in representing the perfect sound for ancient poets; they are meant to
reveal wisdom both implicitly from within the sonic domain and explicitly
through its acoustic channel. Therefore, investigations have to reach beyond
traditional philological methods to establish the link between real acoustic
phenomena and acoustic hallucinations. For archaic Greek epistemology,
Sirens incorporate acoustic features of superior soundings that have musicological relevance. If the *two* Sirens correlate with the double-flute (*auloi*)
as a musical instrument with disharmonic joints, the grammatical *casus
dualis* of Homer's Sirens could thus have been acoustically motivated. This
leads to a musicological hypothesis of an early Greek diaphony based on
enharmony.[2]

The correlation between this acoustic latency, revealed by cold measurement evidence, and a conscious understanding of such reverberations in
ancient times (induced by the semantically heated transmission of the
Siren songs in the vocal alphabet) uses techno-mathematical aspects of
communication to pose challenging questions regarding the nature of
cultural tradition. Any such deduction of sonic significance oscillates
between signal and noise.[3] The inventor of infinitesimal calculus, Gottfried
Wilhelm Leibniz understood the implicit sonic knowledge of waves when
walking along the seashore. This understanding corresponds, eventually,
with Fourier's mathematical analysis of complex waveforms.[4] The prelude
of Richard Wagner's *Rheingold* opera starts with the natural tonal series
(*Naturtonreihe*), which unfolds like a Fourier analysis of superimposed sinus
waves more than a musical melody, sonically expressing the river Rhine
as streaming signal.[5]

When the academic team undertook its archaeoacoustic research at
Li Galli Islands, 'the basic premise was unqualified trust in the ability of

Homer's [...] words to describe Siren songs and a qualified distrust in the ability of human ears to fully understand them.'[6] This premise echoed that of young Heinrich Schliemann, who took a reading of Homer's *Iliad* as a literal account of past reality and in so doing was able to excavate the ancient city of Troy. Does the contemplative vision of gentle waves at the Amalfi coast lead to *aural* hallucinations of acoustic waves when the area is auratically charged with the epic memory of faint Siren songs? After all, these remain distant, in Walter Benjamin's sense, however close they are to experience. Ernle Bradford, who is well known for having tracked Odysseus's naval voyage across the Mediterranean, claims that he had heard the Sirens while serving on H.M.S. Exmoor in early September 1943. During the ship's defensive patrols of the Gulf of Salerno:

> [t]he music crept by me upon the waters [...]. I cannot describe it accurately, but it was low and somehow distant – a natural kind of singing one might call it, reminiscent of the waves and the wind. Yet it was certainly neither of these, for there was about it a human quality, disturbing and evocative.[7]

During the Second World War, the Li Galli islands served as a possible hideout for battleships. It was here that Bradford heard (or hallucinated) the supposed Siren call. While acoustic signals can and must be actually heard, sonic hallucinations do not depend on mechanical vibrations. Bradford had reached a point when the singing started to make sense; it had a direct bearing on his sensation. 'It began to draw on me so that I wanted to join it – and this 'joining it', I knew in some obscure way, meant going back into the past [...]. It meant, I knew, going back in time, retreating in some way or other into a different world.'[8] This world is not simply different in terms of historical distance. Bradford's description of the uncertain zone between natural sounds and intentionally addressed messages with a pseudo-human quality can be interpreted in a more fundamental sense. Meaning here emerges from noise and is reinforced by its coupling to a cultural memory of antiquity. This corresponds in Lacanian terms with the transfer from the real (waves), through the symbolic (symbolically encoded communication), to the imaginary.[9] By preliminary acoustic analysis, this phenomenon can be media-archaeologically located; what can not be decided is the degree of acoustic intentionality in a hermeneutic sense.[10]

According to Homer, Odysseus could hear the Siren song only because a divine power (a *daimon*) calmed the sea around the Siren islands, which ensured a perfect signal-to-noise ratio. If there were waves, they were silent

– ultra-sonic radio frequencies, for instance, do not resonate in human ears
without a radio receiver to demodulate and transmit them as low-frequency
loudspeaker emissions. When addressed by the Sirens, Odysseus was not
only in a boat *on* the sea but immersed *in* a field of waves. The human
ear perceives kinetic impulses of acoustic waves affectively rather than
consciously.[11] The optical regime is about immediate spatial impressions
that preserve physical distance; sound in a different, haptic way seizes
the body with its vibrations. Lacking ear-lids, there is almost no escape
for the human visitor from the acoustic attack of a sonosphere. This sonic
imprisonment takes place on the manifest level when listening to a musical
composition, but on the latent level when what is *seen* turns out to be a
secondary function of sonic eventuality (such as with the ultrasonic or
fully electronic image). The epistemic insight of sonicity is found across
the whole spectrum between mythology and media archaeology, between
the human voice and electronically produced frequencies. The analysis
of sonic memorization goes far beyond simply doing justice to *auditory
memory,* which 'has been largely neglected in memory studies in favour of
visually-oriented arts of memorization'[12] – the rhetorical tradition of *ars
memorativa* with its spatial bias.

'Sing to me, Muse, the deeds of a man called Odysseus', Homer's epic
poem starts. So-called oral poetry, as it is known in cultural tradition,
was sung for thousands of years before being registered and displaced in
writing symbols that 'technologize'[13] the acoustic signal, sacrificing its rich
over- and undertones (tuning, pitch, timbre, rhythm). With the arrival of the
mechanical phonograph that records sound as time signal, such memory is
preserved in its sonicity. This results in a different notion of implicit sound
in its epistemological dimension. In order to be communicated beyond
its physical limits, acoustic sound must be technically transduced to fit a
channel such as the telephone line or electromagnetic radio transmission.
While passing as transduced signal in voltage-controlled current, sound
is in its *sonic* state. The same is true for the transmission of sound across
culturally emphatic time intervals called 'historical tradition': it must be
signal-recorded in phonographic media rather than symbolically coded by
literary or musical notation.[14]

The ancient Greek recalibration of the Phoenician alphabet, i.e. the add-
ing of vocal symbols to the syllabic alphabet to record the musicality of oral
poetry, was symbolically engineered in the period between the formulation
of the *Iliad* and the *Odyssey.*[15] The mythic Sirens are expressions of this
different vocality, just like Hermann von Helmholtz experimented in the
nineteenth century with technical sirens in order to artificially produce

vocal sounds. The media-archaeological difference is between emphatic sound and technically produced soundings, between cultural myth (as an anthropomorphic effect of the symbolic operations of phonetic literature) and its acoustically real articulation as signals in matter.

Julian Jaynes[16] described that in the prehistoric age – that is, prescriptural – the voice of the (dead) king was hallucinated whenever sound took place as a spectral event. 'Sound politics' in Homer's time, therefore, meant gaining control over authoritarian verbal hallucinations using writing as a sound-technology driven by symbolically reproducible vowels. 'Acoustic' writing and sound reading of the sonosphere of language, mediated by the phonetic alphabetic code, was a cultural technique that remodelled the bicameral brain; both hemispheres are cognitively bound together by the phonetic alphabet.[17]

The Homeric mythological Siren is made relevant for media archaeology of sound today by the intervention of the phonograph. With this device the replay of recorded voices and human presence are rendered equivalent for the first time, in spite of the knowledge that recorded sound is channelled *via* dead signals on a storage medium.[18] This affordance is expressed in the chapter on phonographic euphony in Thomas Mann's novel *The Magic Mountain*. Sirens are non-human in terms of such machinic or cyborg sound. Their sweet chant sounds alive, yet the listener knows this may very well be a reproduction of dead signals *via* a storage medium like phonograph or gramophone – and even more with electronic sound processing. Here, the uncanny of the monstrous Sirens corresponds with the irritating imaginary of technology itself. Parikka defines 'imaginary media as shorthand for what can be addressed as the non-human side of technical media'[19] – which in the world of sound processing accelerates to ultrasonic speed. Maurice Blanchot identifies the acoustemic challenge embedded in the Sirens' song with its turning the notion of human singing upside down:

> Some have said that it was an inhuman song – a natural sound (is there such a thing as an unnatural sound?) but on the borderline of nature, at any rate foreign to man; almost inaudible [...]. Others suggested that it [...] simply imitated the song of a normal human being, but since the Sirens, even if they sang like human beings, were only beasts [...], their song was so unearthly that it forced those who heard it to realise the inhumanness of all human singing.[20]

Theodor W. Adorno's writings on phonographic recording accentuate an understanding of Sirenic singing as not human: 'Wherein the more perfectly the machine is able to represent the human, the more thoroughly is the human removed [...].'[21] Therein resides the technotraumatic element of the voice itself as 'the site at which, in the distinction between the cry and the song, the human and the inhuman are differentiated in a state of perennial irresolution.'[22] In the case of acoustic hallucinations and visual imagination of the voice, the 'most human' turns out tohe be the most inhuman. This is richly evident in the twentieth century's success in manufacturing synthesized voices by technological means in its full sense: materially refined electronics (*techné*) and mathematical analysis (*lógos*).

Among others with parallel approaches, Boris Yankovsky actually *computed* the human voice by treating sound matter in a fully formal way. A combination of a mathematical model of the synthetic tone ('syntone') and its implementation in a processing mechanism (Yankovsky's Vibroexponator) turns symbolic abstraction into a media event in physical time. In order to get to the essence of sonic articulation, any imagining of sound must first be suspended. Thus emerges operative sonicity:

> To synthesize the human voice singing a vowel, one would need to choose several templates related to formants (drawn waveforms [...]), to add extra templates as needed [...], to recalculate their sizes according to the desirable frequencies and intensities of formants, and then to mix them. The final waveform would sound like a 'frozen' vowel. This waveform could be used to produce a temporal 'quant' of sound, physically related to one frame of the film. To produce the sound, dynamically changing in time, one would have to calculate the sequence of static frames, in which each frame represents the successive state of changing timbre. In order to produce the final soundtrack one would have to cross-fade successive overlapping frames by optical means to achieve smooth transitions and to avoid clicks.[23]

The notorious *Symphony of Sirens* performance in Moscow on 7 November 1923[24] liberated sound from the culturally emphatic semantics of music as an art form. Sound was liberated in the name of noise but still belonged to the aesthetic of the industrial age – the age of thermodynamic energy exchange. A techno-mathematical (re-)creation of Sirenic voices, though, takes an informational approach. Sonicity thus suspends (if not liberates) the sonic event from sound. Applying an electronic Harmonizer to transform male voices into sweet female singing in digital real-time is a post- or rather pre-human operation.

The frequencies of specific human vocality – once analyzed on a sub-symbolic (alphabetic) level as real micro-signal events – are not simply regular and periodic but happen arhythmically (as made evident by the diagrammatic recording that produces sonagrams). When its 'listening' is transferred into digital reality, a temporal gap opens between rhythm and algorithm. The digital computer requires an exact and periodic high frequency *clocking* in order to be able to synchronize its multiple data processes without internal confusion. Recordings of the human voice reveal irregular ratios in pulsation, while the digital manipulation of such sound recordings by computer programs is genuinely mathematical, resulting in 'algorhythmic'[25] phenomena. Human voicings have become 'the technological shadows of the apparatuses that document them'.[26]

The Siren myth refers to a psychoacoustic reality effect, a shock-like affect within the listener. In the context of modern media experimentation with the human voice, this uncanniness derives from the return, as *other*, of what was previously known (culturally) as Siren singing in a moment of technological sublime. The artifactual correlate for the Homeric Sirens in sound-archaeological terms is the technical siren apparatus.[27] The working assumption of the acoustic archaeology at Li Galli has been the folding of both meanings of the 'siren' – the cultural and the technological. That is why it was almost obligatory to emit across the sea between the ship and the island acoustic impulses generated by the technical double-siren. The siren as *sonic* device (as developed by Cagniard de Latour and refined by Hermann von Helmholtz) delivered vocal formants to techno-mathematical analysis and calculation. This produced a retro-effect regarding the metaphysics of the human voice in occidental ontology: the voice became considered and perceived as a frequency-based vibration event in itself. Once the wonders of the voice are no less mechanical than sounds produced by synthetic machines, de Latour's and von Helmholtz' nomination of technical 'sirens' is no longer metaphorical:

> 'The special twist of this forensic Siren story [...] is the fact that one of the sound producing devices used to disconceal the ancient Sirens was an aerophone, a noisemaker that produces signs by interrupting the air flow – in other words, a modern siren. Sirens track Sirens.'[28]

This is experimental media archaeology of the acoustic, replacing traditional philological hermeneutics with technical analysis. Academic terms like *primary orality* and *oral history* came into existence only with the writing monopoly. Alphabetic vowels symbolically transposed Homer's voice into recording, while the technical siren generates tones by numbered holes in hardware. Numerical frequencies represent the reverse of vocal sine waves. In terms of an archaeology of knowledge, the ancient Greek vowel alphabet implicitly set the agenda for a culture of research based on discretization and analysis of sonic phenomena like speech, which are physiologically perceived as streaming signals. Alphabetising sonic articulation – which is technologizing *logos* – already encapsulates its *telos* as contemporary technology, since it epistemologically preconditioned future discrete sound technologies.

The epistemic irritation induced by s/Sirens goes even deeper into the realm of temporality, since it challenges the historiographical, predominantly linear emplotment of cultural time:

> Kittler mentions the Sirens as [...] example of recursive history 'where the same issue is taken up again and again at regular intervals but with different connotations and results' [...]: from seductive Greek sea nymphs [...] to the nineteenth-century technical use of the term in the form we understand it, i.e. as a signalling device with a sound, subsequently playing a key part in the mapping of the thresholds of hearing as well as the development of radio [...].[29]

An ahistorical short-circuiting of distant times takes place when the technical siren as a sound generator confronts its mythological precursor:

> Recursions fold time and thus enable direct contact between points and events (and S/sirens) that are separated when history time is stretched out on a continuous line. In the case of the Siren-to-siren shortcut we are leap-frogging across millennia.[30]

In order to acknowledge the possibility that an acoustic event other than female voices could have been the origin of the poetic memory of Siren songs, recordings of monk seals were also broadcast from loudspeakers on the main Li Galli island. The anatomy of the vocal tract of these amphibious mammals – common in the Mediterranean in Homer's times – results in vocalizations that might easily have been easily associated with the human voice. The naturalist monk seal explanation represents a traditional mode of explaining ancient myths. However, a truly techno-epistemic approach to modelling such (supposedly imagined) voices is not to imitate the physical human vocal tract by mechanical analogies, but to analyze the voice itself as signal event and wave form. This decisive shift took place in the late eighteenth century as a counter to experiments like Wolfgang von Kempelen's mechanical voice-generating apparatus that imitated human organs. Once techno-mathematically analyzed (e.g. with von Helmholtz' 'Resonators'), the complex sonic colour can be composed by a dynamic composition of single sine waves. The electronic equivalent to *glissandi* in human singing is achieved by condensers that, in an act of electromathematical integration, successively increase or decrease the electric charge. At the same time, changeable frequencies are generated from astable multivibrators.

The flexible coupling of two actual acoustic warning devices (appropriately called 'sirens') results in miraculous effects of additional or subtractive vibrations when their frequencies are close to each other; the so-called *Out of Tunes* (the German term for which, *Schwebung,* has a Hegelian overtone of aesthetic sublation) become psycho-physiologically 'virtual' when they are processed within the human ear/brain-complex. All of a sudden, the Siren singing is not simply poetic imagination any more but a media-archaeologically explainable event. This argument does not refer to the actual singing but to implicit sonicity as the epistemic core of the Siren myth. The seductive *aura* of such artificial voices might be explained by the fact that this addresses deep layers of the epistemological sense of sonicity within humans.

The implicit sonic wisdom of the Siren mythologeme thus goes far beyond apparent seductive pleasures. But it is part of the media-archaeological approach to cultural knowledge to be self-critically aware of the scientific limits of such archaeoacoustic evidence; the Sirenic question can not be determined by measurement and quantitative analysis of musical intervals alone.[31] Further acoustic reasoning will be required at the site under more favourable conditions than the stormy early April days of the German expedition. Media-archaeological research can never definitively reconstruct what has been said (or sung), but rather explores and defines the conditions of possibility regarding what *could have* been enunciated. The sonic evidence thus produces primarily indirect arguments *ex silentio.* Signal-based exploration is twisted into a historical 'source' only when coupled with symbolic records.

Sound, historicity, and the narcissistic impulse of a dialogue with the dead

Thomas Alva Edison's invention of the phonograph (1877) disrupted the familiar occidental logocentrism of both oral and aural presence. From that moment on sound could be technographically recorded (and not just symbolically by alphabetic musical notation), and sound from the past could be preserved for both present replay and future posterity. Apart from this explicit storage of sound, there are more implicit, sublime embodiments of sound from the past as well. This tracing of sonicity leads back to the Sirenuse Islands.

Sonic environments are site specific since the physical character of acoustic waves adapts to local signal run times. Whether intended or not, a sense of place is necessarily encoded in the sonosphere. Within the land- and seascape of the Sirenuse Islands, the optical regime is challenged rather than simply supplemented by its auditory display; immediately what looks like a panorama in fact is transformed into a panacoustic surrounding. Sound from speakers fixed on the shores of the main island in the dark – similar to acousmatic techniques in ancient Greek theatre[32] or Richard Wagner's hidden orchestra in his Bayreuth opera house – directly address and confuse ears positioned between the two small rock-like islands opposite to them. In these experimental settings, certain frequencies are emphasized or vanish when set against a background of audio-visual absence (i.e. as much silence and darkness as could be achieved). Does the past literally resonate when technical sirens emanate strange sounds on such spots? Can past time resonate in the present?[33] At first glance, space cannot be experienced as 'historical' in aural terms, since, by definition, empty architecture is silent. On the other hand, it is through sonic signal runtime differences that the human binaural listening apparatus acquires orientation in space. Space thus becomes itself a function of acoustic waves. Any sound or noise – unless electronically reiterated – starts to perish from the moment it is expressed; by their very nature, acoustic articulations affect the temporal sensation of the human subject, which is G.W.F. Hegel's philosophic argument.[34] Present silence in space may thus be reconsidered as part of a negative (cosine) phase amplitude in what was previously, positively (sine) articulated as audible.

There is an unmistakable desire for sonic communication with the dead: 'If I never believed that the dead could hear me, and if I knew that the dead could not speak, I was nevertheless certain that I could recreate a conversation with them.'[35] This *prosopopoeitic* desire takes place in spite of the knowledge that every dialogue with the past only echoes one's own voice. In ancient Greek mythology, Narcissus is distracted by his own mirror image in the water. What is usually overlooked in this primary scene is that it happens while the nymph Echo tries in vain to seduce him with the acoustic 'mirror' (echo) of his own words. The epiphany of the mirror image differs from the temporal delay implicit in acoustic reflections; sonic belatedness (its perceivable temporality) is superseded by the apparent immediacy of the image. The decisive momentum in the Narcissus myth is that he sees his image mirrored in the water, while the acoustic echo unfolds in time. In the distinction between visual and acoustic space, time makes all the difference. But e/Echo is more than just the simulacrum of one's own voice; it is already a pre-emptive epistemic presentiment of the phonographic voice. In ancient mythology, Echo's body wastes away until only her voice is left, anticipating the disembodied voice of a gramophone recording. The introduction of coupled magnetic recorders in music studios after the Second World War gave rise to micro-temporal echoes, reverberations and resonances that became constitutive of Rock 'n' Roll music as such. These specific, time-critical sound characteristics, such as the slapback echo used by Elvis Presley (among others), performed Husserlian pro- and re-tention by means of electro-technical signal delay operations.[36]

The specificity of such sonic articulation cannot be captured and subsumed by the logocentrism of traditional narrative historiography. Acoustic space is of a different temporal nature: not linear, but synchronous, simultaneously from every direction at once – *echo land*.

Let us take this metaphor literally: Acoustic echo implies delay, the very temporality induced by air or water as channel of signal transfer. It was acoustic delay (the echo effect) that once led Aristotle, in his research on perception (*Parva naturalia*), to discover the medium as a category of delay and resistance in itself, the 'in between' – *to metaxy*.[37] Its translation by medieval scholars transformed the adverb into a noun, and the notion became the well-known *medium*.

Sonic indexicality: Recording sound from the real world

Roland Barthes described his experience of looking at an old photograph of his late mother with the word *punctum*. This concept describes a temporal moment, a short cut between past and present. Its equivalent in acoustic recording by gramophone involves a processual, time-based signal, the re-play of which generates a sense of the past different from Barthes' *punctum*. Ludwig Wittgenstein once confessed that when he imagined a tune recorded for a gramophone 'this is the most elaborate and exact expression of a feeling of pastness which I can imagine'.[38] Such a mechanical recording differs dramatically from an electronic recording of the same sonic event. Sound, when re-generated out of electromagnetic latency, embodies a tempor(e) ality different from the scripturally engraved gramophone groove.[39]

As engraved index (in Peirce's semiotic sense), a sound forms a sharp contrast to its symbolic notation. *Indices* represent their objects 'by virtue of being in fact modified by them', in a truly analog way.[40] The gramophone

groove is literally in-formed by sound, but this is a material, physical shap-
ing, whereas digital information is not a question of matter or energy. The
acoustic signal does not lose its temporal indexicality when recorded, as
exemplified by the long sounding whistle of an approaching locomotive
dramatically changing pitch as the train passes by. This is a confrontation
with a physical event:

> Replicate that same sound on a recording and it will not lose its capacity
> to confront a hearer with the apparent motion of a large body, but will
> continue to index the direction and speed of an apparent object, without
> the train actually being present any more. The sound, taken away from
> the real event, retains its indexing properties.[41]

An aggressive acoustic signal (intrusive on the body through the unsheltered, open ear) even in its media-technological reproduction seems to
retain its physically *effective* and physiologically *affective* reality. Still, the
acoustic signal undergoes a change of being when replayed from a technical
recording, though it is identical in terms of its frequency values. Hearers
of sound from a technical record emitted by loudspeakers no longer immediately search for its source; thereby sound ceases to be narrative and
becomes a hyperspatial and hypertemporal artifact.

Auditory hallucinations (against *prosopopeia*)

The silence of the traditional scripture-based archive has techno-rhetor-
ically been replaced by an aesthetics of the undead: disembodied voices
on audio-visual records sound as if they were still alive. What in classical
Greek was termed *prosopopeia* is the rendering to something not alive of a
live 'speaking' mask. The undead undoes the binary logic of life and death
(recalling René Descartes' comparison of the human body to a clockwork).[42]
But storage time is empty time.[43] Siegfried Kracauer has been pessimistic
about the possibilities of translating the narrative continuity of a novel into
camera-life[44] – since living processes cannot be told, but simply registered
by technical media. What looks *live* to the beholder in visual media, might
as well have been pre-recorded on magnetic tape – an uncanny, undeadly
state of the moving image and of articulated sound.

How can human readers resist the temptation of projecting a face onto
archival files?[45] Instead of giving a voice to archival documents (a prosopopy
resonant in the Etruscan-Latin term *persona*, designating the actor's mask
with open mouth), they might simply be serially grouped into silent entities.
Speech symbolically coded in alphabetic writing or telegraphic transmission

– different from recorded signals – cannot be made to speak, only analyzed and recombined, without ever identifying the physical voice of the author. The archive as uncanny space of symbolic letters is paralleled in the biblical vision of the prophet Ezekiel (Ez. 37), who describes dead signifiers (real bones) that long for eschatological re-animation: 'So I prophesied as he commanded me, and the breath came into them, and they lived, and stood up upon their feet, an exceeding great army.' But only with the introduction of explicit vowels into the alphabet was this hallucination 'technologized.'[46] Ever since, such re-animation has involved *re-reading* aloud or with an inner voice – the historian's symptom.[47] Any historicist impulse to speak with the dead, as Shakespeare's Hamlet does in the graveyard (act V, 1st scene), takes place against the better knowledge that every dialogue with the past only mirrors one's own voice. There is no textual *gramophone*, just phonetic *grammata*, letters of an alphabet. Written letters inevitably belong to the realm of the symbolic, which is the mute order of the archive, different from physically indexical traces such as rays of light traced by photography or grooves of sound on records. These new kinds of technical memories are archives or libraries no longer; the *a priori* of discourse turns into dynamic systems of signal transfer.[48]

The American painter of allegories Elihu Vedder (1836-1923) once expressed with oil on canvas the subject of *Questioning the Sphinx* (1863).[49] This painting depicted a scene in the desert close to the Pyramids of Giza. With his ears close to the Sphinx' sculptural lips, a man in vain tries to listen to her secrets. On the actual archaeological site of the painting's setting, remnants of skeletons can be detected – people who once tried in vain to speak to the Sphinx. Any present enquiry is confronted with an archivally or archaeologically frozen *read only memory* – which is the nature of any mechanically recorded inscription, any material monument. The gap separating a given presence and the absence of the past is unbridgeable. This insight is allegorical, much different from symbolic modes that privilege continuity.

The postmodern painter Mark Tansey has given Vedder's image a media-archaeological turn. Tansey provides the interrogator of the Sphinx with a microphone and thus the option to not only listen to the dead, but also well to record this evidence.[50] Electronic recording is the techno-fiction of reversing death; with the invention of the gramophone the human voice has lost its logocentrist privilege of authorizing true presence. In Walter Rathenau's novel *Resurrection Co.,* the administration of a cemetery in the city Necropolis, after several scandalous cases of people mistakenly buried alive, the administration of a cemetery in the city Necropolis establishes a company called 'Central Resurrection Telephone and Bell Co.' with the aim of connecting the buried to the public telephone network – just in case.[51]

'We associate libraries, collections of knowledge, and systems for memory retrieval with silence [...].'[52] The distant relationship between reader and alphabetic text has been amplified by printing technology that favours the silent reading situation – a sonosphere confronting absences, as opposed to the noisy multimedia phantasies of today. It is exactly this kind of distancing silence that the archaeologist of knowledge defends, resisting the temptation to turn symbolic memory into the phonocentristic imaginary of a dialogue with the past. Reading phonetic writing is not simply a visual activity but a form of displaced orality that results in the hallucination of a conversation with kindred spirits long dead or at great distance.[53] Historians in the archive long for the opportunity to make a textual body resound – a theatrical re-enactment. Jules Michelet, historian of the French Revolution, hallucinated the murmurs of the dead in the archives, as if archival records had always been the logocentric variance of a phonogram (*avant la lettre*). Not yet equipped with technical media of recording and projecting, Michelet made use of the psychic medium of imagination: '*Dans les galeries solitaires des Archives où j'errai vingt années, dans ce profond silence, des murmures cependant venaient à mon oreille.*'[54] Contemporary digital interface aesthetics make use of this mindset, privileging auditory hallucinations. Hyper-media itself becomes a '"talking archive" [...] lost to us in the era of silent libraries.'[55]

The media-archaeological resistance to the prosopopoetics of a 'dialogue' with data instead accentuates the signal-to-noise-ratio (using the language of communication theory) that accompanies electronic data transfer. What was once called tradition is today the technical transmission of signals. Recorded voices from the past can be listened to via CD-ROM or other data carriers. In the presence of scratchy recordings, human ears, not the technical device, make sense out of noise. The prosopopoietic illusion of the sonic media archive is for human understanding only. Let us take, for example, the necessity of compressing audio data streams in order to make them storable and transmittable as *streaming media*. In contrast to the transmission of archived texts in the occidental tradition, where every letter counts (the point of a whole discipline called philology), in the compression and decompression of digital sound files, subtle amounts of data are lost. But this loss is almost undetectable for weak human ears – an organ that is deceived in its perception by almost any acoustic communication.[56] The temporal information of human sound sensation is particularly unreliable.

Sirenic sonicity: Sound politics and sound poetics

Even if the mythic kernel of the song of the Sirens is probably based on specific acoustic conditions of a particular landscape, it remains unclear who or what emitted the song. After all, the very term *mythos* reminds of an acoustic origin. But such an 'origin' (*arché*) demands a media-archaeological rather than anthropocentric interpretation.

Only the vocal alphabet can serve as a link between mute writing practice and 'living' speech, serving as a recording device not just for acoustic (consonants, syllabic alphabet), but also sonic (or even musical) events. Therefore the Sirens address themselves to Odysseus in explicit Greek. Since there is no interpolation of onomatopoetic elements or non-semantic phonetic utterances in the Homeric stanzas of the singing Sirens, this is a media reflection of the sound element in speech (poetry) itself: 'Come hither, Odysseus [...] listen [*akoúses*] to our voices. Never has any man passed by in his black ship without hearing the honey-sweet voice from our lips.' Paradoxically, within the vocal alphabet – which is able to phonographically record Greek language in written form – a reminiscence of the pre-alphabetic age takes place. One cause for the breakdown of the bicameral mind in early antiquity was the advent of writing itself, 'because once something is written you can turn away from it and it has no more power over you, in contrast to an auditory hallucination which you cannot shut out.'[57] The immediate result of this loss of hallucinated voices (emperors and gods) resulted in media-like substitutes: 'the idea of genii or angels as messengers between heaven and earth, the idea of evil gods such as demons – all are new phenomena.'[58]

According to Homer, Odysseus prevented his companions from being seduced by the singing Sirens by though sealing their ears with wax. Wax itself might be read here literally. Not only does honey play a central role in Homer's description of the Siren song language (honey-sweet voices), but bees-produced wax was among the first technical recording media for Edison's phonographic apparatus: the hard wax cylinder. Archaeoacoustics knows about traces unintentionally created by sonic articulations in the past – sound recordings *avant la lettre*. With nano-physical means such traces might actually be (re-)sonified. Sonicity is the name for such unintended (sound) recordings.

Referring to an as yet not pursued thought experiment by the nanophysicist Wolfgang Heckl, Friedrich Kittler imagines that the song of the Sirens might not have vanished as completely as is supposed. Acoustic traces may have modulated ornamental engravings in wet clay produced by the turning disc of pottery in the making.[59] The pioneer of digital computing Charles

Babbage imagined that water and air are capable of a dynamic – though implicit – storage of all propulsive acoustic waves that have ever been articulated. To become explicit memory, a technology of replay is required:

> The air itself is one vast library, on whose pages are forever written all that man has ever said or woman whispered. There, in their mutable but unerring characters, mixed with the earliest, as well as with the latest sights of mortality, stand for ever recorded, vows unredeemed, promises unfulfilled, perpetuating in the united movements of each particle, the testimony of man's changeful will.[60]

Babbage obviously confuses analog sound signals and discrete alphabetic symbols; the 'library' is rather a phonographic recording medium, while the programs written in punched cards for his Analytical Engine constitute what contemporary computing science calls a 'library'. Analog and digital concepts of the universe interlace here. Babbage's contemporary, Jean Baptiste Joseph Fourier, started to integrate both approaches by analyzing wave forms according to their single sine wave components, which can subsequently be converted into numeric frequencies and thus become computable by digital machines. Such numeric values are no longer time signals but measurements that embody temporal information – the most elaborate abstraction of sonicity. If 'no motion impressed by natural causes, or by human agency, is ever obliterated',[61] even the geological formations of a mountain can be deciphered by Fourier Analysis in a sonicistic understanding of times past – an understanding that undoes history.[62] Mikhail Tsekhanovsky actually proposed to taking ancient Egyptian or Greek ornaments for a sound track: 'Perhaps we will hear some unknown archaic music.'[63]

In contrast to philological conjectures, acoustic media archaeology manages to retrieve the memory of sound from cultural artifacts of the past. In a novel called *Time Shards*, Gregory Benford imagines a research laboratory that reconstructs 'fossil voices' out of the grooves of mediaeval pottery. 'Does not a sound fossil as well appear as a density [...] in comparison to a trace [...] as something that accumulates – has an extension in time?'[64] In 1925, Sigmund Freud wrote *A Note upon the 'Mystic Writing Pad'* in which he compared human memory apparatus with a well-known writing toy for children:

> One makes incisions onto a wax tablet, over which has been stretched a thin sheet of cellophane (not unlike the acoustic membrane of a

microphone). When one pulls up the cellophane, the marks on the surface seem to disappear. Yet the traces of the incisions remain in the wax, almost unreadable, yet present all the same.[65]

This discussion of implicit graphics could very well be applied to phonographic form as well.

> If we lift the entire covering sheet [...] off the wax slab, the writing vanishes and [...] does not re-appear again. The surface of the Mystic Pad is clear of writing and once more capable of receiving impressions. But it is easy to discover that the permanent trace of what was written is retained upon the wax slab itself and is legible in suitable lights. [...] this is precisely the way in which [...] our mental apparatus performs its perceptual function.[66]

Wax is an essential medium, because – according to René Descartes and Fritz Heider – it provides a loose coupling of elements, on which a tight coupling (form) can be impressed as in/formation. Did the wax with which Odysseus sealed his companions' ears implicitly record the siren songs? This idea is not so far- fetched for media archaeology. The missing link is provided by Plato who lets Socrates assume that our soul is a block of wax:

> This is the gift of Memory, the mother of the Muses, and [...] whenever we wish to remember anything we see or hear or think of in our own minds, we hold this wax under the perceptions and thoughts and imprint them upon it, just as we make impressions from seal rings; [...] but whatever is rubbed out or cannot be imprinted we forget and do not know.[67]

In Homer's poetry, the beautifully singing muses (*opi kallé*) are transformed from active agents to objects of oral poetry with the muse Kalliope as imaginary of the phonetic alphabet. Jaynes explicitly refers to the *Iliad* to test his thesis on the origin of consciousness and of the narrative 'I'. The mnemotechnical hexametric form made it possible to transmit poetic memory of the fall of Troy from the end of the Mycenean age down to the origin of the vocal alphabet, which was finally able to record and fix such songs. The symbolic 'vocalization' of the Phoenician alphabet happens through the introduction of arbitrary letters for single vowels. Whereas the *Odyssey* displays already the nature of a dictated epic poem (as shaped by the new medium of the vocal alphabet), in the poetic memory of the *Iliad*, except for assumedly later interpolations, there is no trace of consciousness and subjectivity. However, 'whenever a significant choice is to be made, a voice comes in telling people what to do. These voices are always and immediately obeyed. These voices are called gods. [...] I regard them as auditory hallucinations.'[68] This is sonicity of a non-scriptural kind, where vowels have not yet become single symbols in a finite alphabet but instead keep their full acoustic spectrum. The advent of the phonograph in 1877 thus undoes or re-modifies the apparent cut, which, in terms of the cultural *historical* approach, suggests that around three millennia ago modern consciousness came into being by separating people from ancestors who were equipped with a bicameral psyche subject to auditory hallucinations.[69] The media-archaeological approach instead assumes that with Edison's invention, all of a suddenly the bicameral psyche returns as a constant backdrop to our consciousness.

The sound of Sirens can be described as a mental impression, a penetrating sensation, a transmitted disturbance. Human ears as the channel of acoustic signal transmission and processing are always already caught within a double bind of both body and soul, physiology and mind. Human strategies to culturally digest a psycho-physiological experience such as the sound of Sirens – within the realm of uncertainty between actually physio-acoustic event and musical hallucination, between the noisy and the harmonic – can be narrative or non-narrative. The Siren sound is paradigmatic of what can be redefined as a media-cultural state of anthropological uncertainty: Humans can no longert be sure any more whether the sounds they are confronted with are organically or technologically produced. 'Technologies are artificial, but [...] artificiality is natural to humans.'[70]

The constellation of listening to Siren songs is metonymic of a further state of uncertainty: is such a sound meant to be communicative, is it directional (a signal) or rather a pure utterance (acoustic impulse)? How and when did the Siren sound become defined as lyrical rather than noisy? Located between the extreme borders of 'silence' on the one hand and 'noise' on the other, the sono-poetic trope of the sound of Sirens is difficult to define. In other words: is it acoustic, sonic, or musical? These are the three media-archaeological layers for analytic differentiation of sound as event: The acoustic denotes the physical event, the sonic is already technoculturally prefigured and the musical is semantically charged. The theorization of the Siren sound requires a differentiation between sound as acoustic event as opposed to sound symbolically coded as text. One must avoid, however, avoid falling into the trap of a binary opposition, which is anyway undermined by the fact that the transmission of the Homeric poems takes place not just in hexametric writings (an oral poetry memory technique) but in the vocal alphabet, which includes the musicality of human speech as represented and expressed in vowels.

What kind of s/Sirens are at stake? Modern ears, especially with acoustic memory of the Second World War, associate 'sirens' with acoustic warning devices against air raids, just like the working class associates 'siren' with the acoustic signal used to indicate various factory times (e.g. the beginning and end of a working day, and its breaks). Such a sound attacks the body in ways images cannot. Humans keep their eyes shut in order to avoid violent images, but their ears remain open unless somehow externally closed off. Penetrating that channel as real signal invasion,[71] sound addressing the body can be both seductive and dangerous. This is why the 'sirens' have been ambiguously coded from the beginning. Odysseus shelters his companions against the Sirenic seduction not in the visual regime (they can actually see them) but by filling their ears with wax. The Hollywood movie presenting Kirk Douglas as Odysseus does not actually show any Sirens; they are present rather as his acoustic hallucination of Penelope's voice, asking him to come home to the shore of Ithaca. According to Julian Jaynes, voices 'speak' only in bicameral minds; with phonetic writing the silenced voices became replaced by a system of demons. In pre-scriptural society the commanding voices of kings were hallucinated by subjects at their graves even after death. Eventually, vowels in the Greek alphabet replaced auditory hallucinations with symbolic articulation.[72]

From Sirens to PRISM: Surveillance and sonicity

Acoustic real-time surveillance takes place not just for monitoring deep ocean volcanoes or registering seismic waves.[73] The US Navy employed a net of hydrophones in the North Pacific, information that was only de-classified for academic research in 1991. This was a system of several hundred kilometres of submarine cables to which sound pressure measuring devices were attached. The SOSUS net (Sound Surveillance System) had primarily served to detect Soviet Union submarines.

The 'acoustic' (by sonification) re- or dis-places, deconstructs, or even rivals the visual ('panoptical') paradigm of surveillance. Therefore, it is necessary to supplement visual violence studies with acoustic research. The TROIA (Temporary Residence Of Intelligent Agents) project byof media artist Olaf Arndt researched non-lethal sonic weapons and attacks on privacy in public space that operate from hidden places and sources like 'Trojan' horses.[74] After all, it was an acoustic phenomenon that seduced Odysseus – Sirenic songs. When the panoptic landscape is replaced by a pan-acoustic one, all of a suddenly a soundscape is literally re-called; Homer's description of the Siren songs returns.

Read against the backdrop of directed sound, Homer's description of Odysseus confronted with the Sirens oscillates between sono-poetical and sono-political connotations. In Homer's *Odyssey* only the intervention of a demon, who calms the sea to complete silence, enables Odysseus to hear the Siren songs from distant shores. So-called 'demons' return, in sonic terms, as contemporary sound weapons: directed energy weapons (DEWs). 'Demons are weapons with strong directed energy output. The musical overtone of the vocabulary is not accidental.'[75] Sonic hallucinations are here produced by voice synthesis and morphing devices to replicate the voice of a known figure in order to deceive, produce false orders, or gain access.[76] Hypersonic spotlights are built on the fact that, psycho-acoustically, 'no one can escape from the inner voice, the acoustic hallucination has power over the hallucinating'; Arndt continues: 'Ultrasound spotlights which target messages and silently address people. The sound packet, whatever it contains, is only heard in the head of the target person, the skull bones play the role of a resonator, which changes the high frequency waves back into audible sound'[77] – demodulation, just like with radio waves.

In early July 2013, continental Europeans were shocked by revelations about PRISM, the American data communication surveillance and spying program. This elicited critical thoughts on sonicity with unforeseen undertones. The radio signal interception system started by NSA after the Second World War under the name ECHELON is known in German as '*Abhören*,' a term from the auditive field. It does not refer to immediate acoustic channels, such as those with which Athanasius Kircher once proposed to equip palace walls for spying on different rooms,[78] but to radio signal transmissions byof the former Soviet Union. These were to be intercepted by a net of radar stations. Within one of the spectacular spheres that were meant to shelter the actual radar antenna, nothing could be heard but peripheral sounds (like the cooling aggregate). The actual short wave radio signals first had to be demodulated and amplified by special radio receivers in order to be turned into audible articulations that could be decoded by human ears (using earphones). Apart from the connotations of dataveillance (which was known as signal surveillance in analog media days), the presence of sound in such spheres is sublime in Edmund Burke's sense, since one is aware of these sounds and at the same time cannot perceive them directly with human senses.[79] Such sublime vibrations give an idea of what is captured by the concept of sonicity: implicit sound, sound as an epistemic artifact. Sonic intelligence service might hurt our political ears.

Nowadays for such radio transmission, signals are coded in binary impulses. Pulse Code Modulation was developed first for the most secret system of high command telephony, SIGSALY, but the acoustic event here was not the actual telephone conversation (which was encoded in teletyping). Rather, it was the one-time pad consisting of twin records with completely noisy signals – the most secure random key for en- and decryption.

Did the digitization of radio transmission (as practiced almost universally today) actually 'silence' the traditional radio channels? The answer is no, but the audio- (or rather radio-)sphere of digital telecommunication has turned from the explicit to the implicit, from sound to sonicity. Specific detectors of electromagnetic waves (the sonic 'EM Sniffer') act as non-human archaeologists of such knowledge. Shintaro Miyazaki undertook a series of experiments in the sonification of what he termed 'algorhythmic' data processing. The rhythmic dimension of computing (based on its cycles) requires understanding beyond what can be textually expressed; therefore Miyazaki transposed the so-called *Daktylen* (a technical term well known from poetic prosody) in frequency- and time multiplexing of GSM mobile telephony into audible sound.[80]

6. Textual sonicity: Technologizing oral poetry

Re-discovering the sound of 'texts': Oral poetry
Though Florens Chladni was already experimenting with visualizations of acoustic wave figures in sand-covered plates created by the vibrations of the violin bow, 'Goethe's definition of literature did not even have to mention [...] acoustic data flows.'[1] The practices of oral tradition were silenced by the general textualization of the word and 'only survived in written format; that is, under pre-technological but literary conditions. However, since it has become possible to record the epics of the last Homeric bards, who until recently were wandering through Serbia and Croatia, oral mnemotechnics or cultures have become reconstructible in a completely different way.'[2] This difference is dramatic: a change from symbolic notation to signal recording. 'Even Homer's rosy-fingered Eos changes from a Goddess into a piece of chromium dioxide that was stored in the memory of the bard and could be combined with other pieces into whole epics.'[3]

Since Plato's dialogue *Phaedrus,* the media-critical argument repeats: the dead letters of alphabetic recording kill the living memory culture of oral poetry. Textualization is a threat to oral traditions. Is Milman Parry's theory of formulae-based oral poetry itself an effect of analyzing oral poetry in a transcribed and thus textual form? Aristotle gained his insight into the phonetic character of speech only after its visible elementarization by the phonetic alphabet. The alphabetization of phonographically recorded oral poetry in philological studies (Homer studies, Classics) papers over its essential nature: sound. In a somewhat oxymoronic and, at the same time, significantly honest way, the name given by Albert Lord to the impressive archive of recorded oral poetry from the former South Yugoslav countries at Harvard University is the Milman Parry Collection of Oral Literature. But media archaeology recognizes that there is no primary 'text', only recorded voices and sound – even if some of them were transcribed into literature and musical notation.

When the classicists Parry and Lord set off to the kingdom of Yugoslavia in 1934/35 to record epic songs on aluminium discs, their research was driven by the philological impulse to reconstruct the mechanism of Homeric oral poetry by analogy. Thus, the first thing to do after phonographic recording was to transcribe the song as a musical score and poetical text.

Is the relation between oral speech and its 'immortal' recording (starting from alphabetic writing up to the 'dictaphone' function in a smartphone

'app') a transitive one? This question was already posed in Plato's philosophical dialogue *Phaedrus*. Sound, by nature, is temporally transitive. Once
recorded in the analog or digital way, it loses its temporal essence as being-
toward-death. We are confronted with a dilemma when, for the purpose
of analysis, acoustic articulation has to be recorded, thus 'archived'; in the
transcription of audio recordings from former Yugoslav *guslari* songs, the
charme of oral poetry is destroyed by its very notation. The actual performance escaped academic cultural analysis until real-time signal capture
and analysis became possible. The signal-based recording of oral poetry
operates below textuality: subliminally in the neuro-physiological sense
and sublimely in the poetic sense. With signal recording and transmission,
memory in the age of electro-technical media involves more volatility than
ever known by so-called oral cultures (running contrary to the endurance
claim of printed letters). With Walter Ong's famous analysis, a kind of
'second mem/orality' recurs in a techno-temporal fold.

**Technically induced 'secondary orality': Textual dictation *versus* sound
recording**
The misunderstanding starts by mistaking oral poetry for literature. There
is nothing 'literal' in oral poetry, no letters, no alphabet. The message of
the medium is neuro-temporal (real-time poetics), not spatially literal.
The 'musical' aspect of oral poetry performances lies not in its harmonic
(melodic) but in its rhythmic aspect – the chronopoetic and time-critical
aspect of prosodic articulation.[4] With the Edison phonograph, the sound
of language could, for the first time, not only be recorded symbolically
(as withby the phonetic alphabet), but as a real audio signal. 'We can't
understand orality without consideration of sound', and the archaeology
of sound at stake here is 'closely connected to recording technologies that
simultaneously [...] shape our sensory experiences of oral poetry'.[5] In order
to subject (and open) cultural articulations like 'oral poetry' to academic
research, these speech and sound events first had to be symbolically or
technologically recorded and archived in order to slow them down for
careful and detailed analysis. Time axis manipulation ('slow motion')
is the *a priori*, the condition for scholarly analysis of such time-critical
processes as those Edmund Husserl called pro- and retention. In neu-
roscientific terms, these cover the three-second time span ('window of
presence') for a sung verse line (such as an ancient Homeric hexameter).

As explicitly stated by John Miles Foley, the songs collected by Parry and
Lord are grouped

in respect to the actual medium of performance [...]: *sung* texts, performed at customary speed (varying both by singer and within individual
song-texts) to the accompaniment of the *gusle*; *recited* texts, performed
without the instrument; and *dictated* texts, taken down in writing at a
much slower pace by an amanuensis.'[6]

Each of these 'media' sharply differs with respect to their temporal modalities. The situation of an oral poet asked to dictate a song for someone to write
down lacks the kind of servo-motoric feedback thatwhich is characteristic
of the 'musical' performance – revealing the (absent) function of the accompanying string instrument (the *gusle*):

> He is accustomed to composing rapidly to the accompaniment of a musi-
> cal instrument which sets the rhythms and tempo of his performance. For
> the first time he is without this rhythmic assistance, and at the beginning
> he finds it difficult to make his lines.'[7]

Even if he can adapt to this new situation, in terms of the temp/orality of
such performances, a time-critical difference remains at work as long as
the recording is not immediately operated by a phonographic machine;
the poetic mind moves ahead more rapidly than does the human writer's
pen. Because of their different temporal pace, the dictated texts tend to
reveal fewer deviations of all kinds; from such features Lord derived in
(ahistorical) analogy that the Homeric poems as we know them today must
have originally been dictated, probably by Homer himself.

Cultural memory of a different kind: Audio recordings of oral poetry
Inbetween the sonic spectrum and poetic spectres, epic songs in the
legacy of Milman Parry and Albert Lord cannot be reduced to philological
transcriptions, but encompass the audio-visual archive of recordings as
well. Cultural memory (notably oral poetry) is of a particular kind when
it is mechanically recorded by phonograph or gramophone. The latter is
– as its very name suggests – still close to graphical 'writing'. Electronic
recordings on magnetic wire or tape, as performed by Albert Lord on the
same grounds around 1950, are of a different order entirely. Apart from
being of a different technological essence, such recordings stimulate a
different mode of scientific analysis that is no longer simply philological or
musicological, but researches the sub-semantic poetic articulation on the
media-archaeological level (e.g. spectral analysis with electronic measuring
media). Such processes reveal evidence of a different (but still poetic?) kind.

With phonographic recording of the real voice, an irritation of the temporality of cultural memory took place. Challenging traditional notions of archival historicity, the recordability of oral poetry as a physical audio-event (not just symbolically as with the phonetic alphabet) engenders a kind of re-presentation of past performances. This eludes historiography by being invariant to historical time. Media-inherent temporality differs from the established notions of cultural history.

Let us muse about technologies of cultural feedback: What happens when such a recording is re-played today to the local Serbian culture using the same device? Are we (and the oral poets) in Lord's position when we record a contemporary *guslar* performance with a historic Webster Wire Recorder? Furthermore, is the digital processing of such recordings just another technical extension or does it transform the very essence of oral literature? In a crude way, algorithmic processing of poetic rhythms, as genuinely re-generative, might be closer to the 'formulaic' principle detected by Parry than any previous kind of technical reproduction.

The tradition of songs and tales for millennia occurred through mnemotechnics of oral transmission, increasingly accompanied (supplemented, deferred) by notational writing (the vocal alphabet, musical notes). When the twentieth century enabled a media-induced re-entry of orality, it was a derived orality based on analog recording technologies like phonography, magnetic tape, and cinematography. With its reappearance in the late twentieth century as alphanumeric code in computing, symbolic notation took revenge. The digitization of Parry and Lord's aluminium disc and wire spool audio-visual legacy makes a difference to the essence of its cultural content; Plato's primary 'media' critique of writing as an ambivalent memory technology is valid again. From this situation arises the 'archival' question: What happens to the genre of oral poetry when the one-line instrumentation (the *gusle* string) and the one-line recordings (literally Lord's wire spools) become accessible online? Is the media critique of writing as a recording device, articulated by Plato with respect to the ambivalence of technical memories, valid again?

Electromagnetic *versus* mechanical recording: What difference does it make to oral poetry?

Parry's mid-1930s investigations into the non-written memorizing techniques of South Yugoslavian epic singers (the *guslari*) were pursued as a living analogy to Homer's ancient songs. At this time, direct phonographic sound recording on aluminium discs (and its transcription into writing) was the technical condition that formed the analytic basis for the resulting formulaic theory of oral poetry (a theory that proposed that the hour-long oral tales were regenerated for each occasion from a stock of existing formulae). In 1950/51, Parry's assistant Albert Lord returned to the scene to repeat or continue some of the first recordings, sometimes with the same singers. But this time he used a new technology, a magnetic recording device (based on steel wire). What difference does it make if popular song recording no longer takes place gramophonically on aluminium discs but now electro-inductively *happens* on a magnetic medium? Mechanical recording remains a kind of visible graphical writing; recording in magnetic latency, on the other hand, requires a fully electrodynamic re-enactment to be reproduced.

Harold Rhodes developed an electric piano, a mechanism that in spite of its deficiencies led to a sonic aesthetics of its own. The keys strike tuning forks tightly coupled with a resonating tone-bar; the tone itself is picked up by a magnetic device. When Bill Evans used such an electric piano within his ensemble of traditional instrumentation, he declared it a supplementary device: 'No electric instrument can begin to compare with the quality and resources of a good acoustic instrument.'[8] Although in the age of Physical Modelling of acoustic instruments by digital simulation this notion might be debatable, there is a (probably involuntary) epistemological truth expressed here. Any 'e'-instrument electromagnetically transubstantiates (to make use of a term in Christian liturgy) the essence of sound from mechanical vibration into an essentially different, but physically analog form of existence – from explicit sound to implicit sonicity. The very possibility of such transducability is an indicator of an essential co-existence of physical and electronic oscillations that deserves to be declared. Digital sampling and quantizing waveforms into numerical bit values is no longer transduction, but rather a dis-continuous arithmetization with epistemological dimensions.

An electric wire recorder like the 'Webster Chicago' (fabricated in 1948 on thermionic tube basis) used by Lord is not a phonograph, which, as the name suggests, is still part of the tradition of graphical recordings. Instead, such a device transforms the sound memory into a different physical state. The process of electromagnetic recording and reproduction is, however, not a continuation of writing in a new form, but rather a fundamentally different and genuine technical media event born of the very nature of electricity. While phonographic recording (basically working without any electric current at all) somewhat self-referentially belongs to the world of mechanical pressures (the world of the ear), magnetic recording and its electromagnetic replay belongs to a different world of almost non-material elementary particles called electrons. Their behaviour is not only much more sensitive than mechanical cultural physics, but epistemologically demands a different language. This affects the terminology of 'sound' as well, which at first glance is subject to simply two different technologies of recording. While phonographic recording appropriately is explicit 'sound' recording, the magnetic latency of recorded audio signals exists in implicit 'sonicity'.

In September 2006, a Webster Wire Recorder turned up unexpectedly from the vaults of Berlin's Radio Art shop.[9] The device was technically identical to the one used by Albert Lord for his South Yugoslav recordings of oral poetry. I organized a spontaneous research trip to test what happens if such recordings are re-played to the local community on the original apparatus. An attempt was also made to record such songs on the same medium. With the kind assistance of a local Radio and TV station, at the far end of a road near Novi Pazar (now Serbia), an aged *guslar* actually took his dusty one-string *gusle* from the shelf and sang into my microphone.

At this point, let me add a personal supplement that momentarily suspends the media-archaeological 'distant' listening pursued throughout this text. When the singer Hamdo sang into the wire recorder microphone, accompanied by his *gusle*, a knee-held violin, he did not pay respect to the electronic recording device but looked directly into my eyes. I was overcome with a sudden and double astonishment. First, although this moment was one of a symbolic configuration, a combination of body, epic, and instrument, what I was seeing and hearing was not a sound-machine but rather the power of an individual in the state of poetry; a cultural performance that at this moment rose up above all symbolic and technical mechanism and – although a function of the latter – transcended them. At the same time, I was overcome by the impression induced by the almost surrealist proximity of the *gusle* and the wire recorder, and was struck by the mysterious correspondence between the string (horse-hair chord) being bowed and the recording wire made of steel. The most human aspect was expressed precisely in the playing of the instrument, and it was the wire recorder that recorded exactly this momentum: the circle of vibrations in technology and poetry was complete. Thus, the most human was simultaneously the most inhuman – precisely the coldest media-archaeological ear was listening to the most magical of all sound machines.

Technical recording *vs.* symbolic transcription
Even if the Greeks added vowels to the Phoenician alphabet for the explicit purpose of making the musicality of oral poetry (and thus Homer's epics) recordable, this notation is still symbolic – like the musical transcription

that Béla Bartók provided for Milman Parry's recordings of *guslari* songs. These discs also recorded a surplus: non-musical articulations such as birdsong in the background, or even a singer's coughing. Not just oral poetry was recorded but noise as well. However, the process of transcribing a sonic event into musical notation obliterates such acoustic events. The analysis of such transcriptions thus remains within the disciplinary discourse of philology.

Whereas the age of 'analog' electronic media involved passing beyond alphabetic textuality (in McLuhan's sense), ironically textuality reappears even more powerfully within technomathematical machines. A media-epistemologically different alphabet returns as a secondary writing: alphanumeric code, even if it is disguised as 'secondary orality' in mobile telephony. Parts of the audio records preserved in the Milman Parry Collection of Oral Literature have been digitized, and some of them can actually be accessed online – even if the most on(e)line element here is the *gusle* string. Different from the notational transcription of sound into musical scores, technical signal recording of cultural articulations allows for the electro-physical measuring of recorded events (digitally done by 'sampling'). This opens the cultural event to experimentation, enabling a non-hermeneutic analysis of cultural articulation on the sub-philological, even sub-alphabetic level.

Mathematically discovering subsemantic poetic articulation

The documentary records of Milman Parry and Albert Lord were transformed at the end of the twentieth century into digital files (both the textual and pictorial documentation of the Yugoslavian research journeys and some of the recorded *guslari* songs themselves). Does this digitization (by sampling) transform the essence of such a memory? And what is the new 'archive' to which such files online give access? The poetic event cannot be reduced to its semantic verbal and literal level. It makes a decisive media-archaeological (rather than philological) difference for the notion of 'oral poetry' when its notation for analysis takes place not in symbolic writing (whether alphabetic or music notational), but by signal recording media like Milman Parry's aluminium discs and phonograph. Micro-events in performing oral poetry might thus come under consideration: subtle discontinuous changes, probabilities of transitions, re- and protentions that require stochastic rather than simply statistical analysis.[10] The 'real-time' feedback on the sensomotoric level that takes place between the human articulation and the rhythmic *gusle* play turns out to be of a servo-mechanical rather than musical character. In poetic expression, human sensomotorics coupled with resonant instruments create a cybernetic organism of human and machine that is in between subliminal signal processing and arbitrary articulation. Can oral poetry therefore be re-generated by a machine? Can the *formulae* (as defined by Parry) be transformed by algorithms? Recall Claude Shannon: 'artificial languages [...] we merely define abstractly [as] a stochastic process which generates a sequence of symbols'[11] – which is exactly the definition Jacques Lacan gives to the mechanism of signifiers in the human unconscious.

Case study in sono-analytics: Milman Parry Collection of Oral Literature, Harvard University

In the course of their field research on the compositional mechanism of oral poetry in former South Yugoslavia, Parry and Lord collected around 3500 aluminium discs with recordings of epic songs by local *guslari* (as well as a series of literal transcriptions and conventional score notations). One of these compositions was over 12,000 lines long. 'What is a 'line' here? [...] The basic unit is the heroic decasyllable. The basic rhythm of this unit is – u – u – u – u – u. Parry and Lord applied what they learned about oral composition, that is, composition in performance, to the Homeric texts.'[12]

Below philological interpretation, an even closer reading of epic songs on the level of their actual physical articulations (signal analysis) reveals sensomotoric and cognitive processes that are performed by the singer in real-time, in the act of improvisation itself. Ironically, the most inhuman form of analysis of signals – registering minimal deviations of speed and intonation – gives access to individual poetry, part of a *culture* that is not reduced to a symbolic regime (as defined by Ernst Cassirer). 'Performance aspects enclosed in the recorded audio material are likely to bear valuable information, which is no longer contained in the transcription.'[13]

The techno-mathematical 'listening' of the computer leads to results about musical performance on the very level of their operative enactment: their micro-temporalities. To account for temporal variations, time warping techniques are applied to balance out the timing differences between the stanzas.[14] The second edition of Albert Lord's *The Singer of Tales* provides an additional CD with recordings of the songs transcribed or discussed in the printed text. Suddenly, a different analysis is possible, beyond reading, that addresses the sub-literal memory of an oral culture that is not any longer a gift of the Muses but of technological audio media.

But neither Parry, nor Lord were academically interested in the technical essence of their recording media.[15] In order to achieve publication in print, the songs needed to be transcribed from the phonograph records. As classic philologists, they transcribed the audio-signals as soon as possible into musical scores and alphabetic text lines, preparing them for interpretation. This resulted in a methodological asymmetry with the culture of oral tradition where there is no 'script' or other technology of writing required for composition-in-performance. Missing was a media-archaeological sensitivity for modes of audio-visual signal recording beyond (in a temporal sense of cultural history) or rather below (in the signal processing sense) the cultural technology called writing. One notable exception is Avdo Mededovic's early experiment in ethnographic audio-visual recording using sound film. Parry considered Mededovic the most talented of all the singers he worked with, and his attempt to re-experience lost Homeric performances is accessible today on the website of the Parry Collection at Harvard.[16] But since no *guslari* song is ever sung in the same way twice, even cinematographic recording renders a false illusion of presence. Recorded oral poetry misses its specific temporality. Sensually being absorbed by sound and vision when beholding such media-archival evidence, we tend to become trapped by the referential illusion, believing ourselves to be confronted by the original audio-visual event (even if both are slightly out of synchronization). But in fact, discrete bit-strings are being processed in the mode of online re-presencing – a sublime textuality of an alphanumeric data stream, operating on the subliminal level of our understanding. This is an unexpected technical return of what Gottfried Wilhelm Leibniz described as unconscious (*'nesciens'*) mathematical calculating in human *pétits perceptions* when listening to breaking waves at the sea shore.

> It has only been in the last few years that the science of electrical sound recording has given us an apparatus of such a sort that it can record songs of any length and in the large numbers needed before one can draw conclusions, and finally which can make recordings which are so good that the words on them can be accurately written down for the purpose of close study.[17]

Here, Parry confuses mechanical with electric recording. He operated with a mechanical voice recording device himself, the phonograph, which by its very name still refers to the tradition of writing. But when his assistant Albert Lord later applied a magnetic wire recorder, it was not simply a continuation of the same recording method with different technological means. Electromagnetic recording subliminally changes the nature of sound memory, from symbolical notation (writing) or mechanical engraving (phonography) to sonic latency, a field very different from writing.

Sound changes its substantial embodiment to *high fidelity* of a different kind, from sound to sonicity. The electromagnetic field as discovered by Michael Faraday and calculated by James Clerk Maxwell is no longer a traditional cultural artifact. It is now closer to the transient nature of sound itself, something that can only be grasped by mathematical vectors as an aggregation of particles or waves.

The Wire Recorder allows 'fairy electricity' (Lacan) to reign, resulting in different notions of sound and its analysis. Not only different musical cultures, but also sound recording technologies demand adequate interpretation. An adequate rendering of recorded sound signals is their oscillographic co-representation. But the recordings on aluminium discs, once transcribed, were subjected to traditional practices of library classification; as the transcription was carried out, a set of practical indices was devised to replace the rough log of text collected. These assigned a number to each item recorded in the field and also registered the name of the singer, plus the place and date of recording. The symbolic transcription resulted in separate indices: a master index of texts listed numerically, another index of singers with the songs, and an index of the first lines of the songs giving the text number of each version, the name of the singer, and the place of collection. The option of *content-based music retrieval* is an alternative against such logocentristic taxonomy – a technologically 'immanent' notation.

Frequency analysis: Popular music as technical memory
When sampled works from online sound archives can only passively be heard or accessed in transcriptions, the approach is not really media archaeological. Sonicity can only be analyzed by diving into the audio data themselves, by genuinely sound-based audio search and data navigation, resulting in truly techno-mathematical research. This is possible only with digitized, mathematizable signals. When measuring algorithms themselves become 'media archaeologists' of sound (producing spectrograms and other forms of data visualization), the traditional, almost ideological identification of music and mathematics (Pythagorean harmonics) transforms into a dynamic relation. A different kind of involuntary cultural semantics might arise from sonic data once analyzed in such a way. By applying measuring and algorithmic analysis of the recorded signals themselves, a passive archive or collection composed of silent listings of sound carriers can be turned into an active archive. Thereby techno-mathematical tools become 'archaeologists' of sounds past. Why not take the visible image of grooves in a vinyl record literally and analyze them as what they are: wave forms? They embody the *sono-real* (a neologism in the sense of Jacques Lacan)

insofar as this escapes all numerically countable quantization.[18] Once sonic articulation is phonographically recorded, its physical signal registered, measuring devices that are capable of indicating and analyzing vibrations and waves (the oscilloscope and spectral analysis) are able to capture the sonic event on its subsemantic, subcultural level – the realm of sonicity. Only technologies that respond to and resonate with the whole bandwidth of physical acoustics can also account for the noisy sound that interrupts the symbolic order of cultural music. Such devices recognize that the physically *real* corresponds with the contingent pauses and breath taking of an oral poet. However noisy such an acoustic signal is, it remains a function of a variable that can only be expressed in real numbers: time.

The Lomax impulse

An early corpus-based musicology project was developed at Princeton University in the 1960s. Arthur Mendel and Lewis Lockwood generated electronic scholarly editions of the complete works of Josquin, including concordances and relevant related works. From this, statistics for cadential progressions and modal indicators were compiled and subjected to statistical analysis in order to study issues of authorship and stemmatic filiation. However, as it aimed primarily at style analysis, this project never extended to revealing cognitive processes.[19] In folk music research, a more formal approach was developed that corresponds with folk music's tradition of primarily anonymous authorship. This approach involves using computers to extract song features, thus enabling the automatic classification of song melodies according to their musical characteristics. European folk melodies can then be sorted into homogeneous groups by employing Ward's classification algorithm, with essential features derived from the monophonic melodies.[20]

Alan Lomax recorded acoustic signals using mechanic and electronic devices in explicit opposition to 'notebook-orientated scholars.'[21] Lomax captured folk songs more precisely than possible with any of the symbolic score notation systems that had been developed to suit 'harmonic' occidental music. From that practice, Lomax derived the methodological impulse to analyze such sound recordings by electro-technical means – a media-archaeological excavation of latent sonic knowledge.[22]

> Today it may be possible with modern scientific measuring instruments such as the visible speech machine, the electro-myograph and other instruments, to describe the various types of vocalizing in precise scientific terms. […] there seems to be evidence that these unconscious but

culturally transmitted vocal patterns are direct evidence of deepening emotional conditions [...]. Thus, ethnomusicology may bring us close to deep-lying aesthetic forces which have been dynamic in all human history.[23]

Well-known technologies like the Edison phonograph can no longer be understood as the beginning of sound reproduction. Rather, they represent the climax of preceding tools for the analysis of speech, such as Léon Scott de Martinville's mechanical *Phonautographe*. This device fixed phonetic articulation as wave forms in the kymographic method that is proto-archival signal recording literally *avant la lettre*. The scientific application of oscillographic measuring media to phonographic sound recording is not an entirely new method of scientific analysis but a media-archaeological return to its early uses.

Part III
Techno-Sonicity and Its Beeing-In-Time

7. History or resonance?

Temp*aural* memory: Phonographic recall and sonic media temporality
Music lets us experience time. Culture tries to save sound from its ephemeral temporality in favour of cultural memory. The phonographic record as media artifact not only carries cultural meanings like words and music but is itself an archive of cultural engineering. In its very material fabrication, technological knowledge is waiting to be thawed and liquefied. Digital archaeology operates below the sensual thresholds of sight and sound – a level that is not directly accessible to human senses because of its sheer electronic and calculating speed. Synaesthetically, a spectrographic image of a recording provides a straight look into sonic memory. The microphysical close reading of sound, where the materiality of the recording medium itself becomes archivally poetical, dissolves any semantically meaningful unit into discrete blocks of signals to which philosophical or musicological hermeneutics cannot be applied. The media archaeologist suppresses the passion to hallucinate live presence when listening to recorded voices, such as happened to the dog Nipper when confronted with 'His Master's Voice' from a gramophone funnel (an image made famous by the HMV record company). Is it the affinity between the signal-recording phonograph and the musicality of the vocal-cantered Indo-European language that seduces the dog to hallucinate the presence of his human master?[1] In the original painting of that media-theatrical scene, the gramophonic apparatus is actually based on his master's corpse – his coffin.[2] While a dog does not perceive a photographic portrait of his late master as alive, in the case of the phonographic replay of his voice just such a perception occurs. For humans as well, the ear is the organ that is most time-critically sensitive to physical vibrations. To a large degree it is through sonic awareness that the human is addressed by the time-varying world.[3]

Whereas the cinematic and TV image is always perceived as framed and thus contained as a kind of quotation of reality, the acoustic signal is never minimized but addresses itself directly into the ear. The radio voice is not perceived as *representation* of the 'real' (physically present) voice but as identical with the human voice itself. Just like the 'disembodied' radio voice phenomenologically annihilates the spatial distance in live transmission,[4] the undoing of the culturally significant difference between life and death is the epistemic message of the phonographic voice – at the same time, it short cuts the 'historical' distance between presence and past. Ancient phonographic records need archival protection, for sure. But once Enrico Caruso's voice is articulated by replay from beyond the grave, it miraculously emanates against the material entropy of its technical embodiment in the shellac record.[5] Experiencing such a phonetic shining-through, human perception forgets about the artificiality of transmission; hermeneutic understanding that occurs through the hearing apparatus in fact improves the signal-to-noise ratio in communication engineering. Signal-based technologies of memory, addressing human perception on the affective rather than cognitive level, successfully *dissimulate* the archive.

The media-archaeological exercise is to be aware that at any technologically given moment of phonetic reproduction we are dealing with media, not humans; that we are not speaking with the dead, but that an apparatus is operating in an undead mode. Once in operation, technical media are always undead. Sound and music are amongst the most powerful operators and operations of generating presence. Music, by its very binary essence as sound art based on the presence or absence of physical vibrations, has the power to generate presence. Audio recording is able to store time as a mixture of frequencies in the acoustic realm; with the invention of the phonograph, men and women of the past remain ahistorically present. Their existence no longer needs to be written down and narrated exclusively. The dead can talk themselves. 'When I hear Kirsten Flagstad as Isolde [...] the voice of the opera legend is concretely present to my ears.'[6] At that point, media-archaeological knowledge conflicts with phenomenological sensation: 'The intellect tells me that the recording is 72 years old [...], but for my senses, she is with me in space, here and now.'[7] Different from movie projections from the past, in which light flashes are perceived by human eyes as immaterial electromagnetic waves, recorded sound mechanically resonates within the human ear. The temporal experience here is invasive, an almost violent *sonurgy*. If we listen to such a recording – the soprano's song *'Mild und leise wie er lächelt'* (the *Liebestod* motive from Act III of Richard Wagner's opera *Tristan und Isolde*), sung on 22nd May 1950 at the Royal Albert Hall in London, accompanied by the Philharmonic Orchestra and conducted by Wilhelm Furtwängler – there is a direct correlation between the human experience of musical temporality and sound-generating machines like the piano and the phonograph. The one is connected with discrete time (thus close to the symbolic score), the other catches the continuous acoustic signal. Until the electrification of the phonograph around 1925 the recording of harmony and melody was rather restricted by the limited bandwidth of the apparatus; recorded sound was therefore experienced in its temporal structure rather than by timbre.[8]

Research into past sonospheres has emerged as a new branch of cultural memory studies. The term *sonic environment* is commonly associated with industrial and other sources of noise.[9] Complementary to the social *history* of such sonospheres there is a need for an *archaeology* of sonic expressions. Technical sound is not just acoustic pressure on the ear or deriving aesthetic pleasure from musical sensation but addresses the human sense of temporality in unforeseen ways. The 'tuning of the world' (Schafer) is its *timing* as well. What looks physical (acoustic) is temporal in its subliminal affect. If the 'sonic environment' is also extended to so-called Hertzean waves as well, electromagnetism turns out becomes sublime in all ways.

The media-archaeological investigation of sonicity – electronically generated sound, and sound taken epistemologically as emanation of time – provides access to a plurality of temporalities, moving beyond the limitations posed by the historiographical reliance on alphabetic writing and below the threshold of narrative contextualization. So far, historiography has privileged the visible and readable archival records in full accordance with McLuhan's diagnosis of the *Gutenberg Galaxy* as being dominated by visual knowledge. But since Edison's phonograph, sound, noise, and voices can be technically recorded and thus memorized. The phonograph (respectively Emil Berliner's gramophone) registers a whole range of acoustic events. Whereas in discrete musical notation (in analogy to the alphabet) a symbolic registering of music takes place, the phonograph records the physically real signal. The alphabetic symbolism reduces acoustic events to the 'musical' harmonic order, whereas the register of the real encompasses the sonic. The latter includes noise and a-rhythmical temporal phase shifting, such as swing. This generates an *anarchive* of sound in technological storage (through the infolding of sonic signals) that opposes the archival order of musical notation.

The presence-generating power of technically recorded voices differs fundamentally from the imagination of speech by letters in the vocal alphabet, which is *grámma*-phonic only *avant la lettre*. 'The true message of the phonetic alphabet as a cultural technique is its desire to achieve an indexical relationship to the sonic materiality of the voice, but this outstrips the capabilities of symbolic notation. The phantasm is only realized by genuine signal recording technology, the phonograph.'[10]Suddenly, we are carried into Walter Benjamin's media theoretical territory. Benjamin notes that every historic era 'shows critical epochs in which a certain art form aspires to effects which could be fully obtained only with a changed technical standard.'[11] In order to convince the audience of the sonic fidelity of phonographic recording, the Edison Company in 1916 arranged for a

media-theatrical setting by placing a mahogany phonograph on the stage
of the New York Carnegie Hall:

> In the midst of the hushed silence a white-gloved man emerged from
> the mysterious region behind the draperies, solemnly placed a record
> in the gaping mouth of the machine, wound it up and vanished. Then
> Mme. Rappold stepped forward, and leaning one arm affectionately on
> the phonograph began to sing an air from 'Tosca'. The phonograph also
> began to sing 'Vissi d' Arte, Vissi d'Amore' at the top of its mechanical
> lungs, with exactly the same accent and intonation, even stopping to take
> a breath in unison with the *prima donna*. Occasionally the singer would
> stop and the phonograph carried on the air alone. When the mechanical
> voice ended Mme. Rappold sang. The fascination for the audience lay
> in guessing whether Mme. Rappold or the phonograph was at work, or
> whether they were singing together.[12]

A similar staging of human vocal performance *versus* apparative acoustic
operativity was discussed in the pages of the *Boston Journal* from the same
year: 'It was actually impossible to distinguish the singer's living voice from
its re-creation in the instrument.'[13] The Sirenic effect of the phonographic
voice is the illusion of presence induced by signal recording. Once sound
can be recorded, humans can listen to voices of the dead. This has since
been a shock to logocentric occidental culture; logocentrism is no longer
metaphysics but has become actual physical signal recording. This technologically induced trauma has not been epistemologically digested yet – even
if listening to recorded voices and music has become an everyday custom
of media consumption.

Re-accessing transient articulations
In previous centuries, sonic articulation belonged to the most *transitive*
cultural phenomena, as expressed by the saxophone player Eric Dolphy:
'When you hear music, after it's over, it's gone, in the air. You can never
capture it again.'[14] The recall of such listening experience depended on
actual (and thus always unique) bodily re-enactment; thus, the 'sound' of
tradition was in the ahistoric momentum of sonic experience. *Listening*
to modern history is a welcome widening of the scope of source material
of modernity, from writing and visual evidence to past sonospheres. Such
was the aim of the *World Soundscape Project* of Raymond Murray Schafer
and other initiatives to 'archive' the sound of modern life. Still, the fram-
ing of this extension remains within historical discourse in its (literally)

con*textualizing* gesture. But 'discourse analysis cannot be applied to sound archives or towers of film rolls.'[15] There is another, rather ahistorical type of sound and noise source – which is close to what humanities and classical studies have long known as the archaeological object. Karen Bijsterveld reminds of such limits to historiography:

> Hearing the cracks and noises of a phonograph recording may initially enlighten their historical status as 'mechanical' instruments. Yet, the very same sounds complicate our understanding of the 'tone tests' of the early twentieth century in which audiences were unable to hear the difference between performers and records playing [...]. Thus, if we take seriously the historicity of perception, [...] recordings are a far less informative or a much more complex source [...].[16]

In terms of communication engineering, such cracks belong to the kind of 'noise' introduced in the channel of transmission, which here is temporal decay.[17] Media-archaeological listening to the *sonic* past pays more attention to such techno-acoustical signifiers than to the musical signified. Both levels are interlaced; the culturally semantic content of a medium, according to McLuhan, can never be separated from the message of the medium itself. Let us, therefore, extend the sonic understanding of the past to media-archaeological hermeneutics. At first it looks as if past modes of listening – which vary with cultural history – can only be reconstructed by written descriptions. On the other hand, both past and present ears can be coupled to the same media mechanisms – be it Pythagoras's ancient monochord, or the Edison phonograph. The term *sonics* is appropriate for acoustic or musical experience that depends on the technological apparatus (in parallel to terms like electronics). Exactly because sonics is non-human itself, it allows for a non-historical immediacy as an equitemporal situation and position. The media-archaeological hypothesis is that the human auditory apparatus is induced to obey laws imposed by the media device; historicity therefore is suspended by technology. This implies a non-trivial challenge: Can ephemeral sound in its transitive being be caught by historiography at all? Only by reconstructing the 'akroamatic dispositive'[18] as sonic version of the Heideggerean *Gestell* can the epistogenic audiospheres be literally re-presenced.

The *a priori* of the sonic time machine: Listening to the monochord
Is it the happy alliance between musical and mathematical notation within the same alphabet, achieved in ancient Greece, to which our present

alphanumeric code recursively returns?[19] It was, after all, with the mathematical calculation of harmonic sound ratios that the mechanization of
music started, culminating in the Euclidean algorithm (the *sectio canonis*) as
division of the monochord string. The one-string Pythagorean monochord in
fact is a sonic time machine – not for time travelling in the traditional sense,
but rather for tunnelling the apparent cultural-historical distances between
modern times and antiquity, West and East.[20] If we consider the monochord
not simply as an ancient device for Greek knowledge about harmonies
but as an operative medium, it serves to demonstrate an approach that is
surprisingly invariant toward historical change; that is, it demonstrates the
mathematical principles enabled by such simple techniques:

> They short-circuit from their time to ours, *establishing an operational link.*
> Whenever we listen to or play the monochord, we also share at least a bit
> of that past world that is actually not past but non-linearly 'here'. This
> could be seen as a sort of a re-presencing of the past, as Vivian Sobchak
> has argued.[21]

This entanglement between the time domain and the frequency domain,
between analog vibrations and discrete numbers, is the essence of the
sonic time machine that is physical and symbolic at the same time: GO
TO *algorhythmics*. This entanglement between the time domain and the
frequency domain, between analog vibrations and discrete numbers, is the
essence of the sonic time machine that is physical and symbolic at the same
time: GO TO *algorhythmics*. We discover that sonicity is already within
machines. One of the designers of the present day simulator of the archaic
British EDSAC electronic computer (for museological re-enactment) draws
an explicit 'analogy between a computer program and a musical score – once
described as 'frozen music' needing only an orchestra to melt it.'[22] This is
no metaphor. The operations of this Electronic Delay Storage Automatic
Calculator were based on a set of acoustic mercury delay lines – a serial
access memory that (different from the Random Access Memory well known
today) demanded time-critical programming since it necessarily had to pay
respect to the cyclic, ultra-sonic rhythm intermediary storage of data words.

Symbolically encoded information is different from purely material
(archaeological) relics from the cultural past that are subject to physical
erasure and entropy. Symbolically encoded information – which is the
essence of digital computers and has been the cultural technique of preserving musical information despite the evanescence of acoustic articulation
– can instead be almost time-invariantly transmitted to posterity. As with

every operative digital computer, there is implicit music (sonicity) in the functional diagram of the EDSAC. 'Consequently, the EDSAC simulator is textual rather than artifactual in spirit. [...] However, as with musical scholarship, this textual approach permits the informed and explicit filling in of lost textual fragments where this will produce a richer experience for the user.'[23] Thus starts a real media philology.

The best method for understanding a medium is through re-engineering and functional (re-)enactment. Charles Sanders Peirce describes diagrammatic reasoning as such: '[...] similar experiments performed upon any diagram constructed to the same precept would have the same results [...].'[24] When we re-enact Pythagoras's sixth century B.C. experiment with the monochord today[25] – that is, when we pull such a string – we actually share the techno-physical insight of the relation between integer numbers and harmonic musical intervals that once led the Greek philosopher to muse about the mathematical beauty of cosmic order in general (including the rejected experience and fear of deviation of this aesthetic ideology resulting in the 'Pythagorean comma, i.e.: irrational number relations). We are certainly not in the same historical situation as Pythagoras. Our circumstances, even our ways of listening and the psycho-physical tuning of our ears, are different. But the monochord is a time-machine because it lets us share and participate in the original discovery of musicological knowledge, since – in an almost Heideggerean sense – the repeatable *is* the original.[26]

In the Italian *re-naissance* of knowledge from antiquity, Vincenzo Galilei undertook a number of experiments with a lute to investigate the nature of musical harmonics[27] – a kind of media-based archaeology of the acoustic: 'Galilei employed the lute here not as a musical instrument but as a piece of laboratory equipment [...].' Scientific experimentation with sonic artiefacts (different from subjective intonation in musical play) should be almost identically repeatable. On the diagrammatic level, the re-enactment is time-invariant; on the operative level of implementation, the materiality of the medium itself seems to impose certain vetoes rooted in the historicity of the instrument. However, the epistemological operation remains intact in principle (*archaeo*logically):

I [...] set out to replicate this experiment using a lute built in the 17th century by an unknown maker [...]. The present condition of the instrument required the use of some substitutions for the materials originally used by Galilei in his experiment; however, these did not affect the basic tenets of the experiment.[28]

Once their senses are coupled with technological settings (media settings), humans are within an autopoietic temporal field, a chrono-regime with its own dynamics (or mathematics, when data are registered digitally). Such couplings create moments of literal exception: humans are taken out of the human-made cultural world (Giambattista Vico's definition of 'history') and confront naked physics.[29]

On the one hand, in phenomenology the 'event' is a singular and instant act that cannot be subsumed under general terms. On the other hand, in Martin Heidegger's late philosophical work, the fundamental notions of *being* and *time* converge in the notion of the *event*.[30] In this double sense, the experiment allows for a unique experience and, at the same time, for communication across the temporal gap, bridging a temporal distance. In the processual moment of the re-enacted experiment, we share the same temporal *field* – a notion that explicitly refers to the micro-temporal figures of electromagnetism. The analysis of such experimentation can be extended to macro-temporal eventuality as well. At first glance, experimentation does not give access to historic knowledge, since past events can not be exactly re-enacted (except perhaps in experimental archaeology). This is the argument of historians usually applied to differentiate their hermeneutic discipline from the natural sciences. Hermann von Helmholtz, at the peak of historicism in Germany, declared that it is impossible to truly re-enact the experience made with a musical experiment in the past, since the successive layers of tuning our ears blinds this immediate access; therefore we are dependent on historical information.[31] But media-archaeological experimentation (simulation as opposed to historiographic historicism) gives access to the invariant elements of knowledge in time. Such time tunnelling brings us back to Pythagoras's monochord and ancient music.[32] The re-performance of electronic music is a technological equivalent to the re-enactment of Pythagoras's supposed experiment with the mechanical monochord string.

Re-enactment of electronic music

Sound technically emanating from a vintage Edison phonograph cylinder contains physical traces of sound recorded in the past for time-delayed replay. In contrast, a Nintendo *Game and Watch* handheld electronic game from 1981 keeps its contemporary sound as implicit information: 'Its electronic circuitry, its ICs and its loudspeaker enable us to experiment analytically, recreating the same auditive events that the device would have produced when it was first sold.'[33] Such regenerated techno-logical sound differs from simply transductive replay; the device itself allows for an

equiprimordial experience. This makes it media-archaeologically imperative to work with the original (and not just emulated) hardware versions
of the electronic devices.

While sound and speech from past analog and digital storage media up
to Compact Discs have become a growing concern of archival institutions,
'the same cannot be said about obsolete computer programs and electronic
hardware which have become a challenge of conservation.'[34] Simon Emmerson's piece *Spirit of '76* (1976) serves as an example: 'A reel tape machine
is used to create an accelerating tape delay. This effect is realized by letting
one of the two reel tape machines drag an empty tape spool around the
performance floor. Although the sonic effect of the delay can easily be
reproduced with digital means, the theatrical effect or the sliding spool gets
lost.'[35] Just as with the case of musical transcription of epic songs, the score
of such an acoustic event does not tell it all. Even sound or video recording
do not suffice for documentation purposes. In order to reinterpret the same
electroacoustic composition for live performance, a recorded document of
its first performance is both insufficient and inadequate; the recreation of
such a work requires a co-originary approach that is rooted in its proper
technology.[36] Data archaeology, musicological knowledge, as well as direct
technical knowledge of studio equipment and sound engineering is required
in order to re-enact electronic music from the past – either by using old hard-
and software, or by emulating old machines on new computers, and finally
by re-writing the composition with new code. But a patch for Max/MSP
for example can easily have dozens of sub-patches; 'in order to recode the
patch it first must be disassembled and its structure understood' (Berweck).

Off history: Sonic *Eigenzeit* (Heraclitus, Stern)
The analysis of contemporary media culture corresponds with the pre-
Socratic age when it comes to describing virtual, technomathematically
calculated tempor(e)alities. In one of his surviving fragments, Heraclitus
declares that humans, when awake, share one world. While asleep, each
individual moves within his or her proper, self-referential, auto-poietic
world.[37] With the term *ídios kósmos,* Heraclitus correlates the notion of
'*Eigenzeit*' (which might be called *ídios chrónos*). While awake (in cognition
and consciousness) we belong to the world of history, while in the sonic
situation we live in temporal tides (*Gezeiten*). There are idiosyncratic temporal heterochronies of 'proper time' (*Eigenzeit*); one of its most powerful
manifestations is musical articulation.

Only with the emergence of an emphatic philosophy of history in the
age of Enlightenment is musical experience subjected to the order of linear

and progressive time; *before* 'music was simply "in time," it "took time," its successive events had to be somehow arranged one after the other, but the distinction between past and future, between "earlier" and "later," did not much matter to the way it was experienced and understood.'[38] But caution, this *before* risks re-affirming the historiographical master-narrative of the time arrow itself; it should rather be understood as a structural alternative that is re-called by technological media. With phonographic recording sound immediately becomes inscribed into a non-historical, non-human, signal-based archive of a new kind. This archive requires a temporal motion itself (like the turning disc) in order to become re-presenced, de-coupling the past from history:

> The concept of linear, historical time is denied, if not actually eliminated, by the electroacoustic media. If a particular sound can be preserved and embedded within that originating from any other time, the concept of a linear flow of time becomes an anachronism.[39]

Twentieth-century technologies of mechanical reproduction allowed for the suspense of time's pure linearity:

> While a time of modernism exists on the historical timeline, do we have a 'modernism of time' that accounts for the temporal zigzags? What exactly did time mean in the decade that witnessed the distance-defying velocity of Lindbergh's transatlantic flight, the first radio broadcasts, and an increasing addiction to Edison's Duplex Telegraph wire?[40]

Günther Stern, in his unpublished and unachieved habilitation thesis *Philoso-phische Untersuchungen über musikalische Situationen*, differentiates musical Eigenzeit from other temporal 'enclaves' like sleep and shock.[41] It is this being-of-history that correlates operative media time with sonic temporality.[42]

To question the historicity of sound, an archaeology rather than a history of sound is required since To question the historicity of sound, an archaeol-ogy rather than a history of sound is required since, in an archaeology, temporal relations cease to be historiographically linear. In many respects sound – heard, recorded, or transmitted – is radically ahistorical. Serious engagement with the sonic – sound as sound and sound as time – opens up access to a plurality of non-narrative temporalities. When the music band continued playing on deck while the Ocean liner Titanic sank in April 1912, this was not just a katechontic act, a deferral of the end, but the transfer of the listener into another temporal reality.

Stern's phenomenology of such musical temporality resonates with a theory of media time. Since the emergence of signal recording devices like Léon Scott's Phonautograph or Edison's Phonograph, an acoustic event can be re-played invariantly in relation to historical change. Time-based signal processing media share with musical performances the power of generating an affect of presence[43] – while at the same time deconstructing the transitive experience of time by the repeatability of any acoustic record. Sonic temporality thus turns into technical sonicity, just as cinematography (as formal measurement and mechanical analysis) objectified visual live movement through a technical trick.[44]

R. G. Collingwood's notorious claim that historians have to re-enact the past event derives partly from his astonishment that a present performance of a musical piece composed at some earlier time can still be understood at all. Different from historical imagination in its visual sense, '[T]he *sine qua non* of writing the history of past music is to have this past music re-enacted in the present.'[45] This practice of re-presencing (well known in its technological equivalent in contemporary Retro Computing culture's hardware and software replication and emulation) escalated in audio recording media such as the phonograph. A gramophone disc, according to Stern,[46] does not reveal an acoustic image of the *Mondscheinsonate*, but the *Mondscheinsonate* itself – just like the radio does not reproduce speech and music, but actually performs them via signal transduction. To rephrase it in the words of Stern's contemporary Walter Benjamin, the rehearsal of a musical piece from the past transcends its unique historical context by a kind of 'temporal index by which it is referred to redemption.'[47] The 'phonographic situation' (a term coined in accordance with Stern) is a temporal ecstasy, 'off' historical time. What the transposer does to pitches and voices, the phonograph does to acoustic time.[48]

Resonant past: Listening to music as a non-historic form of being-in-time

The temporal relation between presence and past in sonic spheres ceases to be a historiographically linear one and is shaped according to the dynamics of resonance (technologically materialized in the electromagnetic resonance circuit). Sonic situations serve to synchronize the individual with its surroundings: 'From a biological point of view, the function of our sense of time is to tune our behaviour to the environment.'[49] Being tuned in the right temporal mode leads to a different kind of communication with the past – as resonance.[50] Musical tradition is not accumulative but rather resonant. Resonance is a non-linear form of instantaneous energy transfer (Nikola Tesla's vision).

The online accessibility of sonic data in the World Wide Web seems to transform any sonic memory into a memory of the present; or rather: the past becomes a simple extension of the present (analogous to the 'working memory' within the human brain). Still, musical *Eigenzeit* cannot be completely dissolved into historical contextuality. A Baroque fugue is part of the musical rhetoric of its time; at the same time, it is 'absolute music' in its very form of chrono-mathematical temporality.[51] Operative signifiers thereby gain supremacy over the traditional despotic denominator of 'deep time'.

In his opera *Prometeo,* Luigi Nono explicitly refers back to Venetian multi-chorality – which unintentionally anticipated Fourier analysis of composite sound. Sound memory itself might be a synthesis of such tunings. It is an unconscious sonic memory that is activated by Nono's way of evoking (rather than 'quoting') past music.[52] Such musical recalls and recitations are not subject to historical semantics. Nowadays in Hip Hop music a sample can always be recognized in its source, whereas Techno neutralizes the sound bit or dissimulates its source. Hip Hop is 'historicizing' in that sense,[53] while Techno is temporalizing: de-centring the hearing (and dancing) subject by its microrhythms.

There is a remarkable affinity between sonic temporality and operative media time. The 'telephonic' transducability of a sound wave from acoustic to electrical form reveals the essential sonicity that pervades both regimes: the correspondence between a continuous change in pressure and a continuously changing voltage.[54] A further affinity exists between the ahistoric *momentum* of experiencing time in listening to music (affective temporality) and in operative presence-generating devices on the level of chrono-phenomenological *aisthesis*. At stake is not merely an extension of the current understanding of music of the past and of music *within* socio- or cultural-historical time, both of which still remain within historical discourse. Let us rather step out of that discourse for a moment in order to (re-)vitalize alternative strands of thought that have remained latent, such as Stern's. The 'musical situation,' Stern argues, sets the human listener outside his or her biographical lifetime and momentary biological state of existence. Musical existence is ahistorical. Being-in-music is a temporal suspension, the *epoché* of a different temporality. When listening to music 'one falls out of the world'; 'one is somehow somewhere'; nonetheless, 'even in this hiatus, one remains in the medium of time.'[55] While historiographical and biographical time are not repeatable, musical performance is repetition in a literal sense, retaining its temporal shape. In the performance of a piece of music, its inner temporal unfolding is re-enacted.[56]

Music oscillates between its irreducible cultural historicity and its ahistoricity as mathematical aesthetics. As long as music – conceived as theoretical creation beyond its contingent sonic implementation – is strictly coupled to mathematical knowledge, its temporality claims metahistorical invariance. Martin Heidegger, in his lecture on logic at the University of Freiburg in summer 1934, emphasized that numbers remain invariant against the passage of historical time, which links to the anamnestic argument in Plato's dialogue *Menon* on diagrammatical reasoning.[57] As Kittler titles a sub-section in his unfinished monograph *Roma aeterna: Return as recursion.*[58]

In a telegram style note, Harold Innis once remarked: 'Music [is] not the universal medium generally supposed – rather an index of a civilization – Spengler noted shift from unison to counterpoint as significant in west [...] – 22 notes of Indian music – 5 of Chinese – incomprehensible to west.'[59] Even if, according to Stern's theory, musical listening is a fundamentally ahistorical experience, the cultural tuning of the ears (its sonicity) is subject to cultural change: 'Musical listening has its irreversible history, even if the purely physiological act of listening as such may have remained invariable at all times.'[60] *The Science of Musical Sound* (John R. Pierce), however, media-archaeologically listens to the physics of sound and focuses exactly on the physiological level that technologically correlates with electronic media.

Chronological *tempus* and musical temperament may even interfere in an ahistorical retuning of the past. In a double meaning of *temperament* as timing, electronic tuning allows for anachronistic changes in a piano's tuning – both in its micro- and macro-temporal sense. Modern pianos are usually tuned in so-called equal temperament by the division of each octave into twelve equal half-steps. Thereby and therefore the frequency of a note is adjusted up- or downwards, 'sacrificing some harmony in all keys so none are too dissonant.'[61] Different from that modernist practice, many tunings in times past elected for extremely pure intervals in some keys at the expense of others, which were exposed to increased dissonance. Johann Sebastian Bach's notorious *Well-Tempered Piano* pieces gave rise to a tuning scheme that allowed keyboardists to play them all without retuning the instrument. Equal temperament (and its escalation into microtonal systems) is now universally applied, but this compromise sacrifices the literal *understanding* in past musicality of sonic difference. 'Historic temperaments are essential to unlock the emotional charge of earlier music.'[62] In spite of their analog voltage-controlled variability, even electronic synthesizers have thus far been subject to equal tuning. It is only by taking key frequencies at their numerical face value that digital real-time signal processing allows for dynamic tuning; such an organ can re-enact obsolete past tuning systems without physical manipulation – a sonic time machine. The most contemporary digital device here acts as archaeologist of the acoustic – a non-historicist subversion of the distance between present and past sound cultures. The conjunction of musical (symbolical) algorithm and media-technological (physically real) time operation enacts sonicity.

Signal-based reproduction of sound
When listening to musical articulations, humans are locked in a double bind between the historic and the ahistoric sensation, between cognitive understanding and affective listening. Thereby it is possible to experience sonic artifacts from the past both in their difference to the present *and* as presence.[63] The 'musical situation,' as defined in Stern's planned habilitation thesis, is characterized by its very mediality (*Medialität*): contrary to Heidegger's existentialism (*In-der-Welt-sein*) it means a specific not-being-in-the-world (*spezifisches Nicht-in-der-Welt-sein*).[64] 'Being in music [...] is conceivable only as an 'enclave'.[65]

Material entropy versus symbolic endurance of sound recording
With phonetic writing, arbitrary acoustic articulations such as speech, singing, and oral poetry, become symbolically recordable and alphabetically coded for space- and time-independent re-performance (decoding).

The 'archival' permanence of recorded sound signals is almost time-invariant within the interval of a few human generations, sublated from change with time ('absconding from history,' as expressed by Rainer Bayreuther), leading to ahistorical immediacy in the moment of re-play. Bartók, referring to Milman Parry's phonographic recordings of oral poetry (and the corresponding transcriptions into symbolic musical score), commented in a surprisingly optimistic way on the chances of sonic memory in the age of reproducible media recordings:

> The records are mechanically fairly good [...]. Aluminium disks were used; this material is very durable so that one may play back the records heaven knows how often, without the slightest deterioration. Sometimes the tracks are too shallow, but copies can be made in almost limitless numbers.[66]

But the evidence of the physical reality of such storage devices over time is that they are increasingly subject to macro-temporal entropy such as the material deterioration of Edison cylinders or magnetic tapes. Digitized signals at first sight represent the return of traditional music notation (the score), but this time the symbols ('bits') are endowed with operational activity; they are algorithmically executable.

Symbol-based invariance

Music as theory belonged to mathematics in the medieval *quadrivium*. Mathematics, like astronomy and geometry, claims meta-historical validity. Whereas ancient Greek music *theory* was influential for the European Renaissance through its written tradition, actual Greek musical practice was not influential or even renewed in the Renaissance due to lack of knowledge: very little ancient music has been notated for tradition.[67] Signal-induced ahistoricity (coming from the phonograph) refers to the materiality of music, its actual physical sound. As to the conceptual part of music, the composition, another invariance comes into play: the ahistorical symbolic regime. Whereas poetry works just as well when read (even silently) – recall the success of the phonetic alphabetic recording of Homer's epics – a musical score to a much higher degree depends on its actual sonic realization in physical sound bodies.[68] Similarly, algorithms become operative only when implemented in matter, being in the world (and thus in time). Music in its epistemological sense – conceived as a 'harmonic' concept since ancient Greek *music-as-theory* – belongs primarily to the symbolical order (notation/concept). As such, music is invariant against entropic time, and is different from the incorporated sound whose physicality is time-bound (the 'real').

Rescuing the ephemerality of sonic articulation from time: Symbolic notation, signal recording, and a sense of ending

Does symbolic notation of sonic articulation lead to invariance against historic, i.e. entropic temporality? *'Soni pereant, quia scribi non possunt.'*[69] In fact, musical notation 'saves' music from the contingencies of historical time, while sonic articulation is, by definition, ephemeral, time-based, and self-annihilating. According to Leonardo da Vinci's *Trattato di pittura,* painting and sculpture are 'permanente,' while music 'sie va consumando mentre ch'ella nasce.'[70]

While Guido from Arezzo's notation of musical duration allowed for symbolically fixing sonic articulation, the phonograph does it in physical reality. But the event of phonographic recording is not limited to the intentionally recorded signals. There is another entanglement of technical recording and articulation: The recording device (phonograph) has mechanical utterances, the noise of the apparatus, which somehow resembles the consonants of human speech. Musicality resides in periodic vowels; non-periodic mechanical noise is the other side of sonicity.

Listening to a vintage phonographic record, *the audible past* (Jonathan Sterne) is frequently associated with the noise of the recording device (the scratches and grooves of the wax cylinder) rather than the recorded voice or music. In this way, the medium talks both on the level of enunciation and of reference. The cultural content (such as recorded songs) does not hide the medium's message but co-articulates it as limitations in vocal bandwidth. If a close analysis of recorded sound is not limited to the signal but also extends to the sound recording hardware, technological items like electromagnetic pick-ups come into focus as media-archaeological conditions of the sound archive itself.[71] The tempor(e)ality of 'history' microphysically corresponds with the entropic deterioration of the magnetic charge and chemical carrier of the magnetic tape *versus* symbolic, i.e. almost time-invariant coding. To what extent is an archival sound record suspended from historical, entropic time? The traditional endurance of sound records, based on the materiality of their storage media, changes. It becomes the 'enduring ephemeral' (Wendy Chun) when the record unfolds electronically; signal flow (the dynamic essence of electric current) and algorithmic data migration replace the fixed inscription.

'Musical situations' (G. Stern) and technical media essentially share the definition that both come into being only in the process of performance. Since the temporal experience of listening to music is as inner co-performance,[72] its privileged alliance with technical media resides in the common quality of temporal action.[73] At the same time, in listening to music the listener is always aware that the piece, the performance, will end. Once the pick-up of the record player is put onto the vinyl groove, the spiral itself pre-emptively indicates the beginning of its own end. Any sonic articulation has an in-built sense of ending even with un-damped oscillators that are subject to limited energy supply.

Günther Stern's 1927 publication of 'The Phenomenology of Listening' coincided with the publication of Martin Heidegger's *Sein und Zeit*, thus compensating for Heidegger's silence on music.[74] In fact, the notion of attention (*Aufmerksamkeit*) has been primarily oriented toward the model of vision.[75] Marshall McLuhan gave a media-archaeological explanation for this supremacy of the optical sense. With the emergence of the phonetic alphabet the ears from oral culture became deaf in favour of visual recording and transmission of knowledge.[76]

The attention to silence leads to reflection on the relation of time, historicity, and sound in a more fundamental sense. Archival 'understanding' (of the past) is not just a cognitive operation of the mind triggered by reading *via* the optical channel; listening to the past is of a different chrono-epistemological quality. Within humans, the act of listening activates the temporal rather than spatio-visual sense.[77]

The (a)historicity of musical articulation and listening (Riemann)

Since the emergence of scientific acoustics – anticipated by Archytas of Taras in South Italy with the name of *aisthesis* (physiological rather than cognitive perception) and explicitly declared by Ernst Florens Chladni's *Die Akustik* in 1802 – the physical science of sound and the cultural notion of harmonic relations drifted apart. It was Hermann von Helmholtz who then insisted on their interlacing.[78] But in the world of harmonic scales, natural laws and cultural historicism only asymptotically converge. A further indication of the incommensurability of musicological historicism and physical acoustics is Hugo Riemann's search for the (positively impossible) 'undertone.' This project attempted to deploy the prestige of the natural science approach to knowledge (at the same time ignoring its contradicting results): the assumption of ahistorical, time-invariant laws, in an effort to translate this into aesthetic experience. A similar Kantian *Widerstreit* between natural-physical atemporality and irreducible historical indexical-ity takes place with technological media like sound recording. Musical understanding in its mixture of physiological and hermeneutic procedures merges both areas. Any meta-historical approach to the ordering principles of tonal music is deconstructed by the materiality of the sonic event which is contingently embedded in techno-cultural time.[79]

Musical listening for Riemann is primarily 'logical activity,'[80] a mental process; thus, a rather cognitive impression of tones, different from the merely physiological sensation of sound as physical event. From the vantage point of a neo-Platonic concept of music, both symbolic music notation and its concrete acoustic implementation as signal are mere technical opera-tions.[81] Against Riemann's rather ahistorical understanding of harmonic functionality and in favour of a more systematic epistemology, according to Wilhelm Dilthey and Hans-Georg Gadamer, every cultural phenomenon is embedded in a temporal horizon of understanding. This leads to the familiar hermeneutic circle:

> We reconstruct the historicity of a piece of music by reconstructing the time horizon of its epoch. Thus, we write general history and treat music as an element of that general history. Here applies our argument: [...] The predominant manifestation of this spirit is the musical work itself, or to

be more precise: the event of the musical work. There is no other relevant time structure for understanding a piece of music than the time structure of the music itself. The historicity of music is enclosed in the music itself.[82]

This *Eigenzeit* is emancipated from the standard theory of historicism. The archaeological structures that ground the specific vitality of a musical piece are layers such as tuning systems, techniques of building and playing instruments, and singing:

> Music creates its own history which has nothing to do with Dilthey's and Ranke's concepts of an '*Universalgeschichte*'. Nevertheless, we do not believe that music history according to this standard theory is redundant. Classical historical knowledge of music (Heideggerian *Historie*) has its legitimation when the question is how music is embedded in broader cultural textures.[83]

But if we ask for the genuine historicity (Heideggerian *Geschichtlichkeit*) of music, classical historiography can only be the first step. 'The second has to be a reconstruction of the specific time structures unfolded by the piece of music itself. These temporal relations cease to be historiographically linear ones.'[84]

To what degree does the historicity of sound depend on its material embodiment?

Sound is more than acoustics or listening experience, but the question remains as to whether it should be considered a discursive event (an 'enunciation' in Foucault's terms, like alphabetic printing) or a non-discursive articulation. The material embodiment of sound refers explicitly to the naturally given physical media of transmitting pressure waves such as air or water, and implicitly (the sonic 'fold' as discussed by Leibniz and Deleuze) to culturally engineered artifacts that produce technological media such as electronic synthesizers, in fact *sonicity*.

> Is the sound of an existing Roman era bell dating from the third century a more ancient sound? For this to be the case we would have to think of the bell itself as an encoding of some 'sound'; that sound, in turn, would have to include the splashing of the molten brass, the beating by smiths' hammers etc. But the sound the bell produces in its current use is far from being a recording of these sounds.[85]

DeMarinis's hypothetical bell is not the carrier of a more ancient sound but its time-invariant substantiation. Similarly, the phonographic groove is sound in latency waiting to be activated (Heidegger's being-in-time in its sonic expression as *Durchstimmung*). Whereas the ontological status of such recorded analog sound signals, as temporal in between of presence and past, still corresponds with the decay character of human existence itself, the atemporality of digitally sampled sound replaces the wave forms unfolding along a temporal axis (*t*) by its mathematical 'other', which is numerically calculated frequencies. 'The easy repeatability of digital recordings – set against the spectre of a continuous sine wave – masks their intrinsic temporal character, the natural auditory decay of sound.'[86] Against the former impossibility of preserving or recovering sounds from the past, the digital simulation of soundscapes lost to time opens an epistemological window onto a different kind of 'historicity' of sound – though perhaps we should replace this notion with a more appropriate term such as *chrono-sonicity*.

Micro-temporal sonic experience requires even more micro-temporal precision in technologies. This is because human auditory perception has a significantly higher temporal resolution than visual perception and thus requires accuracy in the microsecond range. 'Although this is significantly longer than the nanosecond clock of most current operating systems, the accuracy required to maintain a suitable quality-of-service for audio-visual tasks remains a challenge.'[87]

In fact, the Heideggerian 'being-to-death' that is the temporal experience of human existence corresponds with musical listening where a melody can be mentally experienced as a unity even if acoustically it consists of a discontinuous or fragmentary series of single tones. This phenomenon is discussed in Henri Bergson's philosophy of temporal duration (as opposed to mathematized time) and in Edmund Husserl's philosophy as the experience of subjective time (*'innere Zeiterfahrung'*). Still, it is its finality that determines the aesthetic experience of a melody. Like diagrammatic operations, successive tones unfold in human neuronal perception as harmonic relations only in temporal re- and protention. Such processes are familiar from the intermediary storage and predictive calculation of automated anti-aircraft prediction in the Second World War, as developed by Norbert Wiener's explicit 'harmonic analysis' of time series. G.W.F. Hegel described this sono-temporal logic like an arithmetic *arpeggio*.[88]

This recalls the dilemma in Fourier Analysis between the physically impossible ideal of stationary sine waves and the transient *momentum* of an actually performed sounding. Denis Gabor resolved this conflict by mathematically quantizing sound-as-time itself; his notion of microtemporal windows of the sonic event became a precursor of current wavelet synthesis.[89]

Experiencing the past based on resonance rather than linear history

When figured according to the dynamics of resonance (technologically materialized in the electromagnetic resonance circuit), the temporal relation between presence and past ceases to be a historiographically linear one. Linear writing and printing of alphabet-based historiography, which induces the notion of historic linearity (modelled into the scheme of 'progress') in the unfolding of time ('development' of temporal folds), is replaced by another type of temporal event. Karlheinz Stockhausen expressed this in words that recall McLuhan's model of electronic (post-Gutenberg) media culture:

> Our intellect, our senses, are trained to respond to visual information. Our concepts are visual. We don't even have words to describe sounds, or very few that are not visual in what they express. [...] I want to build a new tradition, an aural tradition, transmitted via the ears.[90]

This kind of tradition does not fit into the linear ordering of history; in fact, emphatic tradition transforms into synchronous transmission.

Sonicity in resonance: Radio and light waves (Heinrich Hertz)

The media-electronic equivalent to the vibrations of the monochord string is electromagnetic waves. But whereas the mechanical reverberations produce audible sound to be perceived by human ears, radio waves as such are implicitly sonic. Their media-archaeological roots go back to early experiments into the nature of wireless communication. In 1879, Hermann von Helmholtz initiated a prize competition from the Berlin Academy of Sciences to answer experimentally the dispute about the true theory of electricity: Is it immediate action, or subject to temporality, to limited speed?[91] Electromagnetic waves, on the micro-temporal level (that is, before becoming known as mass media called 'radio' and 'television'), have a *sense of ending*. Michael Faraday and Heinrich Hertz discovered the relation between electricity and magnetism as being dynamic – which transformed the philosophical question of its *essence* into its perception as *event*. Moving electric charges produce magnetic fields, whereas a changing magnetic field in reverse produces an electric current in a conductor. We are faced here with micro-events that appear immediate but, in fact, unfold in time.[92] It was the temporality implicit in the event named induction, that led to a break with Newton's mechanistic notion of *actio in distans*, and James Maxwell's mathematical equations even suggested visible light as a specific section of the electromagnetic wave spectrum. In 1887, Heinrich Hertz produced ultra-frequent electromagnetic waves and detected them acoustically, rather than visibly, at the other end of his setting (a university auditorium). Experimenting with electromagnetic wave propagation was not simply the prehistory of radio broadcasting in the mass media sense, but its epistemological *a priori*. When Hertz discovered that electromagnetic waves propagate through the high-frequency excitation of an open oscillating circuit, it was the result of a query for knowledge. With his experiments Hertz demonstrated that sparks are, in fact, oscillations. Such sparks have been known since antiquity (Thales of Milet) by rubbing pieces of amber; this is why electricity is named after the Greek *elektron*. These sparks always behaved like 'natural radio', but for a long time there were no means of detecting them as such; there was no electromagnetic wave detector until Eduard Branly's 'Coherer' in 1890, invented as a laboratory device in the Parisian Salpêtrière and further developed by Oliver Lodge. Radio thus was unconsciously invented in the laboratory and only later put together by entrepreneurs like Guglielmo Marconi, who combined the Hertzean apparatus with Branly's device and Popov's antenna to create a functional tool for transmitting wireless Morse code. The experimental system 'knew' radio much earlier than human scientists. In a way, radio transmission discovered itself before it became a subject of human inventors.[93]

This latency is the index of a non-historical temporality that is equally original with each moment of experimentation.

In 1901, communication bridged the Atlantic as electromagnetic waves transported information signals. But 'wireless' has not always been synonymous with radio as a medium of communication. The patent registered in 1904 by John Ambrose Fleming developed an effect detected by Edison in experimenting with light bulbs, in which electricity flowed from filaments to an additional enclosed electrode, in spite of no direct contact. In his patent manuscript of 1884, *A Manifestation of the Edison Lamp*, Edison explicitly describes electricity flowing through the vacuum 'without wires' – literally wireless: radio inside the evacuated, etherless tube.

Let us thus solve the riddle of why Heinrich Hertz did not consider the implied 'radio' content in his experiments. Early radio was closer to Morse code than to what we now know as radio, or, to put it differently: radio was digital before it became, through speech and music modulation, an analog medium. The digital only managed to re-enter through pulse code modulation – with which radio finds its way back to its original potential as telegraphic medium.

Another instance of radio activity in experimentation is found in the Deutsches Museum in Munich's reconstruction of the original experimental apparatus that Liselotte Meisner and Otto Hahn set up to detect nuclear fusion. Central to this apparatus, next to the vacuum tube amplifier, is the counter for nuclear events. Counting brings us to an alternative kind of experimental time that is an extreme of what vibrating media have been considered before: discrete micro-events called 'digital'. Alan Turing's notion of a computing mechanism, which started as a thought experiment, is based on the unconditional assumption that this machine can only exist in 'states'. Experimental media eventuality changes from the continuous (the electromagnetic radio paradigm) to the discrete. The Turing Machine experiments the eventuality of mathematics.

8.   From sound signal to alphanumeric symbol

Signal analysis instead of symbolic notations
After a decade of so-called analog audio media – with its corresponding sonification of memory – the symbolic regime returns within digital sound culture. The binary operation in digital sound by its very electrotechnical essence requires short-time storage of a binary state within the flip-flop unit; the algorithmicized archive is dynamic. This return of textuality into the sonosphere is actually 'musical' in its character.

Signal-based memory like the phonographic record was, in the past, an alternative to symbolic archival inscription; a textual record cannot sound 'alive'. Time-based dynamic storage is sonic by nature; it is no longer subjected to the spatiality of textual arrangements. The analysis of the indexical, physical acoustic traces from the past (as opposed to the merely symbolic nature of notation and writing) provides access to the *anarchive* of soundscapes (including noise, not reduced to music) that is stored in technical recording.

The symbolic order and the indexical signal represent conflicting archival temp*aura*lities. Being of the symbolic order (which according to Lacan always already implies the machinic[1]), archives are not time machines at all. They need external temporalization to generate a sense of history. While the traditional archive consisted of predominantly textual records providing a frozen spatial order that could only be transformed into 'history' by the very act of historiography, the audio record – when operated within machines – takes place in time itself, a regime much different from the scriptural.

Sonic media address humans at the existential level of affective sensation, being, which is essentially temporal. They regenerate human temporal experience by making sensory (aisthetical, physiological) experience radically present. At the same time, mental cognition translates such sensation into a 'historical' con*text*: here, a dissonance takes place, a gap opens. As long as the archival records consist of strings of symbols (i.e. alphabetic writing), a cognitive distance – in spite of the auratic qualities of handwritten manuscripts or autographs – is more or less maintained because an act of decoding must take place using the cognitive apparatus. But once photography and phonography – the first media in the modern sense of this term – entered the archive, the sense-affective, presence-generating power[2] of signal-based media cuts short this distance (which is a prerequisite for *historical* analysis) in favour of mnemonic immediacy – the chrono-electric 'shock'. The archive has to be temporally charged or rather 'biased' in order to become a sonic memory base.[3] Let us identify the 'sound' of such a temporalized archive. In magnetic sound recording, the 'bias' refers to the high frequency pre-magnetization of the tape required to ameliorate the signal-to-noise ratio (dynamics). The proper time signal that is meant to be communicated is thus overlaid or preconditioned by a different *a priori* temporality.

Chronopoetics of the sonosphere
To paraphrase and specify the famous *incipit* of Friedrich Kittler's *Gramophone, Film, Typewriter*: Chrono-poietical media determine our situation in time. When coupled to technical media interfaces, humans are placed in temporal situations that differ from culturally-specific experiences of previous times. In alliance with Stern's thesis from 1930/31, the question arises as to what degree operative media perform *ekstasis* of (or from) historical time.[4] McLuhan coined the term *acoustic space* to refer to the culture without writing of the electric age. But contrary to its immediate impression, this expression does not simply refer to sound and music but designates a specific temporal form that he correlates with the electronic media sphere itself – the sphere of resonances.[5] Thus, a different kind of tempor(e)ality is introduced; in fact, a different *media theatre,* which conceives of space not from the optical-perspective but in its acoustic dimension. In this way, access is opened to the analysis of time-based and time-critical signal processing – the signature of the new media age.[6]

McLuhan defined the 'current' state of electronically induced communication as *acoustic space*, since the ear perceives signals simultaneously (which is also the situation with electromagnetic waves). Such signals are processed in the right hemisphere of the brain, as opposed to the left hemisphere's sequential processing of signals, which has been privileged since the invention of the phonetic alphabet. By heating up writing and reading, the alphabet altered the supremacy of processing information from the ear (in oral societies) to the eye, culminating in the *Gutenberg Galaxy* (as described by McLuhan 1962). Beyond such textuality, non-Euclidian *n*-dimensional Riemann-spaces unfold that correspond to temporal forms like time dilation rather than synchronicity.

Retextualizing audio(visual) records: Digitized sound

'Music' is both within and beyond textuality. As theory, musical harmony has been linked to mathematical ratios since Pythagorean times; in that sense it is symbolically structured. In discrete musical notation, sound becomes text. But as an acoustic event, there are no symbols at work. Rather, there are micro-temporal vectors of pitch and resonance – literally *tonal* tensions and relaxations that are not alphabetic elements, but rather ask for the graphic or diagrammatic notation (in fact recording) of inherent temporal dynamics.[7] Therefore, Phono*graphic* recording differs essentially from alphabetic writing:

> What phonographs and cinematographs, whose names not coincidentally derive from writing, were able to store was time: time as a mixture of audio frequencies in the acoustic realm [...]. To record the sound sequences of speech, literature has to arrest them in a system of 26 letters, thereby categorically excluding all noise sequences.[8]

The arrested symbol cannot articulate time, as in acoustics where there is no sonic 'point' without temporal extension. Sonicity in its time-specific quality here is a metonymy of the temporality of the world as event.

> Of course Europe's written music had already been able to move tones upward or downward, as the term 'scale' itself implies. But transposition doesn't equal TAM. If the phonographic playback speed differs from its recording speed, there is a shift not only in clear sounds but in entire noise spectra.[9]

Recorded sound is temporarily suspended from entropy (in terms of the second law of thermodynamics) and thereby becomes time-shiftable in replay, thus escaping historical time. Sonic events evolving in time might even be time-reversed by immediately sending them back to the source (as long as they propagate without losing too much energy to heat, such as occurs during the random motion of individual air molecules rather than their collective movement in the sound wave).[10]

While it is true that 'inside the computers themselves everything becomes a number: quantity without [...] sound, or voice,'[11] it is only by coupling the binary world of the symbolic machine with physical impulses and time-discrete clocking that mathematics becomes rhythmically operative (biased) and thus implicitly belongs to the chronosphere of sonicity. Only with rhythmically time-structured processing in active electronic elements do sonic mechanisms like modulation, transformation, synchronization, delay, and transposition become techno-logically calculable. Such calculation can even beat time. Active media-archaeological projects in optical scanning and the digital reading of otherwise inaccessible (physically corrupted or fragile) sound recordings retrieves past sound signals by sampling and quantification. What sounds to the ear like the rescued sound in fact becomes the function of a mathematical matrix, transforming the familiar cultural into algorithmic memory. The digital *close reading* of sound dissolves any signal into discrete blocks. Thus, the textual regime returns (in alphanumeric codes) – a new kind of archive. Algorithmic archaeology is the return of textuality in the representation of the past; but this time, the text itself becomes media active – a kind of operativity that the handwritten or printed text never knew. Digitized signals resemble the tradition of music notation; they wait to be algorithmically executed within the central processing unit (CPU) of computers. The CPU is a sonic, highly rhythmical mechanism.

Against the noise of physical decay happening within the material storage medium, digital (literally 'techno-logical') culture poses what is sometimes called a 'negentropic' insistence; that is, a negation of decay. Once digitized with an appropriate sampling rate, sound can be reproduced frequently with stable quality – which had been a rather utopian dream in recent times of analog recording. The secret of this temporal invulnerability is that it is just numbers that are electronically written into the storage medium; even after a thousand copies, a physical representation of a zero stays zero and one probably remains one.[12] Suddenly, a non-literary textuality, a binary pattern, saves the sonic signal, which is an ultimate irony in so-called cultural history.

Signal criticism: First audio recordings
In common histories of technology, the first melodic voice recording is supposed to be the children's song 'Mary had a little lamb' as performed by Thomas Alva Edison himself on his tin-foil phonograph in 1877. But caution, *arché* (the core term in the notion of media archaeology) does not primarily denote a beginning in the history of technologies, but rather a governing principle. Indeed the earliest sound recording was preserved (in Johann Gustav Droysen's sense) as a relic (*'Überrest'*), a phonogram that was never intended to be re-played: Édouard-Léon Scott de Martinville's notational traces of acoustic vibrations produced for phonetic analysis by his 'Phonautographe' on a rotating cylinder. Only media-active, non-human archaeology, which takes technologies themselves as archaeologists (such

as the 'virtual stylus' or the 'variable width' technology), opens this silent archive of sound in order to let it resonate again. Whereas traditional philology undertook to lend speech to those traces that in themselves are not verbal, or which say in silence something other than what they actually say (like Parry's and Lord's transcriptions of epic song recordings), in our time of signal processing, it is necessary to transform *documents* into *monuments*.[13]

Surprising resonifications of phonautographic sound recordings have been achieved by the First Sound Initiative, notably by Patrick Feaster (Indiana University) and by the radio historian David Giovannoni.[14] In such experiments, the archival operation extends from restoration and conservation to re-animation and thus becomes a true media-archaeological operation. In media-active archaeology, the technological apparatus itself turns out to be the archaeologist proper. 150 years after a sonic event, science realizes that with optical 'reading' of acoustic signal lines sound can be re-synthesized and, suddenly, a children's song resonates: '*Au clair de la lune, Pierrot répondit.*'[15]

It is a hybrid technology of sound re-synthetization that makes such oscillation curves vibrate again: optical scanning of acoustic signal lines (as known from sound film). Not by coincidence, one of the earliest of these recordings, deposited by Scott at the French Institut National de la Propriété Industriel in 1859, is a media-archaeological sound itself, originating from a measuring tool: a tuning fork vibrating at 435 Hertz (at that time adopted as the official French reference pitch for musical performance).

What appears as the pick-up of sound images by a 'virtual digital gramophone needle'[16] is indeed a registration of a new kind: digital, time-discrete sampling of time functions (physical signals) and their computational quantization. Exclusively mathematized media technology can trace and reveal such sonic knowledge (*mathesis*). This leads to an extension of the text-critical method gleaned from the philological disciplines, and towards a veritable signal critique that is no longer exclusively performed by human(ist) scholars, but by measuring media and their implemented analytic algorithms.[17]

The earliest known sound recording in Norway was produced on 5 February 1879 by an Edison tin-foil phonograph in Kristiania (the previous name for Oslo). The tradesman of musical scores Peter Larsen Dieseth is supposed to have sung a liturgical psalm. In 1934, Dieseth presented the Norwegian Museum of Science and Technology with a phonographic tin-foil, which was flattened and glued on a piece of paper and enclosed by a picture frame; since then, the artifact has hung silently on the museum wall. Next to the tin-foil piece Dieseth wrote that this was the original of the earliest sound recording. Flattened as a 'document', the tin foil piece – considered the first officially archived record of sound in Norway – itself remained un-playable. Sound archives are the most secret and silent archives.

Recently, in a joint project, the Norwegian Museum of Technology and the National Library in Oslo started to dis-cover the auditive content from this artifact. This was done by applying the method of non-invasive, touchless optical scanning developed by the School of Engineering Sciences at the University of Southampton. Using subsequent digital filters, it is possible to trace past acoustic signals. From such an operation we expect sound. The digital 'reading' of this record led to a resonification wherein human ears wanted to detect something like music or speech but, in fact, heard nothing but noisy patterns. The first act is not listening but measuring the artifact by continuous scanning; even with this radical reading of complex record surface topologies and their subsequent high precision mapping, it is difficult to separate meaningful inscriptions (signals or symbols) from brute physical incisions. Out of several short tracks found on the foil only a few contained significant audio portions featuring music or speech, 'the remaining two tracks were both short and contained negligible content.'[18] Such a technological re-sonification of recorded signals is not just a conventional acoustic replay; the media-archaeological *momentum* is ahistorical: 'probably the first time it has been reproduced since the original recording date.'[19] At the same time, this leads to a new kind of textu(r)al criticism in all its meanings; the real world of recorded acoustic signals finally revealed that the originally enclosed alphabetic commentary was historically untrue to the remaining fragment.[20]

Contemporary ears conditioned by present understanding expect sound from audio restoration operations, but what can primarily be heard is noise.

9. Rescued from the archive: Archaeonautics of sound

Message or noise? Acoustic archaeology

As a very simple kind of psychoacoustic experiment, let us imagine an ancient phonographic recording. Whatever the song might be, one will also acoustically associate scratches in the grooves and noise from the recording device. Such phonographic crackle is an indexical trace of physical time itself (different from its symbolical coding by historiography). True media archaeology starts here: The phonograph as media artifact not only preserves the memory of cultural semantics, but also the technological knowledge of the material past. Such media knowledge is encoded in engineering and waits to be revealed by media-archaeological methods. The noise inherent in a wax cylinder is a non-discursive real event and should not be excluded from otherwise hermeneutic philological analysis of historical recordings. But it is not the only real event revealed by the examination of the phonograph:

> The story of the real phonographic recording offers us much more than the media noise inherent in the wax cylinder. It is the story of severe operational difficulties regarding upholding constant RPM, preserving and storing the recorded material and an extremely delicate and fragile playback mechanism. [...] factors that are extremely important in the media archaeological examination of technical media. The history of operational media is not only the history of the functioning devices, but just as much about the malfunctioning and tenuous machines operating, mediating and recording our reality.[1]

In a truly media-archaeological analysis of sonic articulations, noise is not symbolic but something real that is inextricably linked to the operational machine. The noise from old wax cylinders is not an external accident but an inherent part of such recording media; it essentially constitutes our understanding of these media machines. 'Listening to Technology'[2] firstly of all requires the *close listening* to the noise produced by technology itself. There is a progressive silencing of technical media; that is why an auditory icon simulates the proverbial click of a camera even in digital devices that lack a mechanical correlate. The Museum of Endangered Sounds preserves and takes care of 'dead media' sounds.[3]

In its recommendations from December 2005, the Technical Committee of the International Association of Sound and Audiovisual Archives (IASA) insists that the originally intended signal is just one part of an archival audio record; accidental artifacts like noise and distortion are part of it as well – be it because of faults in the recording process or the result of later damage caused in transmission. Both kinds of signals, the semantic and the *mémoire involontaire*, message *and* noise, need to be preserved in media-archival conservation ethics. Edison wax cylinders from the beginning of the twentieth century may well contain background recordings of environments that were never intended for memory. These now 'recall' (if an earlier event can recall a later one) the Soundscape Project in Vancouver and the admirable and current series, 'Metropolis', produced by Klaus Schoening in the Studio for Akustische Kunst at the WDR.[4] What once were considered undesirable noises may, from a different perspective (or, better: hearing), turn out to be a kind of acoustic cinema. This leads to the counter-historical idea of simultaneity, 'the co-existence of two different times, (or three if you take into account the now-time you are listening in, which is always changing).' The goal of media archaeology is to dig into collections of early recording machines in such a non-historical way (anti-hermeneutically). Out of this archaeological site develops a different 'hearing' of modern history, a notion of the sound of the past based on waves, simultaneous time and shifting soundscapes.

Let us differentiate between the cultural, social, or 'collective' (Halbwachs) memory of sonic events (auditory memory) and the actual (media) recording of sonic articulation from the past. The human auditory sense does not suffice for a proper archaeology of the acoustic in cultural memory. Let us, therefore, track the sonic trace with genuine tools of media studies (which are technical media). One way of pursuing 'acoustic archaeology' is to play a musical partition on historic instruments. But the real archaeologists in media archaeology are the media themselves – not mass media (the media of representation), but measuring media that are able to not only decipher physically real signals techno-analogically, but also represent these signals in graphic forms alternative to alphabetic writing. This requires 'moving' diagrams (sinusoidal sound is articulation in time), such as found with the oscilloscope. The curves of the oscilloscope correspond perfectly and with full (and scalable) temporal indexicality to the needle curves of the phonograph, as preceded by the physiological recordings with the kymograph in the nineteenth century.[5] In the interpretation of minute cultural differences in sonic articulation, phonetic transcription soon reaches its limits. Here, the strength of technical oscillograms presents itself. As Alois Brandl remarked in 1927, the human ear cannot listen as accurately as the visible speech curves are able to measure.[6]

Material entropy *versus* symbolic endurance of sound recording
With the refinement of the Phoenician syllabic alphabet to the Greek phonetic alphabet, acoustic articulation (speech, singing, oral poetry) became symbolically recordable. But symbolic notation in paper archives still differs from signal recording, which rather results in media collections:

> Notation wants music to be forgotten, in order to fix it and to cast it into identical reproduction, namely the objectivation of the gesture, which for all music of barbarian cultures martyrs the eardrum of the listener. The eternisation of music through notation contains a deadly moment: what it captures becomes irrevocable [...] Musical notation [...] kills music as a natural phenomenon in order to conserve it – once it is broken – as a spiritual entity: The survival of music in its persistence presupposes the killing of its here and now, and achieves within the notation the ban from its mimetic representation.[7]

Digitized signals at first sight resemble musical notation, but different from the traditional score they are endowed with operational activity that manifests as algorithmic executability. Symbolic archival permanence is almost time-invariant, sublated from change with time, leading to ahistorical immediacy in the moment of replay. Instead of musicological hermeneutics, the media-archaeological ear is required here, very technically. In May 2011, two black boxes could finally be salvaged from the bottom of the Atlantic Ocean, two years after an Air France plane crashed: the data and voice recorders that preserve not just the last words of the pilots, but also the background noises that retrospectively signal the unfolding disaster. The recordings proved to be miraculously intact. Both data recorders consist of memory chips that keep their magnetic charge, different from the mechanically vulnerable recording media in previous use. Whereas those mechanical records maintained the culturally familiar form of physical impression (writing), electromagnetic latency is a different, sublime, uncanny form of invisible, non-haptic memory. The voices and sounds emanating from such a black box are radically bodiless, resulting in a different temporality than the symbolic time reference in historiography. The 'schizophonic' split between an original sound and its electroacoustical recording[8] results in a temporal disruption as well, a dissonance between the affective sensation and the cognitive awareness of sound-based time experience.

Sonic memory's two technological embodiments: Physical signal and archival symbol

Archival endurance – oscillating between historic and entropic time – is undermined when recorded sound is no longer fixed on a permanent storage medium but instead takes places electronically; flow (the current) replaces inscription. Any rules for record preservation need to be revised with changes to technological conditions (the media-economic dispositive). Digital data need constant updating (in terms of software) and 'migration' (in terms of the hardware that embodies them). Thus, a change is derived from the ideal of archival eternity to one of permanent change – the dynarchive.

When the transfer techniques of audio signals change from technically extended writing on material carriers, such as analog phonography, to calculation (digitization), this is not just a surface change regarding the materialities of tradition, but a complete conceptual change. From that moment on, material tradition is no longer simply a function of linear time (the speed of history), but of a new, basically atemporal dimension (acceleration). This shortcuts the emphatic time arrow and demands for a partial differentiation (just as the infinitesimal calculus was introduced by Leibniz as a measure of non-linear change *within* speed).

A different kind of archive: Sonic memory

The research into past sonospheres and ways of listening has emerged as a new kind of historical knowledge. The economy of knowledge is enriched by the 'sonosphere' or, alternatively, ambient sound. The BBC World Service has launched the 'Save our Sounds' project, looking to 'archivize' sounds that may soon be lost to a post-industrial world. But caution, this is not an archive: if no algorithm is present to enact the transition of sound provenience to permanent storage, the collection remains idiosyncratic and random.

As a research method, an archaeology of listening differs from the concept of 'hearing history'[19]; it does not simply aim to widen the range of source material for historians. It may be conceived instead as a kind of 'diagrammatic listening', with the diagram having a specific indexical relation to sound as it unfolds in time rather than simply the relation of a structural image (German '*Hörbild*'). In contrast As opposed to epistemic listening to implicit sound, explicit listening depends on sound as an event that is transmitted or recorded in matter. With the phonograph, hearing became attentive to all kinds of sounds, regardless of their source and quality, just as the inner ear transduces vibrations in a way analogous to electro-mechanical sound reproduction.[10] With phonographic recording, listening became ahistorical, subject to the time-invariant reproducibility of signals. The phonograph separated sound production from its historical index, which in the language of Walter Benjamin is its unique, 'auratic' moment in place and time.

The Greek term *mousiké* encompassed not only musical articulation in the narrow sense, but dance and poetry as well. The essential operation to create an archive of such moving ('time-based') arts, of course, is recording: either symbolically (by dance notation in the tradition of writing / *graphé*), or by media endowed with the capacity to register the physically real audio-visual signals. Media-active archaeology can be applied to past sound, generating a different kind of audio-archive. The media-archaeological (technical) ear is required here. The media archaeologist, with his or her 'passion of distance',[11] does not hallucinate life when he or she listens to recorded voices; the media-archaeological exercise is to be aware at each given moment that we are dealing with technical media, not humans; that we are not speaking with the dead but beholding dead media in operation. While the recorded voice signal stays remarkably invariant over time, the body from which the song originated ages and might even have passed away. Caruso's voice from an early gramophone recording transcends not only the limited recording bandwidth of his time but temporal decay itself.

> Starting in 1902, Enrico Caruso made a large number of disc phonograph recordings most of which have been re-engineered and released over the last century. It is one of the most persistent (and lucrative) instances of sonic remediation, as Caruso's voice migrated from shellac to vinyl to CDs and iPods, while all around his voice orchestral accompaniments were enhanced, removed and overdubbed. [...] The posthumous career of Caruso is a sequence of archival transformations. All media technologies are 'archives of cultural engineering', and in ways which give a lot of additional meaning to McLuhan's mantra that the content of one medium is always another medium, each archive recursively processes another.[12]

Frozen voices, confined to long-forgotten storage media, wait for their techno-algorithmic unfreezing.[13] 'Media are the new capital-s subjects of media archaeology [...].'[14] Such a reanimation of dead sounds and images does not simply resonate with Walter Benjamin's 'messianic' historical materialism; we might instead phrase it conversely the other way round: Benjamin's awkward formulation is itself redeemed by technical media.

Sound recording does not simply unfold as a smooth, evolutionary technological and historical trajectory. Instead, the phonographic record, the magnetic record on tape, and finally the digital recording represent fundamentally different materialities and non-linear logics in terms of their 'archival' being in time – their modes of registering time-variant signals and time-based forms of reproduction. Electromagnetic induction liberates traditional recording media from mechanical constrains; still, electronic tubes or transistors and magnetic tapes are subject to decay and erasure. The aforementioned 'negentropic' persistence against physical decay over time[15] owes its ahistoricity instead to its different form of registering – not by signals (recording the physically real acoustic event), but by the informational symbolic code.

The difference between mechanical and electromagnetic audio recording is not just technical but epistemological. While the phonograph belongs to what Jules-Étienne Marey once called the 'graphical method' (analog registering of signals by curves), the magnetophone is based on the electromagnetic field. This is a completely different type of recording, in fact a true 'medium'. What used to be invasive writing has been substituted by electronic recording; writing now returns as digital encoding in different qualities. The sampling and quantizing of acoustic signals transforms a complex time signal into its individual frequencies (Fourier analysis), which provides the condition for technical re-synthesis. Media culture turns from phonocentrism to mathematics, liberating sonicity from the conventional time domain.

Is there a 'sound of the archive'?

If sound – heard, recorded, or transmitted – is fundamentally questioned in terms of epistemology and archaeology, it becomes in many respects ahistorical.[16] Its specific temporality can not be totally captured and subsumed by the logocentrism of traditional narrative historiography. Serious engagement with 'the sonic' – sound as sound and sound as time – can open access to a plurality of non-narrative temporalities that move beyond historiography's reliance on symbolic structures of narrative contextualization. Historians will likely respond with reservations on this point, stressing the cultural context of sound's perception, production and consumption, and suggest that sound history, as any other, should guard against the persistent chimera of an unmediated access to the past.

In official institutions of sound preservation, the term archive refers to the symbolic order or metadata rather than to the recorded signal content. Is there a sound of the archive? Different from script-based 'archival' storage where information coded in alphabetic symbols can be more or less faithfully copied and migrated, sonic memory from signal recording is confronted with material entropy: message confronts noise. But noise itself enriches the narrow limits of harmonic sound (i.e. 'music') to the infinite variance (sonicity) of possible wave forms.[17] In contrast to the archive as symbolic order composed of records in alphabetic, discrete notation, there is a para-archival modality of subtextual, signal-based recording: the sound of times past. *Silentium* is indicated by the inscription above the entrance to the Vatican Archives in Rome. But this silence might be literally *understood*[18] by listening to the temporal implications of the archive, rather than simply regarding its spatial 'layers'. The media-archaeological ear is trained to actually listen to archival silence, gaps, and voids. While an empty space within a painting positively endures with time, silence in acoustics is always a temporal (though negative) event. Albert Mayr who calls himself a 'time designer' composes music with silence as the essential element; there are different physically real, culturally symbolic, and historical imaginary qualities of silence. With recording, silence itself can become part of the archive. The software for the sound-processing program Audacity actually provides an algorithm called 'Silence Finder'.

With digital sampling, filtering, processing, and compressing of audio signals, analog noise is usually significantly filtered – thus, silenced. IBut instead, an even more subtle kind of noise arises: 'quantizing noise' on the very bit-critical (technical) level of signal sampling. This is not just a technical question; it but extends to epistemological dimensions as well.[19]

The endurance of vibrating matter is Bergsonian time that passes – silent sonicity. Historians will always insist that there is no unmediated access to the past. But as the negative sound of the archive, silence is the truest articulation of times past. Let us pay respect to absence instead of converting it into the spectre of a false memory. Whereas the scripture-based classical archive is a static array of documents on the macro- and letters on the micro-scale, brought in motion only through the human act of line by line reading, the Edison phonograph appears to be the first form of an auto-mobile archive. Its recording operation is based on a rotating, technically moving apparatus – both in recording and in replay, parallel to early cinematographical practice. And when a Datassette (external tape memory) is loaded into the ROM of a Commodore 64 computer, we can actually listen to data music. What we hear is not memory content as with old percussion-assisted songs,[20] but rather the rhythms of sequential computer memory itself – a software program. We are listening to the data archive, which is not sonic memory but sonicity.

Active media archaeology: Sonic revelation (articulation) from the past (*Au Claire de Lune*)

Sonic media archaeology is concerned with directly audible knowledge that is latent, implicit rather than manifest, and that is kept *within* the material dispositive. Until the electronic age, sonic memory, its storage and transmission, was until the electronic age the most 'immaterial' cultural articulation. It has been long neglected by the primarily text-based academic discipline of history. But recent developments in signal science have opened a new field of research that is not simply an additional source for historical inquiry; with photography, the phonograph, cinematography, and electronic communication technologies, an alternative field for cultural inquiry has been set.

So-called Humanities (as defined by Wilhelm Dilthey) has for the longest time not been concerned with physical realities – due to the limits of hermeneutics as text-oriented method, to the privileging of narrative as dominant form of representation and because of an essential lack of non-symbolic recording media of the real. Battles have been described and interpreted, but the real noise and smell of combat could not be transmitted until the arrival of the Edison phonograph.[21]

A tradition active since pre-Socratic Greek philosophy holds that music is not primarily a practice of acoustic pleasure and entertainment, as it is to modern ears, but a model of knowledge – *mousiké epistéme*. More specifically, in the absence of signal measuring media, musical analysis served as a substitute for insight into time-based processes. As such, the science of music both enhanced and hindered the insight into acoustic media, as in the case of Galileo Galilei. With his experiments of generating sound by rubbing patterned surfaces, Galileo unwittingly involuntarily came close to inventing the phonograph.[22] But instead of crossing that border, the son of the theoretician of music Vincenzo Galilei remained imprisoned in Pythagorean understanding. In accordance with his tendency to interpret natural laws in geometrical terms, in sonic articulations Galileo detected primarily musical (not 'audio') proof of the connection between numerical proportionality in tonal pitch and the impulse theory of sound. As long as the chrono-physical actuality of sound remained subjected to conceptual music, actual sound recoding technologies remained undiscovered. They remained so until a truly non-Pythagorean mind arrived: Thomas Alva Edison simply listened to the noise produced by his Embossy Telegraph.

Phonography did not just provide historical research with a new kind of source material; it rendered different, ahistorical forms of tempor(e)alities derived from the physical and mathematical realities of technology.

This, in turn, generated new ways of 'listening' to the past. Archaeo-acoustics deals with modern – that is, technological – hearing in the sense that it is the sonic media (as active 'archaeologists') thatwhich reveal the sounds of the past. In one of his media artistic projects, the sound archaeologist Paul DeMarinis translates 'illustrations and engravings of sound vibrations from old physics and acoustics texts, many of them predating the invention of the phonograph,'[23] *back* into sound files. DeMarinis finally adds a 'technical note': 'The traces were scanned on a flatbed scanner, extracted and isolated by a number of processes in Photoshop, then transformed into audio files via a custom patcher in Max/MSP. The sounds were then presented [...] as aiff files played back on a conventional CD player.'[24]

The first recording of sound in its media-archaeological sense has been preserved as relic (Droysen's 'Überrest'), which is as unintentional tradition – a Proustian *mémoire involontaire*, a Bergsonian 'counter-archive' as defined by Paula Amad. It originates from Scott's Phonautographe on a turning cylinder (the Kymograph as universal epistemological recording medium of the nineteenth century), invented not for purpose of replay or for transmission to posterity, but for immediate phonetic analysis (techno-linguistics). In media-active archaeology, the technological apparatus itself turns out to be the archaeologist proper. When, 150 years after Scott, computational science realized that with technical 'reading' of such acoustic signal lines sound can be re-synthesized, what metaphorically looks like the pick-up of sound images by a 'virtual, digital gramophone needle,'[25] in fact is something media-epistemologically different, a picking-up of a completely new kind: digital sampling.

Let us get tuned to this non-canonical epistemology, not using texts or the spoken word, but through a French children's song: *Au Claire de Lune, Pierrot répondit.* In an act of active media archaeology, a computer achieves the re-transformation into acoustic articulation of Scott's analyzes of the human voice, originally a graphic recording. By means of the optical scanning of signals and application of digital filters, it is possible to digitally trace past acoustic signals from records. From such an operation we expect sound, but really what we hear is noise – just like the first (archived) recording of sound in Norway, a tinfoil flattened to a 'document' and annotated with a remark by a former collector who claims this as the first Norwegian recording of music on Edison cylinder. The digital reading, algorithmic filtering and final re-sonification of this record by a laboratory in Southampton fell on contemporary ears that wished to detect something like music or speech. In fact, actually such ears hear nothing but noisy patterns.

Past sound is not just 'restored' through the application of digital filters, but has to be remembered with all the traces of decay that have been part of its tradition. Its media-temporal, entropic characteristics deserve to be digitally archived as well, such as the scratches of a vintage phonographic cylinder. Close to the physical record, digitized sound from the past deserves not just to be emulated but actually simulated, preserving its temporal marks as well by over-sampling and physical modelling. The chemical corruption of an Edison cylinder is an essential feature of the techno-sonic record. By means of ferrofluid colouring, the implicit sonic signal from a physical record like a magnetic tape can be made visible; such evidence can then be scanned and algorithmically processed into sound again.

As with any transmission channel, when sound is emitted in its proper surroundings it tends towards increasing noise. Once mechanically re-corded, such sonic noise increases with each act of replay. The signal-to-noise ratio, as described in Claude Shannon's 1948 mathematical theory of communication, can be applied to transmission of sound in time as well – that is, sonic tradition. The devastating mechanical invasion of the gramophone needle on the record groove is familiar from Baroque allegories that display the nagging 'tooth of time' – an articulation of physical entropy as a manifestation of the temporal arrow. According to the Second Law of Thermodynamics, each energetic system tends, over time, to increasing disorder, against which the digital code is, by definition, timeless informa-tion. Cultural efforts devoted to fighting the physical noise of tradition resulted in discrete codes – which range from early alphabetic writing up to techno-logical, i.e. 'digital' alphanumerics.[26] This type of (almost) lossless reproduction of information by identical symbols was previously the realm of Gutenberg printing technology (as opposed to handwritten copies of manuscripts). The Gutenberg media mechanism used negative types to reproduce letters positively in identical numbers – a form of reproduction later reinvented by the photographic negative, the Talbot Kalotype (dif-ferent from the unique Daguerre positive). Such developments led Walter Benjamin to remark that reproduction technology both disconnected and redeemed the reproduced object from the realm of tradition, by replacing the unique event (the condition for its 'auratic' character) with its mass multiplicity. Temporal tradition is thus replaced by a rather topological dissemination.[27]

The media-historiographically canonized primary scene of technical voice recording (Edison's voice on his tinfoil phonograph in 1877) was later re-enacted by the elderly inventor himself to preserve the scene for cultural memory. But the body from which the voice originated apparently aged, being strictly subjected to what we call historical time. The tempor(e)al-ity of 'history' corresponds with the entropic deterioration of the electric charge and chemical carrier of the magnetic tape *versus* symbolical, i.e. almost time-invariant 'tradition'. Whereas an analog sound carrier, which is in-formed physical material, can still be identified according to the criteria of the historical method, digital signal transfer is information in its communication engineering sense – that is, unbound from energy and matter by coding (as Norbert Wiener in his 1948 *Cybernetics* insists).

Media-archaeological voice analysis (case Hitler)
In terms of historical discourse, the message of the past is symbolically coded in the printed record and thus accessible only to the cognitively reading mind. But in actual archival research, the indexical – the immediate material link to the past – is found in the individuality of the handwriting, or in the auditive or visual recording ('signal'). Sound is not political on the semantic level only, a point made evident by Goebbels's *Volksempfänger* radio. This device had to be tuned in order to get the program demodulated – always accompanied by AM noise, the message of radio waves themselves. A notorious case of sonic latency is a recording of Hitler's voice on an AEG magnetic tape. This infamous voice was recorded by microphones installed in the train car that carried Hitler and the Finnish General Field Marshall Carl Gustaf Emil Mannerheim during Hitler's visit in 1942, on occasion of Mannerheim's 75th birthday. Eleven minutes were secretly recorded by Thor Damen, a sound engineer of the Finnish Broadcasting Company (*Yleisradio*) on 4 June 1942. Though Hitler rarely allowed himself to be photographed, filmed, or phono-recorded in private situations, all of a sudden, he speaks in private tones from the secret (media) archive. 'The voice on the tape is low-pitched and somewhat hoarse, with sentences rambling, and breaking off repeatedly into pauses for thought.'[28] But there are dramatic pauses as well; the recording was suddenly cut off when Hitler's security men spotted the cords coming out of the window. When the recording of Hitler's conversation with Mannerheim breaks off, suddenly music can be heard – the previous recording of the tape for radio use. At least *Yleisradio* was allowed to keep the reel, after promising to keep it in an archival condition: a sealed container. One of the tapes ended up in the hands of the head of the state censors' office Kustaa Vilkuna, who later passed it to *Yleisradio* in 1957. The second tape was found in 1992 by Damen's son Henrik, hidden away in his father's garage. The German Central Criminal Police undertook in its acoustics laboratory a study of the tape's authenticity in its acoustics laboratory, during the same period of an ongoing controversy about the

forged memoirs of Hitler (as Lasse Vihonen, head of the *Yleisradio* archives, reminds). Sonic signal memory drastically differs from symbolic records; the protagonist in Samuel Beckett's play *Krapp's Last Tape* (1959) trusts his annual memories to a magnetophone rather than to a traditional written diary.[29] The forensic voice analyst Stefan Gfrörer compared the train car recording to a speech Hitler had just previously delivered and which was recorded using the same technical system as in Finland. While this analysis proved that it was Hitler talking,[30] his personal assistant, present during the train journey, could not recognize the recorded voice as specifically Hitler's; the gap between neuronal and electronic memory opens wide. Technomathematical *forensic* speech recognition of recorded (thus bodiless) voices, by frequency spectrum analysis, is truly *sonic* media-to-media communication, whereas the human ear recognizes nothing but *sound*.

The authentication of the recorded voice as Hitler's, rendering a name to an acoustic wave form, is itself is a media-archaeological act, based on non-human spectrographic signal-detection and analysis by electronic measuring instruments. What flashes is the physically 'real' of acoustics. Different from Roland Barthes' definition of the photographic *punctum*, the signal here is a dynamic one, revealing its evidence only when moving forward. It is, a kind of *punctum*-in-becoming, like the cathode ray, which creates the impression of an electronic image on the inner side of the video monitor that, in fact, consists of nothing but 'Bergsonian' time.[31]

The tape has been used in Germany by actors playing the role of Hitler, such as Bruno Ganz, who 'initially felt that a monster such as Hitler simply cannot be portrayed'[32] – here is the other side of Sirenic sonicity that reveals the monstrosity of the human voice when analyzed (and re-synthesized) as a techno-physical event. A There exists a gramophone recording exists of Heinrich Himmler's 'secret' speech to SS leaders on the *Endlösung* in Posnan, 4 October 1943. The filmmaker Romuald Karmaker produced a 'documentary' film that incorporated a version of Himmler's speech read by the actor Zapatka rather than replaying the original recording that is preserved in the Federal Archives of Germany. But sound recording media do not differentiate between good and evil voices. Even if Himmler in his secret speech declared programmatically the erasure of all traces of the attempted genocide,[33] the technological voice recording deconstructs this statement. There is sonicity even in silence.

Sonic re-presencing: Acoustic archaeology

Walter Benjamin identified an 'optical unconscious' that reveals itself only to the camera eye. Does something analogous exist for sonic phenomena?

From the beginning, phonographic records – however they are part of discursive, ideological, aesthetic, and technical formations – have unintentionally co-registered a whole world of additional information, i.e. background noise. So much noise comes from replaying vintage audiotapes that to remove it would cause the loss of too much audio content. Sound recording is not just a new type of archive that adds to the memory culture of written records, but a real anarchive.

Media-active archaeology can be applied to past sound, generating a different kind of audio-archive in graphic forms alternative to alphabetic writing. This process requires 'moving' diagrams as sinusoidal articulations in time, such as the oscilloscope. Today, listening again to the otherwise inaccessible recordings of early Edison cylinders is possible by image scanning and sampling – a process of opto-digital *close reading*.[34] Sound from the past is accessible for detailed human analysis only by means of operative techno-mathematical diagrams.

This is an analytic form of deciphering the sound of the past, a sonic disclosure. It requires a media-archaeological ear to generate knowledge from such new techniques, which provide an alternative to the cultural emphasis on musical semantics. But to the media-archaeologically sharpened mind, a figure produced on a computer screen by image scanning and sampling will never be confused with a 'live' sound, since such a mind is aware of the algorithms by which this animation is a technomathematical, processual function. This is the epistemological difference to the phonoarchival phantasms in the Romantic tradition, which were triggered almost immediately after the invention of the Edison phonograph, as announced in the journal *Scientific American*:

> That the voices of those who departed before the invention of the wonderful apparatus [...] are for ever stilled is too obvious a truth; but whoever has spoken or whoever may speak into the mouthpiece of the phonograph, and whose words are recorded by it, has the assurance that his speech may be reproduced audibly in his own tones long after he himself has turned to dust. [...] A strip of indented paper travels through a little machine, the sounds of the latter are magnified, and our great grandchildren or posterity centuries hence hear us as plainly as if we were present.[35]

Natural sound is evasive, liquid, in itself unrecordable beyond the bodily range, but technical media are able to thaw recorded voices in almost all frequencies (that is, the Lacanian 'real' of the voice) by re-play. After two millennia of practicing the phonetic alphabet as cultural technique, which filtered the human voice by a very limited symbolic code, phonographic sound recording achieved sub-cultural memory. There is a vocal testimony of emperor Franz Joseph I of Austria-Hungary in the Vienna Phonograph Archive – a recording from Bad Ischl, 2nd August 1903, inscribed deeply into the wax cylinder. For such cases, sound recording has already developed a true media memory that differs from the remembrance of its 'historic' content. The experiment is very simple: if one imagines the phonograph recording of His Majesty's voice without actual replay, whatever one thinks the timbre of his voice sounds, one will almost certainly for sure acoustically hallucinate as well the scratching as well, i.e. the noise of the recording apparatus. True media archaeology starts here: the phonograph as media artifact does not only preserves the memory of cultural semantics but stores past *technical* knowledge as well, a kind of frozen media memory embodied in engineering and waiting to be listened to by media-archaeologically tuned ears.

Getting one step further with this auditory experiment, it is time to quote emperor Franz Joseph's actual statement, which is one of the first voice recordings ever preserved at all. Significantly, this statement turns out to be the pure message of the medium. When a new, technical medium emerges, humans are very aware of its technicality (which afterwards, when it becomes mass media, tends to be forgotten in favour of so-called 'content'). The emperor expresses his joy to literally 'incorporate' his voice into the Vienna phonograph archive.[36] Indeed we are able, today, to listen to human voices that ceased speaking hundreds of years ago, using laser readings of wax cylinders that do not destroy the fragile recording surface in the act of re-play. But what do we hear: message (the emperor) or noise (the scratch)?[37] The noise of the wax cylinder itself, which the record articulates whenever it is re-played, is not discursive (cultural), but rather media-archaeological information of the physically real event. Let us listen to this attentively and not exclude it hermeneutically as occurs in the proverbial cocktail party effect of auditory communication between humans.

Different from passive symbolic writing systems like the phonetic al-phabet or even short-hand 'phonography',[38] which still require the human mind and imagination to become 'alive', the power of signal-based technical media lies in their ability to actively (re-)create real presence. Let us quote once more from Bartók's comment on his transcriptions of recordings of Yugoslav oral poetry from the 1930s: 'You really have the feeling of being on the spot [...]. It gives you a thrilling impression of liveliness, of life itself.'[39]

Media as active archaeologists

The application of the phonograph by ethnologists not only established a new scientific field (music ethnology), but also resulted in large collections of wax cylinder negatives (galvanos) (located e. g. in the Phonogram Archive in the Ethnological Museum of Berlin). These archives require media archaeology of a special kind. Nowadays, digital image processing of sound tracks on early Edison cylinders allows for listening again to otherwise inaccessible sound recording, by a hybrid of mechanical stylus (haptic transitivity) and optical scanning. When media decoders become active archaeologists of past sounds, audio recordings are no longer simply archival objects. Frozen voices from the analogue, vulnerable storage medium of Edison wax cylinders can now be thawed by digital means; what was a pre-phonographic metaphor of writing in earlier times thus becomes technologically true. The Berlin Society for Applied Informatics has developed a method to gain acoustic signals from negatives of Edison cylinders (galvanos) by endoscopic 'reading' – scanning combined mechanical/optical information into sound.[40] Restoring stored acoustic waves to actual sound does not demand rhetoric imagination; but on the contrary, it demands a hermeneutically distant gaze, an exteriority of interpretation that only the aesthetics of the technical scanner can provide.[41]

'The central part of SpuBiTo is the height detection algorithm measuring the height of the tracks, computing the movement of the diamond stylus and reconstructing the acoustical information.'[42] The real archaeologist of sound, here, is here the techno-mathematical apparatus. Thus, one can listen again to the recordings taken by the ethnologist Selenka who went to India in 1907. She made the natives speak or sing into a phonograph before immediately playing the recording back to them. This resulted in a moment of joyful recognition.[43] The recordability of the physical reality of sound is a media mystery by which humans experience an acoustic mirror effect (in Lacan's sense), undoing the clear-cut difference between presence and absence, present and past. It is possible today to listen to such a playback in nearly the same quality as the Indian natives could in 1907.[44] The media-archaeological operation of opto-digital reading and decoding of inscribed traces makes audible otherwise inaccessible sound. Synaesthetically, a spectrographic image of such sonic memory provides a straight look into the archive. 'Where auditory analysis necessarily takes place *in time* and thus *takes* time, the audiospectrograph stabilizes time through combination and scaling.'[45]

10. Sonic analytics

Below the logocentrism of metadata: Kurenniemi's case
As distinct from cultural analysis, sonic analytics in its strictest sense refers to sound analysis performed by technology itself. Technological media provide modes of signal reading that do not immediately aim at understanding. The archaeological method adapts to this ascetic approach to signals, resisting the temptations of premature narrative contextualization. A shift of emphasis takes place from cultural interpretation of audio content towards its *analytics* or even *spectrogrammatics*.[1] Sonic signal analysis and data processing is at work for commercial and monitoring uses already – even if automated music analysis mostly still results in generating metadata. With a focus on audio-as-signals, non-logocentristic search engines emerge that by digital sampling randomize what has to this point been known culturally as music.

From 1972 to 1974, the Finnish electronic engineer and research artist Erkki Kurenniemi recorded private entries on audio cassettes, leaving a heap of such records to the Central Art Archives of the National Gallery in Helsinki. How to cope with such a sonic bequest? Algorithms that sort according to spectra similarity can correlate phonetic signals according to loudness and dynamics in decibel in order to find out, for example, the moments when Kurenniemi's dictation switches to singing.[2] Significant speech segments can be derived below the philological fixation on semantics. In additionAs well, the actual location where the articulation took place might be derived by signal-to-noise ratio analysis separating the speaker's voice from background noise.

Kurenniemi developed the electronic music synthesizer DIMI-A (Digital Music Instrument, Associative Memory, 1969), which was equipped with the remarkable option to retrieve digitized audio signals according to 'content' rather than by first addressing the storage cells – sonic hashing. The sonic archive requires the development of *specific* search tools that differ from those used for text search in traditional archives. Sonic memory does not consist of single symbols or characters but of micro-tonal objects that lead to an associative memory rather than order from metadata.

Philological hermeneutics knows how to make sense of texts – but how to make sonicistic sense of signals that are addressed to ears? It is a different kind of memory that speaks to the ear when an individual becomes archive in electro-acoustic devices.[3] Once digitized, archival records can be algorithmically activated – a status beyond preservation. Michael Murtaugh and

Nicolas Malevé developed such an experimental online archive of Kurenniemi's work that focuses on his sonic legacy.[4] The file system itself (which
represents media-archaeological access to bit-level organization) serves as an
interface to perform operations like read/write/execute, erasure, find, tree.
Algorithmic navigation through the audio files requires accepting various
signal-technical properties and interacting with audio streams as such. The
experimental experience of such sonic knowledge is conditioned by the *a
priori* of specialized algorithms like the Fast Fourier Transform.[5] As a basic
tool for signal-based computational sound analysis, this operation breaks
any kind of digitized sound down into discrete time slices. When algorithms
listen to recorded sound, they detect multiple correlations that defy the
fixed taxonomy of archival classification. Not single sound files but the
bits within are the basic record units, revealing micro- and cross-relations
within big sound datascapes, and resulting in a *diagrammatic* sonic archive.

Within such a sonic field, human auditory perception is no longer the
primary hearing theatre. Just as contemporary humanities are moving
away from traditional hermeneutic interpretation in favour of so-called
Digital Humanities,[6] the relation between music, time, and sound is being
transformed. While the supremacy of visual perception (be it seeing or
reading[7]) for informational purposes has for a long time neglected the acoustic channel; the optical representation of acoustic articulation continues
with audio analysis software that creates predominantly visual interfaces
– waveforms and spectrograms. Algorithmic annotation of speech acts
using software derived from computational linguistics results in their
microtemporal analysis, and the discovery of phonicity as fundamental
category of sonic articulation.[8]

Experimentation with the *a priori* of data organization refers to search
algorithms. Sufficiently intelligent software for sound analysis is currently
available;[9] still lacking is their confrontation with innovative media-theoret-
ical questions. From that, an active specification of available software might
arise beyond the current emphasis on automatic generation of semantic
metadata, in favour of learning how to navigate *within* the audio signal
space itself. With algorithmically driven ('automated') tagging (mark-ups),
a kind of metadata derived from within the sonic signal event reveals its
inner temporality. Such digital archaeonautics of sound may be combined
with external 'social tagging' in Open Access Web 2.0 circulation, which is
non-classificatory in similar ways. This finally results in a hybrid of order
and random access, of technological and social sound-based memory.

Intelligent software also enables the automatic tagging of both intentional and non-intentional (even traumatic) 'silence' in audio files. Such

inaudible sound, where nothing but time (and the recording medium) speaks, can be found in the 'Analysis'-toolbar of the audio software Audacity under the explicit term of 'Silence Finder'. The 'Effects' tool, on the other hand, allows for 'removing silence' or to create 'echo' from audio signals, which is manipulation of the sonic time event on its most minute level. The 'Beat Finder' looks like a re-entry of computer clocking itself; the dominant tool, though, is still frequency analysis in diverse 'algorithms'. The archive here becomes a temporary existence: in order to be analyzed, a sound file musthas first to be literally 'loaded' into the Audacity software so that it may be processed for (re-)search. Sonic analytics does not happen in real-time; rather, there is rather a numerical time lens, as indicated by the option to up- or downgrade the sampling rate.

New options of sound retrieval: Accidental sorting by signal- and symbol-based similarity

A decisive requirement for sound analytics is to describe the audio signal *from within*. This reminds us of the MPEG-7 standard once used to describe multi-media content, particularly its low level descriptors that are both temporal and spectral. Computer-augmented algorithmic cluster analysis, as applied by Classical Archaeology (among the first Humanities disciplines to do so), leads to stochastic data distribution instead of historical narrative, to pattern-matching *versus* hermeneutics, to new forms of search that replace traditional statistics (an approach that still refers to the classical archive). Both challenges to traditional scholarship, and new opportunities, emerge. Dynamic algorithmic access, as practiced by Google's search engine, replaces the static classification of the traditional catalogue in libraries. From this results the need for a flexible tool that allows for the coexistence of different orders without destroying the material structure – *relational* databases and *random search* in the administration of computer storage, a kind of *order in fluctuation,* which is the radical temporalization of order itself. This leads to discovering, reflecting and techno-mathematically realizing new technologies of memory by flexible access. The most immediate media in which this can take place are content management systems that include the option of signal-based search functions that are not limited to alphabetic address.

As long as there have only been symbolic, alphabet-based archives, the phantasma of recording the acoustically real signal (predominantly the human voice) has generated only imaginary forms. Even the systematic collection of phonographic records has been predominantly subjected to forms of inventory and administration that were developed in the *longue durée* of paper-based archives. But with the necessity of digitizing phonographic records – in order to preserve them against physical, media-archaeological entropy – new options of signal navigation emerge that deserve episte-mological attention. Dealing with large quantities of sonic data requires a different set of practices than traditional literary scholarship. Hidden within are messages that were never meant to address posterity, and yet information can be extracted from them.

Media archaeology points out the discontinuities that arose with the invasion of audio-visual records in traditional archives, libraries, and mu-seums in the twentieth century, resulting in a rethinking of the options of retrieval under digital media conditions – transcending the notion of the archive itself. The technical and cultural generation of stochastic order out of media-immanent signal disorder is associated with search operations such as similarity-based sound retrieval.

Whereas genuine signal recording media, such as the phonograph, posed a challenge to text-based archives, with the symbolically encoded electronic records of digital media, the archive as symbolic regime returns – though now in a post-Gutenberg modality. With sonic analytics, soft cultural analy-sis is replaced with a media-archaeological method. Revelations of sonic knowledge arise from search algorithms themselves. With so-called audio *data mining*, the media-archaeological element is addressed quite directly. Browsers like the Databionic MusicMiner, developed at the University of Marburg, allow researchers to identify the similarity of songs. Features include automatic parsing in specific collections based on sound.[10] The predominant tools for audio analysis, though, are still data visualization: diagrams such as wave forms and oscillograms.[11]

In between media archaeology and cultural semantics: Automatic music transcription

The application of techno-acoustic devices for phonetic analysis makes particular sense for certain dialects, which that contain nuances that which easily escape the harmonically tuned ears of occidental scholars and are difficult to transcribe in alphabetic notation.[12] Measuring media have a better understanding here, a more sensitive hearing, resulting in a more delicate writing – be it actual acoustic traces in phonographic *grooves* or their analytic diagrams. The vocal alphabet as writing system emerged as an attempt to *analyze* and thereby literally dis-connect continuous oral speech into individual elements – thus creating the linguistic notion of phonemes as such. For his research onf acoustic distortion (relevant for communication under warfare conditions), J.C.R. Licklider concentrated on the proto-semantic realm. Acoustic listening does not equal tonal hearing: 'In order to discuss intelligibility [...] it will be necessary to work with elements: phonemes, syllables, words, or sentences.'[13] This requires a balancing 'back and forth between the level of functions and the level of elements.'[14] When algorithmic search is applied to sound analysis and the measuring of melodic similarity by sonic parameters, a semantic gap opens between the hermeneutic approach of cultural 'understanding' as practiced by musicology and the explicit measuring approach that is enhanced by appropriate instruments.[15]

In French, the writer of musical scores is called *copiste de musique permanent*. Musical notation aims at the endurance of ephemeral sonic articulations, making them invariant against the contingent moment of re-performance and its implementation by varying orchestrations (instruments and human beings).[16] But a phonographic recording of a jazz performance registers the individual moment of performance and interpretation for identical re-play – the 'historical index' becomes metahistorical, reversing the traditional relation between archive (permanent storage) and history (the passing of time).

The technographic record not only allows for co-originary replay, but for measuring the signal as well – different from philological transcriptions. Even for very old recordings, sonagrams can be produced in order to conduct Fourier Analysis of their sonic nature. In previous times, sonic signals needed human decoders to turn them into musical scores. But for the media-archaeological ears of data processing devices, audio signals can be automatically transformed into digital samples, with the digital audio signal representing a transformed time signal. The sampled audio signal can then be processed into visualization formats like the spectrogram, and, alternatively, be printed as conventional musical score (the digital Score Generator). What was first developed for automated speech analysis is here extended to the musical field. The 'Onset Detector' recognizes the beginning of regular notes; but this automated analysis gives access to the temporal realm of the sonic event by identifying micro-temporal structures, beats, and rhythm. These can then be retranslated (remediated, in fact) into culturally familiar categories of musical time structures such as Harmonic Analysis. Denis Gabór proposed 'acoustic quanta' as subliminal temporal elements from which sound can be calculated in the processual time domain. This corrects a tendency, such as in classical Fourier Analysis, to metaphysically pre-suppose eternally periodic wave forms.

Contrary to traditional musicology, which is based primarily around semantic analysis, a signal-oriented archive will no longer list songs and sonic sequences according to their authors, subject, time, and space of recording. Instead, digital sound data banks will allow acoustic sequences to be algorithmically systematized according to genuinely sonic (i.e. wave-based) notions and computing (techno-mathematical) criteria, rather than traditional musical *topoi*. Such a change reveals new insights into the non-symbolic characteristics of music as sound.[17] Sonic expression, while easy to hear intuitively, is difficult to describe adequately or to remember solely through verbal description. Predominantly script-directed occidental culture still lacks a genuine *acoustic dictionary* such as was made possible long ago for the video analysis of body movements or facial expressions.[18] A sonic equivalent for similarity-based pictorial matching in the dynamic field (the *archive in* motion[19]) is the music finder *mufin,* which chooses a cluster of songs in the data bank according to the requested preferences regarding tempo, style, instrumentation, and so forth. This results in generally surprising and unexpected combinations. This is genuine info-aesthetics, according to which the degree of surprise corresponds with the measure of informative quality.[20]

Commercially- driven software has here been the avant garde. Applications like Last.fm learn to detect and then to automatically propose individual preferences. Another music search machine, the MusicIP Mixer, generates fingerprints from which songs can be identified by their genuinely acoustic signature. But even this music analysis technology is still oriented toat recognizing what is meaningful according to *human* musical perception. Once more, the very term 'music' seems almost identical with human, culturally trained listening. According to ancient Greek mathematics, however, musical knowledge (*mousiké epistemé*) is not the exclusive purview of humans; it may also be conceived as detached, even independent of human listening, such as with the Platonic music of the astronomical spheres. With strictly media-archaeological, machine-based analysis, this conception reoccurs.

Most online cultural web portals like *Europeana* so far restrict the search options to names, titles, places, or dates, and do not allow for content-based search in more anarchi(vi)c modes of retrieval. When advanced search techniques known from the visual field – such as image query by example or visual similarity search[21] – are extended to the under explored *sonic* dimension, this will finally enable a process of navigating *within* the sonic medium. The sonically algorithmicized archive will thereby transform from a passive memory to media-active subject of search. The search engine itself becomes an archaeologist of sonic knowledge. Automated feature description as a media-archaeological tool corresponds with the methods of Systematic Musicology rather than to Historical Musicology. Instead of sono-cultural historicism, it identifies statistical regularities or stochastic correlations in explicit or implicit music- related articulation. Large electronic collections of music that are in symbolically-encoded, computer-readable form[22] enable theories that can re-define the ancient alliance between music and mathematics in more dynamic terms. In a shift from explicit sound analysis to implicit sonicity, 'symbolic formats can be contrasted with audio formats which, instead of capturing notes explicitly, encode the sonic aspect of a musical performance by representing sound as a complex waveform.'[23]

While semantic listening concentrates on *musical objects* like a melody, the media-archaeological 'ear' focuses on the *sonic time object*. If melodies, rhythms, and harmonies are mentally represented in a form comparable with symbolic encoding formats, this is a direct function of the way that musical material is conditioned by cultural and historical modes of understanding.[24] In conceiving a melody as a contour kept and recognized in memory 'over time' (in both senses), the time-critical approach of media archaeology can concentrate on non-harmonic micro-figurations of temporality within the sonic event. Thus, special algorithms are needed that identify such temporal qualities (such as dynamic time warping[25]), or robust and efficient algorithms 'for extracting the repetitive structure of an audio recording.'[26]

'Distant' statistical analysis of massive sound data enables new kinds of techno-mathematical interpretation. But at the borderlines of the *semantic gap*, an automated, algorithmic archaeology of such sound clusters does not explain or evaluate emphatic *musical* relationships. Detailed analyzes of the originality or idiosyncrasies of single artistic works is still dependent on traditional music analysis: 'The quantification [...] is a statistical one and [...] it is cognitive experiment and musicological reasoning that must prove the final arbiter of the system's performance.'[27]

Sonic search 'within its own medium': Content-based retrieval

Efficient sound analysis software has been developed for either copyright protection purposes or as early commercial 'apps'. The obsession with copyright issues in the music industry led to the development of techno-mathematically innovative software; mighty algorithmic tools have been developed for such copyright identification (locating metadata for audio content without metadata annotation). Most advanced mass-applicable content-based search engines for audio data can be implemented in a mobile smart phone to identify and annotate a musical source. The song is almost immediately recognized, and the user might be presented with the recommendation for purchasing a download. The software application recognizes melodies that are accidentally heard and compares it to a large data bank of songs on request, in order to generate a message that provides the user with appropriate metadata such as title and artist.[28]

Traditional modes of audio or image retrieval involved the manual annotation of such data in text form, resulting in a text-based management and retrieval system. Such a literal transcription of audio-visual evidence into symbolic notation is an asymmetrical transformation, reducing the richness of aesthetic signals to semantic signs. The alternative way (e.g. content-based retrieval systems according to the MPEG-7 standards) is to retrieve audio-visual evidence *in its own medium* (that is, aisthetic regime): 'based on audio analysis, it is possible to describe sound or music by its spectral energy distribution, harmonic ratio or fundamental frequency,'[29] allowing for a comparative classification of sound into general sound categories.

Sonic media culture is neither strictly posthuman, nor simply a technological extension of humans. 'Both human users and automatic systems that process audiovisual information are within the scope of MPEG-7'[30]; both may query the MPEG-7 descriptions stored in a database. When such low- or high-level descriptions are (automatically) extracted from the audio-visual record itself – displaying the variation of properties of audio over time or frequency – it makes sense to call the resulting database an archive rather than a library-like catalogue (the latter provides the basis for meta-classification of audio content). But once it is possible to identify identical, similar or dissimilar audio content, the symbolic order is replaced by fuzzy criteria that demand for a different theory and policy of sonic memory.

The time domain description (by the audio waveform descriptor) represents a genuine affordance of multi-media archives, media-archaeologically revealing characteristics of the original music signal in its very sonic existence: the harmonicity of a signal, its tone quality (timbre), down to discrete segments of sound (a phonographic alternative to alphabetic symbolic 'elementarization', that is: analysis). Spectral audio description is derived from the time-frequency analysis of an audio signal; – that is, from within the signal (as sampled into digital values). Media-archaeological ears listen to the endogenic evidence and learn from acoustic surveillance algorithms as have been developed for online copyright violation detection for the popular music industry.[31]

The audio identification software TRM creates an acoustic fingerprint of the first 30 seconds of a piece of music – a sonic kind of *incipit*. The Fraunhofer Institute for Integrated Circuits developed a similar software for identification of MP3 files with the telling name Audio ID. Driven further, such knowbots can navigate the internet itself – resulting in counter-strategies like voluntary distortions of the music piece in question, close to tactics of cryptography. As was described by Michel Foucault for power mechanisms, paranoia can be regarded as productive. For a long time, only songs indexed by their title or performers could be identified on the World Wide Web. This led to curious arbitrary deformations of metadata geared toward escaping such monitoring, e.g. the automatic deformer program Napcameback. Without explicit logocentric identification, digitized sound files remain media-archaeologically naked, like pure alphanumeric URLs on the Web itself.[32] Algorithms that show the way (in the sense of Descartes' *Discours de la Methode*) to the 'content' of a sound file simultaneously at the same time transform the hermeneutic notion of content into a function of mathematical procedures.[33]

The search engine *FindSounds* allows for non-semantic, sound-oriented audio search – even if the criterion is still typed in words ('enter one or more words in the search box').[34] Digital signal processing in combination with psychoacoustics, speech- and contour recognition, computer music, and multimedia data banks leads to a different culture of de-classifying sound and navigation: 'audio based on the characteristics of the audio rather than by resorting exclusively to keywords.'[35]

Such an approach is a hermeneutic hybrid since this content-based sound retrieval application explicitly offers algorithmic tools in combination with traditional text queries. 'It is now possible to select or sort or classify sounds from a database using the distance measure. Some example queries are: Retrieve the 'scratchy' sounds,'[36] which maintains the non-human sonic memory of the recording device itself. This allows for an aesthetic sonicity – a quality that is generated by technical media themselves and could not have been registered in the alphabet before the arrival of gramophone and electromagnetic media.

For a long time, only the textual records of bequests donated to the archives have been on display. But from the magnetic tapes belonging to the 'papers' of the conductor Hermann Scherchen in the Central Archives of the Academy of the Arts in Berlin, the research artist Christina Kubisch extracted segments where Scherchen tests different types of microphones by singing with varying intensity and from different distances the beginning of the *Ode an die Freude* from Beethoven's 9th Symphony. Sonograms of these test recordings produced by Kubisch[37] make such para-musical sonicity graphically visible.

Since the 1970s, R. Murray Schafer has collected endangered sounds, such as the noise of outdated technologies and machines. Similarly, the Phonogram Archives in Berlin and Vienna were established around 1900 to save the music of endangered ethnic cultures from around the world. Not just musical content can be identified and analyzed from such source material; in the same manner, noise analysis from historical recordings allows researchers to identify the recording technology itself (Edison cylinder, gramophone, magnetic tape). These are media-archaeological indices: sonicity from within the technology.

From audio signal analysis to the *signal-to-noise ratio* of communication engineering there are only a few steps. Unusual sonic events can be identified from the frequency spectrum of an audio signal for information.[38] The characteristics of phonetic articulation encompass the whole range between vowels and noise.[39] By making this dichotomy sonographically visible, a formal approach to such phono-cultural content is possible, just as Heinrich Wölfflin in his *Kunstgeschichtliche Grundbegriffe* (1915) identified oppositional contours for different styles in art history.[40]

'While the specific analysis algorithms [...] for audio differ from those found in image or video analysis systems, the general techniques employed bear some resemblance to non-audio content-based retrieval systems, for example, the Query by Image Content (QBIC) system [...].'[41] Is sound analysis subjected once more to the visual-centrism of Western epistemology when its electronic and digital measuring and signal processing monitors translate the audio input into *visual evidence* (to put it tautologically), or when audio browsers displaying text strings in list views? Different from spatial typography, audio signals are essentially one-dimensional functions of the time axis. The visual regime serves to abbreviate temporal extension, with diagrammatic sonicity as condensed sound: 'Waveform and spectral displays are sometimes useful, but only to the highly trained eye (and ear). Visual displays of the n-dimensional search space [...] would be appropriate for browsers of large sound databases.'[42]

Case study *Lautarchiv*
The target of sonic analytics is not individual speech in terms of meaningful content, but subsemantic insights that can be derived from the very materiality of sono-cultural articulation: *phoné* (German '*Laut*').[43] The phonographic collection of early voice recordings (*Lautarchiv*) based at Humboldt University, Berlin is an ideal subject for such a sonic archaeology. The Lautarchiv encompasses three groups: a) Famous voices (which for political reasons were partly neutralized or even destroyed after 1945); b)

truly archival recordings of local speech dialects, based on a set of artificial word sequences in order to achieve formal comparability (so-called Wenker-sentences). The speed of these recordings is controlled by a supplementary oscillographic time code; and c) recordings for musical ethnology (mostly Africans and Indians from the French and British Army in the World War One *Halbmond* prisoner camp at Wünsdorf south of Berlin).[44] The phonological target was inscribed into the Lautarchiv by its promoter Wilhelm Doegen from the beginning – notwithstanding the circumstances of its coming-into-being with recordings in a prisoner camp. While cultural analysis concentrates on this ambivalent historical and discursive context, with a different epistemological vantage point, media archaeology lends its ears to knowledge that can be derived from the actual media articulation contained in the technical archive itself.

In April 1920, these recordings became integrated as the Department of Phonetics (*Lautabteilung*) into the Prussian State Library in Berlin to be reproduced on shellac discs and as transcription for educational distribution. This caused the original relation between spoken orality and its *grama*-phonic derivative (the phonetic alphabet[45]) to be reversed again. The intrusion of real audio signals into the symbolic order of the librarians' Gutenberg world of letters resulted in a kind of animated phonetic library.[46] Printed text starts to speak from an analogue gramophonic storage medium that (contra the coding and filtering of meaning in alphabetic inscription) does not discriminate between signal and noise. The *Lautabteilung* consequently accumulates natural and artificial noise such as the sound of tree leaves in the wind. What had started as interlinear auditory hallucinations in romantic literature becomes real in sub-symbolic recording media. The gramophonic recording method for waveforms in the so-called *glyphic system* on wax discs inscribes even the sound of war into the new cultural memory as *écriture automatique*.[47]

The limits of handwritten phonetic transcription became obvious when it came to the detection of minute variances and the elimination of subjective inexactitudes in listening to the recordings of foreign dialects and voices. This lead instead to the application of visual oscillograms and Fourier Analysis of the phonetic wave forms.[48] When the technographical measuring of sonicity replaces explicit listening, a gap opens between cognitive musical understanding and physical recording (the material, tonally *integrative* engraving of a musical event in the phonographic groove). Just like the point of the gramophone needle can make only one movement at one time,

the illuminated disk of the oscilloscope shows only one line, no matter how many tones are sung into the microphone simultaneously. [...] what the apparatus registers as *one* wave, we *hear* as *multiplicity* of tones – and as an organized multiplicity. [...] mathematical analysis of the shape of the line permits us to deduce the individual waves that are combined in it.[49]

Even the much more detailed spectral voice analysis that had just been developed in Zuckerkandl's generation subjected the complex dynamics of sonic events once more to the visual knowledge regime. Sonagrams, though expressing delicate micro-temporal variations, seem to invite graphic decipherment analogous to alphabetic writing.[50] But the tempor(e)ality of sonicity can never be caught in a frozen state; it always points beyond the moving still – as discussed in Bergson's critique of chronophotography and the cinematographic illusion of 'movement'.

Today, such early phonetic oscillograms represent the truest media historiography of that time. At the same time, they challenge the historical narrative of their recording context. The real archive of sonic articulation emanating from such recordings is no longer literary stories but numerical analysis. The result is digital sampling of analogue records – the transduction of ghostly voices into computability. It was in the linguistic field that effective algorithms for recognition were first developed to transform physically measurable waveforms of speech signals into electric impulses. The operation is based first on electronic transduction and then the transformation of the time signal to its frequency number.[51] Thus, sonicity cannot be reduced to the dynamics of waveforms, but encompasses mathematical operations and subsequently their machinic computing as well. Once a series of digits can represent waveforms, sound is liberated from its acoustic phenomenology. The statistic tools from corpus-based linguistics have been adopted for music analysis:

> While the basic elements and features (or tokens) over which statistics are computed naturally differ between linguistics and musicology, the statistical concepts that allow us to infer regularities within the specific domain are quite similar or nearly identical. Among the chief statistical concepts that can be derived from frequency counts of tokens / features, and that are employed in both fields, are Markov models, entropy and mutual information, association measures, unsupervised clustering techniques, and supervised classifiers such as decision trees.[52]

Sonic analysis in a *Lautarchiv* focuses on the materiality of sound, equally valuable in its acoustic and its technological sense. In modern Greek, radio broadcasting is called *radiophonia*. It is not speech or music as semantic

content that is named here, but an analog to telephony: the phonetic materiality (ancient Greek *phoné*/German *Laut*) of any kind that is transmitted
by a neutral medium called radio. In terms of a media archaeology of
acoustics, the nature of sound is spectral, thus undermining the symbolic
(Pythagorean) order of harmonic tonal relations in integer numbers. Similarly, the letters in an alphabet only symbolically relate to the physicality
of actual speech phonemes that are as 'differential' (Arseny Avraamov) as
the *glissandi* of the Theremin Vox constructed by Leon Theremin as the
first mass-reproduced electronic music instrument in revolutionary Soviet
Union.[53] Evgeny Sholpo's Mechanical Orchestra was an electro-mechanical
synthesizer that used a set of Helmholtz tuning forks as sine wave oscillators.
It was constructed with adjusted frequencies to form a discrete microtonal
scale 'covering the whole audible range with intervals between successive
pitches unperceivable to the human ear.'[54] With sound production that is
subliminal to human perception, sonicity – different from sonority – begins.

Media Time: Technomathematical options of sound-based query
Phonography has been the media-archaeological precondition for new
kinds of academic sound analysis. Mechanical analogue recording media
made sound memorable on the signal level (which addresses the auditive sense) for the first time. This -*graphy* led to a new kind of scriptural
memory that stood apart from alphabetic notation because of its capacity
to record and replay the temporal axis itself using audio-visual signals.[55]
But only electromagnetic signal registration allowed for processing sound
with the intelligence of electronics. When, in an additional sono-analytic
transformation, sound records are digitized, they allow for algorithmic
research. Digitization makes sound memory culture accessible to operations unthinkable in analog days – such as genuinely *sound-based sound
retrieval* and research by means of genuinely acoustic parameters, leading
to a 'semantic' search of a new kind.

'During the last [...] decades, numerous attempts have been made to
develop taxonomies of sounds, including musical and environmental
sounds.'[56] But sonic analytics ought not to be confused with so-called Sound
Studies. Dynamic sonicity teaches us to navigate within the alphanumerics
of digitized sound instead of subjecting them to classification by phenomenological or anthropological metadata. Sonicistic search in sound archives
is understood strictly from the perspective of its technomathematically
conceivable parameters (*sound-based sound retrieval*), suspended from
the questions of philological hermeneutics or sociological contextualization. The algorithmic tool of a Self Organizing Map (SOM), as developed by

Teuvo Kohonen, enables within the computer what Gilles Deleuze and Félix Guattari once conceived as a cartographic linkage of knowledge (Rhizome): an interrelation of purely formal, contingent relations of neighbourhood, analyzed media-immanently and based on digital stochastics, liberated from cultural – that is, semantically and cognitively – burdened metadata.

It is a necessity not just for preservation but also for future transmission of cultural heritage that signals stored in audio archives are digitized. The data pool resulting from that rescuing operation can be used creatively for different purposes: to experiment with archival orders that differ from traditional logocentric and metadata-based classification in favour of genuinely different options for sound retrieval. It is the real challenge of the digital archive to become algorithmically productive, uncovering the mathematical sonicity of dynamic articulations that are otherwise hidden in epistemological silence. This latent knowledge redefines the traditional mathematical character of music[57] and reveals implicit sonicity in any algebraic function. Such sonicity has until now been romantically understood as a vibrational force called 'time'.

Notes

Preface

1. Sound as a way of knowing has been termed 'acoustemology'; see Feld (2011), also Volmar (2012), 71-83.
2. For a well-defined list of sonic effects (especially the entanglement of sound and time, such as 'drone' or 'resonance') see Augoyard and Torgue (2005).
3. See Ernst (2004).
4. See the special issue X (2008) of the online journal PopScriptum curated by Peter Wicke.
5. See Wolfgang Ernst, *Im Medium erklingt die Zeit* (2015). For a brilliant genealogy of technologies to visualize sound and the human voice (in terms of signal recording and its spectrographical analysis) see Mills (2010).

Foreword

1. This Foreword is a revised and expanded version of my review, 'Under the Hood of Wolfgang Ernst's Media Archaeology', which first appeared in *Reviews in Cultural Theory* 4.2 (September 2013). Reprinted with permission from *Reviews in Cultural Theory*.
2. Sean Michaels, *Us Conductors* (Toronto: Random House Canada, 2014), 16.
3. Ibid, 18.
4. Edmund Carpenter and Marshall McLuhan, 'Acoustic Space' in *Explorations in Communication: An Anthology*, edited by Marshall McLuhan and Edmund Carpenter (Boston: Beacon Press, 1960).
5. References to the present text, *Sonic Time Machines,* are indicated with in-text parenthesis. References to *Digital Memory and the Archive* are, as with other external sources, cited using footnotes.
6. It is worth noting that there is no general agreement about what constitutes 'media archaeology'. The most appropriate entry point into media-archaeological debates is the eclectic mix of studies in Jussi Parikka and Erkki Huhtamo's 2011 edited collection *Media Archaeology: Approaches, Applications, Implications* (Berkeley CA: University of California Press, 2011). Parikka himself has done the most work towards unpacking the question of *What is Media Archaeology?* (London: Polity, 2012). He understands it as – among other things—an example of what Mieke Bal calls a 'travelling' concept or theory: a wandering, generative matrix of approaches, concepts, and activities that account for the discursive, technical, and poetic dimensions of media objects and networks both 'new' and 'old' (on traveling concepts, see Bal, *Travelling Concepts in the Humanities: A Rough Guide,* Toronto: University of Toronto Press, 2002). If we imagine that these varying approaches exist on a media- archaeological continuum, Ernst's emphasis on the technical aspects of media (exemplified in the present text and *Digi-*

tal Memory and the Archive) might approach one pole, while a figure like Siegfried Zielinski, who emphasizes media poetics and 'variantology', would approach the other (see Zielinksi, *Deep Time of The Media,* Cambridge MA: The MIT Press, 2006). And yet, the impossibility of such an imagined continuum—which dissolves immediately in view of both thinkers' privileging of the relation between media and time—tells us more about media archaeology than the initial comparison.

7.   See e.g. Lev Manovich, *Software Takes Command* (New York: Bloomsbury Academic, 2013); and Wendy Hui Kyong Chun, *Programmed Visions: Software and Memory* (Cambridge MA: MIT Press, 2011).

8.   See e.g. John Durham Peters, 'Calendar, Clock, Tower' in *Deus in Machina: Religion and Technology in Historical Perspective,* edited by Jeremy Stolow. (New York: Fordham University Press, 2013): 25-42; and Ned Rossiter, 'Logistical Worlds', *Cultural Studies Review* 20.1 (2014): 53-76.

9.   Matthew G. Kirschenbaum, *Mechanisms: New Media and the Forensic Imagination* (Cambridge MA: MIT Press, 2008).

10.   See Jonathan Sterne, *The Audible Past: Cultural Origins of Sound Reproduction* (Durham: Duke University Press, 2003).

11.   Wolfgang Ernst, *Digital Memory and the Archive,* edited and introduced by Jussi Parikka (Minneapolis: University of Minnesota Press, 2013), 55.

12.   Ibid, 25.

13.   Ibid, 59.

14.   Jussi Parikka, 'Archival Media Theory: An Introduction to Wolfgang Ernst's Media Archaeology' in Ernst, *Digital Memory and the Archive,* 9.

15.   See Friedrich A. Kittler, *Gramophone, Film, Typewriter,* translated by Geoffrey Winthrop-Young and Michael Wutz (Stanford: Stanford University Press, 1999).

16.   Sybille Krämer offers the definitive take on Kittler's discovery of time-axis manipulation in 'The Cultural Techniques of Time Axis Manipulation: On Friedrich Kittler's Conception of Media', *Theory, Culture, and Society* 23, nos. 7-8 (2006): 93-109.

17.   Ernst, *Digital Memory,* 30.

18.   For an indispensable discussion of processing—the oft-neglected function of Kittler's famous trifecta—see Hartmut Winkler, "Processing: The Third and Neglected Media Function", presented at *MediaTransatlantic: Media Theory in North America and German-Speaking Europe,* University of British Columbia, Vancouver BC, Canada (8 April 2010). Transcription at: http://homepages.uni-paderborn.de/winkler/proc_e.pdf.

19.   See Shintaro Miyazaki, 'Algorhythmics: Understanding Microtemporality in Computational Cultures', *Computational Culture* (Sept. 2012): http://computationalculture.net/article/algorhythmics-understanding-micro-temporality-in-computational-cultures.

20.   Ernst, *Digital Memory,* 59.

21. See Ernst, 'Telling versus Counting: A Media-Archaeological Point of View' in Ernst, *Digital Memory,* 147-157.
22. Ibid, 149.
23. Ernst, *Digital Memory*, 71.
24. Alexander John Watson, 'General Introduction' in Harold A. Innis, *Empire and Communication* (Toronto: Dundurn Press, 2007), 17.
25. The project of revealing the hidden contours of (being in the) modern world unites Heidegger's 'early' and 'late' periods, though it did not crystallize as specifically modern until the later writings on technology. In *Being and Time,* the problem of being is one of universal human being, by the time of 'The Question Concerning Technology' and 'Only a God Can Save Us', the problem is oriented around humanity's confrontation with the modern technical world (i.e. *Gestell*) and the systems of thought which underpin it (i.e. *Bestand*). See Heidegger, *Being and Time,* translated by Joan Stambaugh (Albany: State University of New York Press, 2002); Heidegger, 'The Question Concerning Technology' in *Basic Writings,* edited by David Farrell Krell (San Francisco: Harper Collins, 1993): 307-342; Heidegger, '"Only a God Can Save Us": *Der Spiegel's* interview with Martin Heidegger', translated by Maria P. Alter and John D. Caputo in *The Heidegger Controversy: A Reader,* edited by Richard Wolin (New York: Columbia University Press, 1991): 91-116.

1.   Introduction: On 'sonicity'

1. Only after transduction into the loudspeaker do such vibrations become sound again, as a German dictionary of electronic music in its entry '*Welle*' ('Wave') insists. See Enders (1997), 363.
2. Somewhat in-between is Alvin Lucier's early sonification of brain waves, *Music for Solo Performer* (1965). From the media-archaeological point of view, the main performer here is the electronic vacuum tube. The transistor allows micro-voltage to be amplified up to a level that can be coupled with a loudspeaker in order to emit acoustic, thus sensitive, waves.
3. Bogatirov quoted and translated in Smirnov (2012), 129. Nikolai Bernstein's 'Kymocyclograms' of the bodily movement of piano players (within Alexei Gastev's biomechanically orientated Central Institute of Labour in Moscow) analyzed micro-movements in terms that are familiar from the Fourier analysis of complex sound.
4. See Deleuze (1985), 80.
5. As described in *The Time Machine* (1895). The sonic time machine is closer to Bill Fontana's sound sculpture project *Acoustic Time Travel*, which listens to the (sonified) enunciations of the Large Haedron Collider at CERN (the European Organization for Nuclear Research) in Geneva.
6. See programmatically the protagonist of electronic music Karlheinz Stockhausen (1957), 13-42.
7. Peters (2004), 193.

8. A kind of 'historage' *sit venia verbo*.
9. See Bergson, (1948 [1907]), 304 f.
10. Jussi Parikka translates the German noun '*das Sonische*' as 'sonicity' in his introduction to Part III of Ernst (2013), 144.
11. For a related media-epistemological approach to sound see Goodman (2009), 81 ff. According to Goodman, sound is merely a thin slice of a wider spectrum of sonicity, those vibrations audible to humans.
12. Yankovsky, quoted and translated by Smirnov (2012), 210.
13. See Zakharine and Meise (2013).
14. This argument refers both to Marshall McLuhan's central argument ('the medium is the message') in *Understanding Media* (1964) and to Martin Heidegger's epistemology of technology's essence in *The Question Concerning Technology and Other Essays* (1977).
15. '[...] aliam vero extensionem habet [sonus, et] motus, a tempore, que nunc vocetur longitudo ipsius soni', Oresme in Clagett (1968), 306.
16. See Hentschel (2000).
17. McLuhan (1962).
18. Such was the impetus of a conference in Amsterdam (29-31 March 2005) under the title of *Sonic Interventions*.
19. Subotnik (1996), 148-176 (161f).
20. See Thompson (2002).
21. As remarked by Angerer (2007), 35. Most current studies on 'affect' almost completely miss the acoustic dimension while privileging visual evidence. See as well Ott (2010).
22. See Snell (1992 [1924]), 96.
23. Letter to Barbara Ward, 9 February 1973, in McLuhan (1987), 466.
24. But caution, a term like 'sonic epistemologies' itself is awry; ancient Greek *epistemé* is already triggered by a visual bias that is rooted in alphabetic writing (a reminder of Ani Goh, Berlin).
25. Davis (1999), 390.
26. Kay in Packer and Jordan (2001), 124, referring to McLuhan (1964). See also Alt in Huhtamo and Parikka (2011), 278-301 (297f). In analogous words Vilém Flusser defined the 'gesture' of listening to music (1991), 193-203.
27. Schrödinger's quantum mechanical wave function, though, does not describe actual vibrations but the implicit propagation of probabilities to locate particles in the spatio-temporal grid. See Schwartz (2011), 650.
28. Such sonic temporality is a necessary factor in Superstring theory, which assumes one *time* dimension in addition to 10 otherwise spatial dimensions.
29. Viola (1990), 44. One way of generating electro-acoustic tone with synthesizers is to start by filtering noise right away.
30. The term 'sonality' has been proposed to name such concepts. See Moebus and Wilke (2011), 12 and 705.

31. In that sense, John Durham Peters writes of 'sonic revelations' of the vibrational qualities of the human eardrum by Hermann von Helmholtz' artifactual resonators (*Resonatoren*), Peters in Rabinovitz and Geil (2004), 185.

32. Derivation is also meant here in its sense of mathematical differentiation, where the derivative of a sinusoidal function describes its rate of change near a chosen input value. On the close ties between mathematical abstraction and phonocentricity in early Indian science see Moebus and Wilke (2011), 227.

33. As was achieved in the eighteenth century with Euler and d'Alembert; see Siegert (2003).

34. For the sonic results from his spectro-morphological Mechanical Orchestra, Evgeny Sholpo declared that 'any possibility of theoretical analysis is suppressed,' in Smirnov (2013), 35. See also a somewhat idiosyncratic mathematical formula expressing the vibrations of a violin string under the action of the bow, Avraamov in Smirnov (2013), 29.

35. On the interrelation between musical notation and marks for prosodic pauses (*prosodiae*) see Saenger (1997), 53 and 74f.

36. Heidegger (1977), 12.

37. 'Matter thus resolves itself into numberless vibrations, all linked together in uninterrupted continuity, all bound up with each other, and travelling in every direction like shivers through an immense body,' Bergson (1950), 276.

38. McLuhan (1987), 177.

39. Viola (1990), 44. See also well Viola's videotape *Information* (1973), which, in the artist's own words, used a video switcher 'as if it were a musical instrument [...] to "play" this nonsignal,' in London et al. (1987), 24.

40. Viola (1990), 44.

41. 'The telephone sparked an anticipatory interest in visual systems [...],' Uricchio quoted in Mills (2012), 39.

42. See Rheinberger (1991), esp. chapter IV 'Das "Epistemische Ding" und seine technischen Bedingungen,' 67ff.

43. This is the training and task unique to Media Studies as a discipline within the Faculty of Humanities and distinct from the engineering and mathematical disciplines.

44. E. g. the Nipkow-Televizor (30-line), produced by the Tratri Novakove Company in Prague, 1934, on display in the *60 Years of Television Broadcasting* special exhibition at the National Technical Museum, Prague, May-December, 2013.

45. When such shellac records recently returned from the archive, they were mistaken for musical sound recordings. On the digital archaeology of these archaic TV images, see the announcement in the online presentation: 'Not until the computer era came on us could we study these images': http://www.tvdawn.com/recording.htm.

46. As can be listened to in the digitally restored video recordings contained on the CD edition: *The Dawn of Television Remembered. The John Logie Baird years: 1923-1936*, conceived, written and produced by Donald McLean (2005).

47. See deForest (1923), 61ff (61).

48. For an online re-presencing of the moving image sequence see Donald McLean (2005), *The Silvatone Recording: 1933:* http://www.tvdawn.com/earliest-tv/the-silvatone-recording-1933.

49. McLean (2000), 211f.

50. The media philosopher Vilém Flusser also well defined a dialectic synthesis of the audio-visual divide – the *sounding image* ('tönendes Bild') of the electronic image in implicit sonicity. See Flusser (1985), 138.

51. Viola (1990), 44. A similar message was conveyed by Nam June Paik's pathbreaking media-artistic exhibition *Exposition of music – Electronic television* at the Parnass Gallery, Wuppertal 1963; Paik had originally been trained in electro-acoustic engineering. It was during an experimental music workshop in Chocorua, New Hampshire, in summer 1973, that Viola's awareness not only of electronic theory and circuit design, but also of time-varying sonicity and sonic perception of space was focused. See London (1987), 11.

52. See Van Eck (1985).

53. An argument developed in Sebastian Dierksen's paper in Media Studies at Humboldt University, Berlin: Elektromagnetische Emissionen von Computer-Bildschirmen als Sonifikation (September 2013).

54. See Hausmann in Niebisch (2013). This device originally emerged as a reading machine for the blind in 1913 with Edmund Fournier d'Albe's Optophone, to convert text into tones and vibrations, as explained by Borck in Daniels and Schmidt (2008).

55. Yankovsky in Smirnov (2013), 209. In a parallel acoustic approach, Rudolf Pfenninger in Munich synthesized sound, while Oskar Fischinger in Berlin derived sound from arbitrary graphic patterns. See Levin (2003).

56. Yankovsky in Smirnov (2013), 209.

57. Fourier (1822), 15.

58. See Schnebel (1963).

59. Herwig Weiser made this split sensuality the message of his installation *Ambiguous Cut into Space of Conjecture*, as expressed by Marcel René Marburger (2011): 'The high-frequency sound is unperceivable to the senses. The work is a sound sculpture whose aural expression is not perceptible. Though the ultrasound produces an effect, human sensorial inadequacy prevents its passing through into the viewer's consciousness. [...] The piece simultaneously reveals and conceals.'

60. Pias in Huhtamo and Parikka (2011), 167.

61. Piggott (1972), 29.

62. Viola (1990), 47.

63. Similarly, digital television signal processing can be traced back to the inside of an electronic time-critical device for otherwise analogue image

recording – where the line- or framewise synchronization of electronic images is implicitly sonic (in the sense of Viola 1990): 'Transforming the signal into numbers, recording them into memory, recalling them at the right moment, and transferring everything errorless back to the analogue signal first appeared in 1974 in the Ampex AVR-2 recording facility', as its digital Time Base Corrector is described in the special exhibition on 60 years of television in the National Technical Museum, Prague (fall / winter 2013).

64. Kurenniemi (2004), 34.
65. Kohl (1983), 148.
66. See Wyschnegradsky (1996); and Barthelmes, Raum and Klang (1995), 68.
67. Viola (1990), 46.
68. Apparently Fourier got the intuition for decomposing complex periodic signals into sine components (*Théorie de la Chaleur*, Paris 1822) when perceiving the vibrating air in the heat of the Egyptian desert during Napoleon's expedition. This is another resonance with Bill Viola's understanding of the electronic image, especially his videotape *Chott el-Djerid* (1979). At a salt lake in the Tunisian Sahara Desert, the intense midday heat 'manipulates, bends, and distorts the light rays to such an extent that you actually see things that are not here. Trees and sand dunes float off the ground, the edges of mountains and buildings ripple and vibrate, colour and form blend into one shimmering dance.' Viola in London et al. (1987), 37.
69. Ong (1982), 72.
70. Ibid.
71. Dated 17 April 17, 1969. McLuhan (1987), 367.
72. According to Norbert Bolz, with the simultaneity of electromagnetic waves the concept of history itself has come to an end. See Bolz in: *First Europeans. Frühe Kulturen – Moderne Visionen,* exhibition catalogue Schloß Charlottenburg, Berlin (1993), 90.
73. McLuhan (1987), 466.
74. See Mackenzie (2001). For a general analysis of online temporality, see Rushkof (2013).
75. See Pias in Huhtamo and Parikka (2011), 173 ff.
76. Abstract to Jussi Parikka (2013).

2.   Beeing as '*Stimmung*'

1. On that term see Levin in Levin, Frohne, and Weibel (2002). On disrupted temporality in current sound culture, see Reynolds (2012).
2. See Ernst (2012).
3. Gregory Kramer et al., Sonification Report. Status of the field and Research Agenda (2010).
4. See Gozza (2000).
5. On 'sonic' time, see chap. 9 'Toward a Media Archaeology of Sonic Articulations' in Ernst (2013), 172-183.
6. As paraphrased by Lenoir's 'Foreword' to Hansen (2004), xxvi.

7.   As expressed by Shintaro Miyazaki in his published Ph.D. thesis: *Algorhyth-misiert. Eine Medienarchäologie digitaler Signale und (un)erhörter Zeitef-fekte*, Berlin (Kulturverlag Kadmos) 2013.
8.   Davis (1999), 387.
9.   See Jenny (1972), 139. (Referring to Wunderlich 1966).
10. Davis (1999), 387 and 390.
11. Media archaeology accentuates the (infra-)structurally time-invariant prin-ciples of *archai* rather than its historicist meaning as origin(s) as expressed in Neckenbürger (1953), 4.
12. Trenholme (1994), 128.
13. See the chapter 'The Resonating Interval' in McLuhan and Powers (1989).
14. Blanchard (1941), 415. This context is discussed in the examination thesis of Johannes Maibaum (2013).
15. The interrelation and recursions between music and mathematics were the focus of the late Friedrich Kittler's magnum opus, *Musik und Mathematik* (2006).
16. Lomax, Bartenieff, and Paulay in Cohen (2005), 278.
17. Lomax et al. (2005), 277f.
18. Anderson (2004), abstract.
19. See Heidegger (1994), 179f.
20. In the time domain humans are mortal, while in the frequency domain they become immortal, as expressed in Kittler (2012), 48.
21. See Cage (1961), 8.
22. As quoted by Diederichsen in Bieber et al. (2002), 432f.
23. See Heidegger (2005), 125.
24. Bayreuther in Thomä (forthcoming), esp. chapter 2.2 'Auf dem Weg zu einer Akustik des Seyns': 'Stimmung', 'Schwingung', und 'Harmonie' nach Sein und Zeit'. Sonic and mental *tuning* merge into one.
25. Listen e. g., to SUNN O))), *The GrimmRobe* demos, track 2 'Defeating: Earth's Gravity', SUNN 37 Southern Lord (LP), CD BMI 2004.
26. Viola (1990), 46.
27. As expressed by Markus Gammel in his radio feature *Das große Summen* (2012).

3.   Sonic re-presencing
1.   See Goodman in Fuller (2008), 256.
2.   See Kirkegaard (2006).
3.   For more information on *AION*, see http://fonik.dk/works/aion.html.
4.   See Fuchs (1994), 175.
5.   Blesser and Salter in Sterne (2012), 195.
6.   As an exemplary study see Weinzierl, 2002.
7.   An operation well known from echo delay by magnetic tape players.
8.   Here the artist de-couples what is known from the cinematic *dispositif* – in which (since the age of the sound film) the relationship between sound and

image is dramatically and technically coupled – to violently merge both sensual modalities in the audience's perception.

9. As has been analyzed by Chion (1994).
10. This art of media-induced differentiation was developed as far back as 1766 in Gotthold Ephraim Lessing's treatise *Laocoon*.
11. See Cooper (2006-2008).
12. Link in Zielinski and Link (2006), 30.

4. The sonic computer

1. See Kittler (2015).
2. See Turing in Carpenter and Doran (1986).
3. Bijsterveld (2008), 148, referring to Antheil (1925).
4. Montfort et al. (2013), 87, referring to Gombrich (1994), 10.
5. See Montfort et al. (2013), 87, referring to Gombrich (1994), 10.
6. On the neuro-processual time frame ('window of simultaneity') that counts as the human experience of 'presence' see Varela in Petitot, Varela, Pachoud and Roy (1999), esp. 272f and 276f.
7. See Hansen (2004), esp. chap. 7 'Body Times', 235-268.
8. See Kittler (2000), 117, for a discussion of having constructed his own electronic music synthesizer.
9. The first social web application of such a device (the 'Pennywhistle-Modem') was developed by Lee Felsenstein for the Community Memory project in San Francisco in 1973. See Höltgen in Reichert (2014).
10. Hear sound samples from the online presentation of Miyazaki (2013) at http://ssl.einsnull.com/paymate/search.php?vid=5&peid=935.
11. As expressed in chapters one and two of Truax (1984).
12. A term coined by Johannes Kroier, Berlin, in his ongoing dissertation *Archäologie des nicht-pythagoräischen Klangs: zur Kulturalität sonischer Medien*.
13. See e. g., Adrian (1932).
14. Licklider in Cherry (1956), 254.

5. Resonance of siren songs: Experimenting cultural sonicity

1. See Frommolt and Carlé in Fastl and Fruhmann (2005), 797 f.
2. See Carlé in Ernst and Kittler (2006).
3. The borderline between culturally intended sound and implicit acoustic settings separates 'prehistoric' sonic articulation from its cultural history not only in a temporal but in a structural sense. See Scarre and Lawson (2006).
4. On the subconscious analysis of distinct waves from the overall noise of the sea see Leibniz (1904), 431.
5. Kittler in Dotzler and Müller (1995), 96.
6. Winthrop-Young (2015), 84-85.

7.   Bradford (1963), 130.

8.   ibid.

9.   Winthrop-Young (2015), 84.

10. See Thomas (2014).

11. 'Not because I count "one" to a tone [...] do I know that I am at the beginning of a measure, but because I feel that, with this tone, I have reached the wave crest and at the same time have been carried beyond it, into a new wave cycle.' Zuckerkandl (1956), 205. This argument is discussed in Sheperd and Wicke (1977), 132ff.

12. As defined in the call for papers to the workshop *Auditory Memory and Sound Archives from the Late-Nineteenth Century to the Present*, University of Amsterdam, 18 February 2013.

13. In the sense of Ong (1982).

14. See Peters (2004), 188.

15. See Powell (1991).

16. Jaynes (1976).

17. As expressed in Martin Carlé's lecture *Psychoacoustics and Simulation – Breakdown and Reconstruction of the Bicameral Mind* at the 10th Transatlantic Dialogue conference *Acoustic Surveillance* on 8 April 8, 2005, at Bard College, New York.

18. 'Presence' in sound engineering is the term for the degree of clarity in instrumental and vocal sound, which can be increased by use of the Equalizer within the frequency ranges of around 18 Hertz to 16 kHz.

19. See the chapter 'Non-human media', in Parikka (2012), 62.

20. Blanchot (1982), 59.

21. Engh in Dunn and Jones (1994), 126. See as well Levin (1990).

22. Engh (1994), 134.

23. Smirnov (2012), 215, referring to an unpublished manuscript by Boris Yankovsky, *Teorya i praktika graficheskogo zvuka. Akusticheskiy sintez muzikalnih krasok* [The Theory and Practice of Graphical Sound. Acoustical Syntheses of Musical Colours], Leningrad (between 1932 and 1940), in the Archives of the Teremin Center, Moskow. See Smirnov in: Zakharine and Meise (2012), 163-185.

24. Described by Fülöp-Miller (1926).

25. See Miyazaki (2012).

26. Kittler (1999), 7.

27. The explicit harmonic analysis of acoustic vibrations (in adoption of Fourier's mathematical analysis) for the sensation of hearing 'tones' was achieved by Ohm (1843).

28. Winthrop-Young (2015) quoting Bradford (1963), 132.

29. Parikka (2012), 67, quoting Armitage (2006), 33.

30. Winthrop-Young (2013).

31. For an integrative approach of media-archaeological experimentation and historical contextualization see Howard and Moretti (2009).

32. On the 'musical' tuning of ancient Greek theatre architecture, see Canac (1967), esp. 14: '*Il est alors absolument nécessaire de ne pas être gêné par les bruits parasites, que ceux-ci proviennent de l'extérieure ou de l'intérieur sous forme d'écho. D'ou des conditions parfaitement bien définies qui peuvent se traduire en language mathématique* [...]'.

33. A question posed by the resonance theory of evolution; see Sheldrake (1988).

34. The exteriority of the tone, while in being, already annihilates itself ('*So ist der Ton eine Äußerlichkeit, welche sich in ihrem Entstehen durch ihr Dasein selbst wieder nichtet und an sich selbst verschwindet*'): Hegel (1970), 134f.

35. Greenblatt (1988), 1.

36. See Doyle (2005), 40ff and 178ff.

37. See Alloa (2009).

38. Ludwig Wittgenstein quoted in Ulmer (1985), 110.

39. See Adorno (1984).

40. Peirce in: Eisele (1976), 887.

41. Cumming (2000), 90.

42. See René Descartes' treatise *Les Passions de l'âme* (1649).

43. While the concept of 'historical time' in its continuity is bound to the medium of the book, technical storage represents empty and dead time, according to Großklaus (1995), 47.

44. Quoted in Seitz (1981), 413.

45. As has been performed by a permanent media installation of Christian Boltanski in the Art Room at the University of Lüneburg, called *The Archives of my Grand-parents*.

46. In allusion to Ong (1982).

47. See, for example, the metaphor of the historian's task in Lamprecht (1910), 4.

48. See Kittler, Schneider and Weber (1987).

49. Reproduced in the exhibition catalogue: *Ägyptomanie: Ägypten in der europäischen Kunst 1730-1930* (Milan: Electa 1994), 262f.

50. Tansey, *Secret of the Sphinx*, oil on canvas (1984). Reproduced in Bolz et al. (1996), Fig. 30.

51. As reported in Kittler (1987), 23.

52. Marcus (2000), 24.

53. See Svenbro (1993).

54. Michelet (1974), 24.

55. Marcus (2000), 27 f.

56. See Sterne (2012).

57. Jaynes (2004), 18.

58. Ibid.

59. As proposed by Kittler in Ebeling and Altekamp (2004), 260.

60. Babbage (1989), 36.

61. Ibid., 37.

62.   Beyond the entropy involved in Babbage's vision of the air as a sound recorder, the German inventor of digital computing imagined electromagnetic waves, once transmitted into space, as principally enduring forever – unfading sound, resulting in a multilayered temporality of quasi-acoustic space. Zuse (1969).

63.   As reported by Avraamov in Smirnov (2013), 175.

64.   The painter Ksenija Čerče, e-mail message to the author, June 29, 2011.

65.   As paraphrased in Dreyblatt (2005), 32.

66.   Freud (1950). See also Dreyblatt (2005), 32.

67.   Plato in his dialogue *Theaetet*, § 191.

68.   Jaynes (2004), 18.

69.   See Sokolowski (2004), 6.

70.   Ong (1982), 83. This challenge returned in digital culture with the *Turing test* and the cybernetic question addressed to the *electronic brain*: Can computers think, and *vice versa*: Are humans in a machinic state when they calculate?

71.   The ear is '*im Feld des Unbewussten die einzige Öffnung, die nicht zu schließen ist*' and thus unsheltered against sonic violence. Lacan (1978), 178. As soon as phonographic recording became practicable, in reverse it was asked if sound leaves traces in bodily memory like gramophone grooves: see Guyau as quoted at length in Kittler (1999).

72.   Such auditory hallucinations return, though, with present non-lethal sonic weapons that precisely beam voices into a distant listener's ear.

73.   See Rademacher (1997), N3.

74.   A research project funded by the European Union *Kultur 2000* program.

75.   Arndt (2004), 38.

76.   Ibid., referring to the *Dictionary of Non Lethal Weapons* edited by John B. Alexander.

77.   Ibid.

78.   Kircher (1650), esp. book IX: 'Magia Phonocamptica.'

79.   An example of artistic (mis-)interpretation of the soundscape within such radio antenna spheres is the audio field recordings produced on the former radar detection station on Teufelsberg in West Berlin, under the title *Radarstation 2* by the media art group Fantomton (2009).

80.   An audible version of such digital communication rhythms can be heard on the publisher's website of Miyazaki's book *Algorhythmisiert*: http://ssl.einsnull.com/paymate/search.php?vid=5&peid=935.

6.   Textual sonicity: Technologizing oral poetry

1.   Kittler (1999), 7.

2.   Ibid., referring to Ong (1982), 27 and ('more reasonably') 3.

3.   Ibid., 7.

4.   See Chafe (1994).

5.   McMurray (2010).
6.   Foley (1991), 40. In the case of the outstanding *guslar* Avdo Mededovic, Parry and Lord recorded 45,000 poetic lines on phonographic discs and 33,500 lines in manual transcription.
7.   Lord (1953), 132.
8.   Quoted in Shadwick (2002), 150.
9.   Probably left by an American soldier from the period of Allied control of Berlin sectors, as could be deduced from the voice traces that resounded – for perhaps the first time in a half century – from the wire spools. Special thanks to Horst Dieter Schmahl.
10. For the difference between statistics and stochastics in Claude Shannon's analysis of dynamics, described as 'Mathematical Theory of Little Juggling Clowns', see Roch (2009), 163f.
11. Shannon (1993), 5.
12. From the entry '"Avdo Kino." From the Milman Parry Collection', http://chs119.chs.harvard.edu/mpc/gallery/avdo.html.
13. Müller, Grosche and Wiering (2010), 247. See also Müller (2007).
14. See Turner and Pöppel (1983).
15. Powell (2002), 8.
16. Online: http://www.chs.harvard.edu/mpc/clips/avdo.mov.
17. Parry as quoted in Lord (1987), 469f.
18. See Kittler (1991), 68.
19. Muellensiefen et al. (2013), 136.
20. Ibid.
21. Lomax, Bartenieff and Paulay in Cohen (2005), 275.
22. For a further discussion of Lomax's early media archaeology, see Svec (2013). Svec posits Lomax's unique approach to sound recording and computational technologies as a *rapprochement* between folk revivalism and medium theory.
23. Lomax in Cohen (2005), 134.

7.   History or resonance?

1.   On the specific affinity between the sound spectrum accessible to recording and transmitting media and the human voice see Zakharine in Zakharine and Nils Meise (2012).
2.   See chapter 3 'The 'Physics' of the Voice' in Dollar (2006), 58-81. This configuration works both ways: Edison was struck by the phonographic recording of the barking of his dog. See Peters (1999) chap. 4 'Phantasms of the Living. Dialogues with the Dead', 137-176.
3.   'Durch das Ohr kommt die Welt zum Menschen.' Hellbrück and Ellermeier (2004), 19.
4.   On the theatricality of the radio voice see Kolb (1932), esp. chap. 'Die Stimme als körperliche Wesenheit', 48-69.

5.   The 'cocktail party effect' of focused listening (well-known in *Gestalt* psychology) holds for recorded voices as well: 'Caruso's sonorous voice rises above the ambient resistance, and becomes a focus of musical expression in a rough field of noise.' Nyre (2005), 90. See also Pfeiffer in Kolesch and Krämer (2006).

6.   Jakobsen in Røssaak (2010), 134.

7.   Ibid.

8.   See Wicke in Scott (2009); also Papenburg in Schulze (2008).

9.   See Bijsterveld (2008), 11f, referring to Schafer (1994).

10. Ernst in Ofak and Hilgers (2010), 182. Translated here by Winthrop-Young.

11. Benjamin (1968), 237.

12. "'Edison Snares Soul of Music'", *New York Tribune*, 29 April 29, 1916, 3.

13. Quoted after Thompson (1995), 132. See also Wicke (2008).

14. As quoted by Diederichsen in Bieber et al. (2002), 432f.

15. Kittler (1999), 5.

16. Bijsterveld (2008), 26.

17. See Parikka in Huhtamo and Parikka (2011).

18. Volmar (2007), 366.

19. See Kittler (2006) and (2009).

20. On such experimentation with sono-mathematical divisions of the mono-chord in ancient China see Fei in Zielinski and Fürlus (2008).

21. Parikka in Ernst (2013), 145 (emphasis added), referring to Sobchak in Huhtamo and Parikka (2011).

22. Campbell-Kelly in Rojas and Hashagen (2000), 399.

23. Ibid.

24. Peirce (1976), 48.

25. Collingwood (1993), 217f., explicitly compares the endurance of Pythagoras' discovery concerning the square on the hypotenuse with the equal possibil-ity of sharing the political ideas of the ancient Roman Republic today. It is just that the historian's mind must be somewhat tuned in the same cogni-tive mood.

26. See Heidegger (1986), 385. A similar argument is expressed in Jacques Der-rida (1997).

27. As described in Galilei (1988), 203-205.

28. Palisca in Gozza (2000), 195.

29. Another 'instantiation' of this argument concerning oscillatory and rever-berative physical events is the pendulum as experimented by Galilo Galilei and Christiaan Huyghens. See Kassung (2008).

30. See Heidegger (2003).

31. Von Helmholtz (1919), 411.

32. On the method of experimentally simulating the sonic past where musical knowledge re-instantiates itself see Carlé (2007), 313f.

33. Braguinski, abstract (2013) of his ongoing dissertation project *The aesthetics and semantics of electronic toy sound.*

34. See Camia (2012). See also Emmerson (2006).
35. The composer Sebastian Berweck in his dissertation (2012).
36. See Bonardi and Barthélemy (2008).
37. This corresponds with today's being almost continuously online by means of mobile smart devices. But the gap between *koinos kósmos* and *ídios kósmos* is a complementary *harmonía* at the same time. See the thematic *exposé* of the Club Transmediale Festival *The Golden Age*, by Andreas L. Hofbauer (2013).
38. Berger in Berger and Newcomb (2005), 14. As quoted by Trippett (2007), 526.
39. Truax (1984), 115.
40. Trippett (2007), 526, referring to Berger (2005).
41. Günther Stern (son of the psychologist Wilhelm Stern who himself developed a non-historicist model of experience) became known under his later name Günther Anders. I owe my awareness of Stern's habilitation thesis to Veit Erlmann's (2010) book *Reason and Resonance*.
42. '*Die Musik hat also in Abhebung von der historischen Zeit ihre eigene Zeit, die 'abgesperrt' ist.*' Ellensohn (2008), 66 (paraphrasing Stern).
43. See Gumbrecht (2004).
44. As criticized by Henri Bergson in the final chapter of his *Évolution créatrice* in 1907. The difference between continuous phonographic and discrete cinematographic machine time is sublated once the acoustic event is addressed in numeric frequencies and the technical image electronically unfolds in one-line scanning.
45. As expressed in Collingwood's 1928 lecture 'Outlines of a Philosophy of History', in Collingwood (1993), 441. For Collingwood, this is true of other time-based arts as well like the reading of old poetry and the historiography of past war battles (ibid.).
46. As quoted in Ellensohn (2008), 64.
47. Benjamin (1968), 254.
48. See Stern (1930-31), 59, note 1, on *Transponierung*.
49. Snyder (2000), 212.
50. On Heidegger's notion of *Gestimmtheit*, see Erlmann (2010), 327, and Heidegger's lecture on logic (*Logik-Vorlesung*, 1934), 129 and 135.
51. About historicism in music see Richter (1995), N5, referring to Nägele (1995).
52. Struck-Schloen in Holtmeier, Polth and Diergarten (2004), 342.
53. See Diederichsen (2002), 439.
54. Truax (1984), 138. This correspondance is drastically broken by analogue-to-digital conversion (numerical sampling).
55. Stern (1930-31), as quoted and translated in Erlmann (2010), 325.
56. As expressed in Stern (1930-31), 60.
57. By contrast, Friedrich Kittler, on the contrary, accentuates the context-dependency of mathematics in history – while himself, in recent work, referring to figures of 'recursion' in occidental knowledge systems – a non-historic argument itself. See Kittler (2000), 115.

58. Chapter 5.3.1.3, 'Die Wiederkehr als Rekursion' of Kittler (2015).
59. Innis (1980), 235.
60. Hammerstein (1966), 20. Translated here by the author.
61. Hafner (2000). For realtime chromatic transposition ('tuning') of the an-
     cient lyre, according to Aristoxenos's intrumental diagramatics, see Carlé
     (2007).
62. Hafner, ibid.
63. An argument quoted from Elliot (1949), 64, in Hammerstein (1966), 23.
64. Stern (1930-31), 34.
65. Erlmann (2010), 326, referring to Stern (1930-31).
66. Bartók (1942). For Bartók's transcriptions of melodies of the songs in the
     Milman Parry Collection see http://chs119.chs.harvard.edu/mpc/gallery/
     bartok_transcrpt.htm.
67. Hammerstein (1966), 3, note 7.
68. Ibid, 2.
69. Isidor from Sevilla, as quoted by Hammerstein (1966), 4.
70. Quoted after Hammerstein (1966), 1.
71. See no. 9311 (type 'Plastisches Objekt') in the *Lautarchiv* at Humboldt Uni-
     versity, Berlin.
72. 'Mitgehen' and 'faktischer Mitvollzug der Bewegungen' according to Stern
     (1930-31), 66.
73. See Augustinus's definition of music as *ars bene movendi*, paraphrased by
     Erlmann (2010) as 'the auditory *Mitvollzug*', 328.
74. See Bayreuther in Thomä (2013).
75. Stern (1927), 612.
76. See Macho in Liessmann (1992), 90.
77. It is taken for granted that humans do not provide a proper 'temporal'
     sense in the physiological way. The acoustic channel (cochlear hearing and
     its time-critical processing within the brain) serves as substitute for this
     chrono-aesthetic lack.
78. Helmholtz remarks that tuning systems are not based on unchangeable
     natural laws but depend on the variable cultural aesthetics (1863), 358. See
     also Rehding in: Holtmeier, Polth and Diergarten (2004), 378.
79. For a metahistorical approach see Lehrdahl and Jackendorff (1983).
80. '*Logische Aktivität*'. Riemann (1914-15), 2.
81. For Riemann, the musical idea is different from its symbolic mediation or
     sonic communication; ibid., 2.
82. Bayreuther and Carlé (2012).
83. Ibid.
84. Ibid.
85. DeMarinis in Beirer, Seiffarth and Himmelsbach (2010), 247.
86. Trippett (2013).
87. Sorensen and Gardner (2010), 828.
88. Hegel (1990), 413.

89. Gabor (1947). See also Hubbard (1996).
90. Stockhausen, as quoted in Maconie (2000), 25f.
91. See Hagen in Maresch and Werber (1998) and Hagen (2005), esp. 30.
92. See Sprenger (2012).
93. See Kahn in Fölmer and Thiermann (2006).

8. From sound signal to alphanumeric symbol

1. See Kittler (1991).
2. See Gumbrecht (2004).
3. 'Bias' was originally a technical term used in electronic engineering to describe the minimum current necessary for circuitry work, an electric *a priori*. For a media-cultural extension of that term, see Innis (1991).
4. See Erlmann (2010), 325f.
5. For an interpretation under the influence of McLuhan's approach as applied to radio and television broadcasting, see Schwartz (1974).
6. Hartmann (2003), 35.
7. See Lerdahl and Jackendorff (1983).
8. Kittler (1999), 3.
9. On Time-Axis Manipulation, see Kittler (1999), 35.
10. Fink (1999), 92. Fink extends this time-mirroring function to sonicity: 'Time-reversal techniques may also be extended to types of waves other than sound waves' (97), notably the quantum wave functions that describe all matter itself.
11. Kittler (1999), 1.
12. Taschner (2005), 77.
13. This argument is based on Michel Foucault (2002), 7.
14. See http://www.firstsounds.org.
15. For a digital version of Scott's recording from 8 April 1860 at Paris, see http://www.firstsounds.org/sounds/1860-Scott-Au-Claire-de-la-Lune-09-08.mp3.
16. Harald Haack (2008).
17. On forms of media-archaeologically augmented textual criticism see Kirschenbaum (2008).
18. Boltryk, McBride, Gaustad and Weium (2010).
19. Ibid.
20. The extracted audio was not the expected psalm singing as documented in the contemporary sources but a mixture of shorter extracts.

9. Rescued from the archive: Archaeonautics of sound

1. Riis (2012), 8of.
2. See Bijsterveld (2008).
3. See the Website 'Museum of Endangered Sounds': http://savethesounds.info.

4. Announcement of the course 'Time waves goodbye' directed by Anthony Moore and Peter Kiefer in the Sound Laboratory of the Academy of Media Arts, Cologne, summer term 2000.
5. See Klotz (1998), 205.
6. Brandl (1928).
7. Adorno (2001) as quoted in Mazzola (2010).
8. See Doyle (2005), 19, referring to a term coined by R. Murray Schafer.
9. See Smith (2004).
10. Sterne (2003), 33.
11. Nietzsche (1886), § 257, 227.
12. Winthrop-Young (2013).
13. See Ernst in Huhtamo and Parikka (2011), 248.
14. Winthrop-Young (2013).
15. According to the Second Law of Thermodynamics, the energy disorder of any closed system tends to increase and tends to a final equilibrium sometimes called 'heat death'.
16. As was argued by the author at the conference *Hearing Modern History: Auditory Cultures in the 19th and 20th Century* directed by Daniel Morat, 17-19 June 17 to 19, 2010, Berlin.
17. Once more, the term 'sonicity' mustis needed here to be differentiated from a reduced concept of sound as *Klang*: '*Es ist ein Verhältnis von 1:1 Million, mit der sich das Universum in der unendlichen Vielzahl von Schwingungsmöglichkeiten für harmonikale Schwingungen – und das heißt: für Klänge – entscheidet [...].*' Berendt (1985), 116.
18. German *verstehen* refers to auditory perception as well as to cognitive understanding.
19. For a creative coupling between archive-technical expertise and theory of cultural memory see Fossati (2009).
20. For an analysis of the interplay between technical memory and affective remembrance see Anderson (2004).
21. See Siegert in Pias (1999), 175.
22. See Cohen in Gozza (2000), 222.
23. DeMarinis (2010), 247.
24. DeMarinis (2010), 252.
25. Haack (2008).
26. See Carpo in Carpo and Lemerle (2008).
27. Benjamin (1968), 217-251.
28. Moring (2004).
29. The last remark in Beckett's script declares: 'Tape runs on in silence' – against which engineers developed the auto-stop of the reels. The real time-critical challenge to biographic voice recognition, though, is not only grounded in distortions of the signal and noise induced by the environment or the recording apparatus itself, but in the change to which the same

person's voice is subjected in a life-time – the autocorrelation of acoustic signals across temporal distance.

30. See http://www.ww2f.com/topic/1497-the-conversation-between-manner-heim-and-hitler.

31. For a dynamic reading of the Barthean *punctum* see Barker (2010), 294f. See also Lazzarato (2002), who updates Bergson's concept of time for the age(s) of electronic images.

32. Moring (2004).

33. '*Dies ist ein niemals geschriebenes und niemals zu schreibendes Ruhemsblatt unserer Geschichte.*' Trial Main War Criminals (Prozeß Hauptkriegsverbrecher), Dok. PS-1919, 64ff.

34. See http://www.gfai.de/english/projects/image-processing-industrial-applications-projects-/spubito.html.

35. *Scientific American* (1877), 304; see also Sterne (2003), 287-334, esp. 297.

36. '*Es hat mit sehr gefreut, auf Wunsch der Akademie der Wissenschaften meine Stimme in den Apparat hineinzusprechen und dieselbe dadurch der Sammlung einzuverleiben.*'

37. '*Freud a fait des énoncés verbaux des malades, consideérés jusque´là comme bruit, quelque chose qui devait être traité comme un message.*' Foucault (1994), 559.

38. See Pitman (1840).

39. Bartók (1942).

40. See Stanke and Kessler in Simon (2000).

41. See Sconce (1998).

42. SpuBiTo is the German acronym for: 'Spur – Bild – Ton'. See 'SpuBiTo – From Image to Sound': http://www.gfai.de/english/projects/image-processing-industrial-applications-projects-/spubito.html.

43. Quoted after Wertheimer (1910), 300.

44. See http://www.gfai.de/projekte/spubito/index.htm.

45. Bruyninckx in Pinch and Bijsterveld (2011), 144.

10.   Sonic analytics

1. For research across large amounts of digitized visual data (notably cinematography), methods and software of statistical sorting have been developed under that name of *cultural analytics* (Lev Manovich).

2. As currently tested by Constant Association for Art and Media (Brussels) in its media-experimental project *Erkki Kurenniemi* (*In 2048*) (*preliminary work towards*) *an online archive*; see http://kurenniemi.activearchives.org.

3. Kurenniemi's private recordings are currently pre-deposited at the Central Art Archives of the Finnish National Gallery (Helsinki) to be catalogued and digitized.

4. Murtaugh and Malevé are members of the Constant Association for Art and Media, based in Brussels.

5.   As presented and discussed by Murtaugh and Malevé during the Workshop
      Online Archive: Erkki Kurenniemi (In 2048) 7-8 June 7-8, 2013, at the National
      Library in Oslo. Computational Fourier Analysis can be sonified by applying
      amplifiers and loudspeakers to the computer itself, as demonstrated and
      recorded by Nijenhuis from the PASCAL main frame computer in the Eind-
      hoven research laboratory of Philips enterprise. See Nijenhuis (1962-63).

6.   See e.g. Berry (2012).

7.   Etymologically, the old German term for knowledge *wizzan* is related to
      Latin *visum*. See as well the visual implication in ancient Greek *theoria*.

8.   See Boersma (1993).

9.   Such as Sonic Visualizer (developed at King's College, London) and Praat
      (developed in the Netherlands for doing phonetics by computer).

10.   See Moerchen, A. Ultsch, M. Thies and I. Loehken (2006).

11.   For an example of a software tool capable of visual analysis of sonic signal
      events see http://www.sonicvisualiser.org/screenshots.html.

12.   See Grieger (1989), 13 (referring to Hermann Gutzmann).

13.   Licklider (2003), 203.

14.   Ibid.

15.   See Müllensiefen and Frieler (2004).

16.   When Messiaen notated acoustic articulations of birds as elementary inspi-
      ration for his own musical compositions, he could rely on the repetitive na-
      ture of such sequences, which transcend the individuality of a single bird.

17.   For such an interactive, open access digital sound archive, see the Free-
      sound Project (https://www.freesound.org/) and more media-archaeologi-
      cally, the Museum of Endangered Sounds (http://savethesounds.info/).

18.   'VID-R builds a visual dictionary by utilizing the procedures described
      for temporal reorganization.' Ekman and Friesen (1969), 242. See further
      Ekman, Friesen and Taussig in: Gerbner, Holsti, Krippendorff, Paisley and
      Stone (1969).

19.   See Røssaak (2010).

20.   See Moles (1958).

21.   See Manovich in Berry (2012).

22.   See the M⁴S project (Modelling Music Memory and the Perception of
      Melodic Similarity), hosted by the Computing Department of Goldsmith
      College, University of London.

23.   Müllensiefen, Wiggins and Lewis (2008), 133, referring to the WAV and AIFF
      formats used primarily in computers and iPods, and MPEG-1 Audio-Layer 3
      (MP3) as a compression format used for web-based and portable applica-
      tions.

24.   Ibid., 136.

25.   See Müller (2007), 69.

26.   Ibid., 165.

27.   Muellensiefen, Wiggins and Lewis (2008), 139.

28. Such as the application 'Contentus', developed within the THESEUS program by the Fraunhofer Institute in Germany. For a media-artistic application see *Dumb Angel* by Klaus Gasteier (developed at the Academy of Media Arts, Cologne), as described in the popular music journal SPEX in issue no. 9/1996: 'Dumb Angel. Brian Wilson wird interaktiv'.
29. Kim, Moreau and Sikora (2005), 2.
30. Ibid., 3.
31. Such as MusikDNA or the software *audentify* (created by the computer scientist Michael Clausen at the Friedrich Wilhelms University of Bonn). In this case, digital patterns of music files are matched against an index. See Bolz (2001), 39.
32. It is in the actual playing that an MP3 file reveals if it is a piece by Monteverdi or by Metallica, as pointed out by Borcher (2001), 46.
33. On algorithmic identifiers of musical mood see Borchers (2000), 30.
34. http://www.findsounds.com/types.html.
35. Blum et al. in Maybury (1997), 113-135.
36. Ibid., 121.
37. *Versuchsreihe – 103 Arten Beethoven zu singen*, published as brochure no. 5/9 on occasion of the exhibition *Künstler.Archiv* at the Academy of Arts, Berlin, August 2005 (Walther König).
38. Such as the Smart Home Noise Classificator (SoClaSim), developed at the Institute of Informatics, University of Potsdam.
39. '*Vokalisch, stimmhaft, sonant, (ex-)plosiv, geräuschhaft*'. Schnelle (1964), 210.
40. See Ernst and Heidenreich in: Schade and Tholen (1999).
41. Blum et al. in Maybury (1997), 114.
42. Ibid.
43. For several socio-linguistic and computer-based analyses in the techno-culturally variant coding of human voice frequencies see Zakharine and Meise (2013).
44. See Lange in Wegmann, Maye and Reiber (2006), 335f. An almost complete list of the both phonographically and symbolically registered recordings is provided online: http://www.sammlungen.hu-berlin.de/sammlungen/78.
45. The architectural front of the German Library at Leipzig (Deutsche Bücherei), founded in 1913, still displays a monumental quote from a Schiller poem: Writing renders body and voice to silent thoughts ('*Körper und Stimme leiht die Schrift dem stummen Gedanken* [...]').
46. According to Doegen, the 'dead letters' in printed texts become alive by the accompanying phonetic recordings (1921), 253.
47. Such as gunfire for a theory of sonic explosion, and the sonoric noise of air planes. See Doegen (1921).
48. Brandl (1928), 72-84.
49. Zuckerkandl (1956), 333f.
50. See Potter, Kopp and Green (1947), and Boris Yankovsky's sound spectrography (as mentioned above).

51.   Schnelle (1964), 211.
52.   Muellensiefen, Wiggins and Lewis (2008), 140.
53.   See Smirnov (2013), 44.
54.   Ibid.
55.   As emphasized in the introduction to Kittler (1999). For a microtemporal analysis of the actual interpretation against the written score in Western music by analysis of electro-mechanical piano recording, see Gottschewski (1996).
56.   Blum et al. in Maybury (1997), 115.
57.   For a clear differentiation between the symbolic regime of pure musical mathematics and its physical – thus, temporal – implementations as electronic sound see Vilém Flusser's lecture 'On modern music' delivered in 1965 at the Brazilian Institute of Philosophy in Sao Paulo, typescript (Flusser Archive at the University of the Arts, Berlin). See Flusser Studies 17 – Music and Sound in Vilém Flusser's work (May 2014).

Works cited

Works cited (English)

'A Wonderful Invention – Speech Capable of Indefinite Repetition from Automatic Records'. *Scientific American* 17, November 1877.

Adrian, Edgar Douglas. *The Mechanism of Nervous Action: Electrical Studies of the Neuron.* London: Milford, 1932.

Alloa, Emmanuel. 'Metaxu: Figures de la médialité chez Aristotle'. Revue de *Métaphysique et de Morale* 62, no. 2 (2009): 247-262.

Alt, Casey. 'Objects of Our Affection'. In: *Media Archaeology: Approaches, Applications, and Implications,* edited by Erkki Huhtamo and Jussi Parikka, 278-301. Berkeley, CA: University of California Press, 2011.

Anderson, Ben. 'Recorded Music and Practices of Remembering'. *Social & Cultural Geography* 5, no 1, (March 2004) 3-20.

Armitage, John. 'From Discourse Networks to Cultural Mathematics: An Interview with Friedrich A. Kittler'. *Theory, Culture & Society* 23, no. 7/8 (2006): 17-38.

Augoyard, Jean-François and Henry Torgue. *Sonic Experience: A Guide to Everyday Sounds.* Montreal & Kingston: McGill-Queen's University Press, 2005.

Avraamov, Arseny. 'Upcoming Science of Music and the New Era in the History of Music'. *Musical Contemporary Magazine* 6 (1916).

––. 'Sinteticheskaya Muzika'. *Sovetskoya Muzika* 3 (1929): 67-75.

Babbage, Charles. *The Works of Charles Babbage vol. 2,* edited by Martin Campbell-Kelly. London: Pickering, 1989.

Barker, Timothy S. 'The Past in the Present: Understanding David Claerbout's Temporal Aesthetics'. *Time and Society* 20, no. 3 (2010): 286-303.

Bartók, Béla. 'Parry Collection of Yugoslav Folk Music. Eminent Composer, Who Is Working on It, Discusses Its Significance'. *The New York Times*, 28 June 1942.

Bayreuther, Rainer and Martin Carlé. 'Absconding from History'. Presentation at the Conference on Interdisciplinary Musicology (CIM.12), University of Göttingen, 4 September 2012.

Benjamin, Walter. *Illuminations*, edited by Hannah Arendt. New York: Schocken, 1968 [new edition 2007].

Berger, Karol. 'Time's Arrow and the Advent of Musical Modernity'. In: *Music and the Aesthetics of Modernity,* edited by Karol Berger and Anthony Newcomb, 3-22. Cambridge, MA: Harvard University Press, 2005.

Bergson, Henri. *Èvolution créatrice* [1907]. Paris: PUF, 1948.

Berry, David M. *Understanding Digital Humanities.* Basingstoke: Palgrave Macmillan, 2012.

Berweck, Sebastian. *It Worked Yesterday: On (Re-)Performing Electroacoustic Music.* PhD dissertation, University of Huddersfield, 2012.

Bijsterveld, Karin. *Mechanical Sound: Technology, Culture, and Public Problems of Noise in the Twentieth Century.* Cambridge, MA: The MIT Press, 2008.

Blanchard, Julian. 'The History of Electrical Resonance'. *Bell System Technical Journal* 20, no. 4 (1941): 415-433.

Blanchot, Maurice. *The Sirens' Song: Selected Essays,* edited by Josipovici. Bloomington: Indiana University Press, 1982.

Blesser, Barry and Linda-Ruth Salter. 'Ancient Acoustic Spaces'. In: *The Sound Studies Reader*, edited by Jonathan Sterne. 187-196. London and New York: Routledge, 2012.

Blum, Thomas et al. 'Audio Databases with Content-Based Retrieval'. Intelligent Multimedia Information Retrieval, edited by Mark T. Maybury, 113-135. Cambridge, MA: MIT, 1997.

Boersma, P. 'Accurate Short-Term Analysis of the Fundamental Frequency and the Harmonics-to-Noise Ratio of a Sampled Sound'. *Proceedings of the Institute of Phonetic Sciences (University of Amsterdam)*, vol. 17 (1993): 97-110.

Boltryk, P.J., McBride, J.W, Gaustad, L. and Frode Weium. 'Audio Recovery and Identification of First Norwegian Sound Recording'. Presentation at the 2010 Joint Technical Symposium (JTS): Digital Challenges and Digital Opportunities in Audiovisual Archiving, 66th FIAF Congress, Oslo, Norway, 2-5 May 2010.

Bonardi, Alain and Jerome Barthélemy. 'The Preservation, Emulation, Migration, and Virtualization of Live Electronics for Performing Arts: An Overview of Musical and Technical Issues'. *Journal on Computing and Cultural Heritage* 1, no. 1 (2008).

Borck, Cornelius. 'Blindness, Seeing, and Envisioning Prosthesis: The Optophone between Science, Technology, and Art'. In: *Artists as Inventors. Inventors as Artists*, edited by Dieter Daniels and Barbara U. Schmidt. 109-129. Ostfildern: Hatje Cantz, 2008.

Bradford, Ernle. *Ulysses Found*. London: Hodder and Stoughton, 1963.

Braguinski, Nikita. *The Aesthetics and Semantics of Electronic Toy Sound*. PhD dissertation, Humboldt University of Berlin (ongoing).

Bruyninckx, Joeri. 'Sound Sterile: Making Scientific Field Recordings in Ornithology'. In: *The Oxford Handbook of Sound Studies*, edited by Trevor Pinch and Karin Bijsterveld, 127-150. Oxford: Oxford University Press, 2011.

Cage, John M. *Silence: Lectures and Writings*. Middletown, CT: Wesleyan University Press, 1961.

Campbell-Kelly, Martin. 'Past into Present: The EDSAC Simulator'. In: *The First Computers: History and Architecture,* edited by Raúl Rojas and Ulf Hashagen. 397-416. Cambridge, MA: MIT Press, 2000.

Camia, Chiara Marchini. *Digital Art Works: The Challenges of Conservation*. Karlsruhe: ZKM, 2012.

Canac, François. *L'acoustique des théâtres antiques*. Paris: Centre national de la recherche scientifique, 1967.

Carpo, Mario. 'Alberti's Media Lab'. In: *Perspective: Projections and Design,* edited by M. Carpo and F. Lemerle. 47-63. London: Routledge, 2008.

Chafe, Wallace. *Discourse, Consciousness, and Time: The Flow and Displacement of Conscious Experience in Speaking and Writing*. Chicago: University of Chicago Press, 1994.

Chion, Michel. *Audio-Vision: Sound on Screen*. New York: Columbia University Press, 1994.

Cohen, H. Floris. 'Galileo Galilei'. In: *Number to Sound: The Musical Way to the Scientific Revolution,* edited by Paolo Gozza. 219-231. Dordrecht: Kluwer, 2000.

Collingwood, R.G. *The Idea of History* [1946], revised edition. Oxford UK: Oxford University Press, 1993.

Cooper, Douglas J. 'Dead Time is the 'How Much Delay' Variable'. In: Douglas J. Cooper, *Practical Process Control: Proven Methods and Best Practices for Automatic PID Control*. E-textbook (2006-2008). http://www.controlguru.com/wp/p51.html.

Collingwood, R. G. *The Idea of History* [1946], revised edition. Oxford UK: Oxford University Press, 1993.

Cumming, Naomi. *The Sonic Self: Musical Subjectivity and Signification*. Bloomington: Indiana University Press, 2000.

Davis, Erik. 'Subject: Acoustic Cyberspace'. In: *Readme! Filtered by Nettime. ASCII Culture and the Revenge of Knowledge*, edited by Josephine Osma et al. 387-391. Brooklyn, NY: Automedia, 1999.

DeForest, Lee. 'The Phonofilm'. *Transactions of the Society of Motion Picture Engineers* 16 (1923): 61-75.

Deleuze, Gilles. *Cinema 2: The Time Image.* New York and London: Continuum, 1985.

DeMarinis, Paul. 'According to Scripture'. In: *Paul DeMarinis: Buried in Noise,* edited by Ingrid Beirer, Carsten Seiffarth and Sabine Himmelsbach. 247-252. Heidelberg: Kehrer, 2010.

Dollar, Mladen. *A Voice and Nothing More.* Cambridge, MA: MIT Press, 2006.

Doyle, Peter. *Echo and Reverb: Fabricating Space in Popular Music Recording 1900-1960.* Middletown, CT: Weselyan University Press, 2005.

Ekman, P. and W.V. Friesen. 'A Tool for the Analysis of Motion Picture Film or Video Tape'. *American Psychologist* 24, no. 3 (1969): 240-243.

Ekman, P., Friesen, W.V. and T. Taussig. 'VID-R and SCAN: Tools and Methods in the Analysis of Facial Expression and Body Movement'. In: *Content Analysis,* edited by G. Gerbner et al. New York: Wiley, 1969.

Elliot, T.S. *Selected Essays,* 3ʳᵈ Edition. London: Faber, 1949.

Emmerson, Simon. 'In What Form Can "Live Electronic Music" Live On?'. *Organized Sound* 11, no. 3 (2006): 209–219.

Engh, Barbara. 'Adorno and the Sirens: Tele-phonographic Bodies'. In: *Embodied Voices: Representing Female Vocality in Western Culture,* edited by Leslie C. Dunn and Nancy A. Jones. 120-135. Cambridge UK: Cambridge University Press, 1994.

Erlmann, Veit. *Reason and Resonance: A History of Modern Aurality.* Cambridge MA: The MIT Press, 2010.

Ernst, Wolfgang. 'Media Archaeography: Method and Machine versus History and Narrative of Media'. In: *Media Archaeology. Approaches, Applications and Implications,* edited by Erkki Huhtamo and Jussi Parikka. 239-255. Berkeley, CA: University of California Press, 2011.

––. *Digital Memory and The Archive,* edited and introduced by Jussi Parikka. Minneapolis: University of Minnesota Press, 2013.

Fei, Xu. 'The Exploration and Achievements of the Acoustics of Yuelü: The Theory of the Tone System in Ancient China'. In: *On Deep Time – Relations of Arts, Sciences and Technologies in China and Elsewhere (Variantology 3),* edited by Siegfried Zielinski and Eckhard Fürlus. 257-292. Cologne: Walther König, 2008.

Feld, Steven. 'Acoustemic Stratigraphies'. *Sensate: A Journal for Experiments in Critical Media Practice* (2011). http://sensatejournal.com/2011/03/steven-feld-acoustemic.

Fink, Mathias. 'Time-reversed Acoustics'. *Scientific American* 281 (November 1999): 91-97.

Flusser, Vilém. 'On Modern Music'. Lecture at the Brazilian Institute of Philosophy, Sao Paulo, Brazil, 1965. Typescript (Flusser Archive at the University of the Arts, Berlin).

Foley, John Miles. *Traditional Oral Epic: The Odyssey, Beowulf, and the Serbo-Croatian Return Song.* Berkeley, CA: University of California Press, 1991.

Fossati, Giovanna. *From Grain to Pixel: The Archival Life of Film in Transition.* Amsterdam: Amsterdam University Press, 2009.

Foucault, Michel. *The Archaeology of Knowledge,* translated by. A.M. Sheridan Smith [*1972]. London and New York: Routledge Classics, 2002.

Freud, Sigmund. 'A Note upon the 'Mystic Writing Pad'', translated by James Strachey. *International Journal of Psycho-Analysis* 21, vol. 4 (1950): 469-74.

Frommolt, Karl-Heinz and Martin Carlé. 'The Song of the Sirens'. Unpublished paper (2005).

Gabor, Denis. 'Acoustical Quanta and the Theory of Hearing' *Nature* 4044 (May 1947): 591-594.

Galilei, Vincenzo. 'A Special Discourse Converning the Unison', translated in Claude V. Palisca, *The Florentine Camerata. Documentary Studies and Translations.* New Haven, CT: Yale University Press, 1988.

Gombrich, Ernst H. *The Sense of Order: A Study of the Psychology of Decorative Art*, 2nd edition. Oxford: Phaidon, 1994.

Goodman, Steve. *Sonic Warfare: Sound, Affect and the Ecology of Fear*. Cambridge, MA: MIT Press, 2009.

Gozza, Paolo, ed. *Number to Sound: The Musical Way to the Scientific Revolution*, Dordrecht: Kluwer, 2000.

Greenblatt, Stephen. *Shakespearean Negotiations: The Circulation of Social Energy in Renaissance England*. Berkeley, CA: University of California Press, 1988.

Gumbrecht, Hans Ulrich. *Production of Presence: What Meaning Cannot Convey*. Stanford, CA: Stanford University Press, 2004.

Hafner, Katie. 'Piano Tuners Have Built a Bridge To 18th Century'. *The New York Times*, 17 February 2000.

Heidegger, Martin. *The Question Concerning Technology and Other Essays*. New York: Harper and Row, 1977.

Hofbauer, Andreas L. 'Discourse Groundwork: Digging Deeper into the Golden Age'. Thematic Overview of Discourse Program, CTM – Festival for Adventurous Music and Arts, Berlin, 2013. http://www.ctm-festival.de/archive/festival-editions/ctm13-the-golden-age/feature-teaser-2013/the-golden-age/.

Howard, Deborah and Laura Moretti. *Sound and Space in Renaissance Venice: Architecture, Music, Acoustics*. New Haven, CT: Yale University Press, 2009.

Hubbard, Barbara Burke. *The World According to Wavelets: The Story of a Mathematical Technique in the Making*. Wellesley, MA: AK Peters, 1996.

Huhtamo, Erkki and Jussi Parikka, eds. *Media Archaeology. Approaches, Applications, and Implications*. Berkeley, CA: University of California Press, 2011.

Innis, Harold A. *The Idea File of Harold Adams Innis*, introduced and edited by William Christian. Toronto: University of Toronto Press, 1980.

––. *The Bias of Communication*. Toronto: University of Toronto Press, 1991.

Jakobsen, Kjetil. 'Anarchival Society'. In: *The Archive in Motion: New Conceptions of the Archive in Contemporary Thought and New Media Practices*, edited by Eivind Røssaak. 127-154. Oslo: Novus, 2010.

Jaynes, Julian. *The Origin of Consciousness in the Breakdown of the Bicameral Mind*. Boston: Houghton-Mifflin, 1976.

––. 'Consciousness and the Voices of the Mind' [1986]. *BABEL* 4 (May 2004): 10-31.

Kahn, Douglas. *Noise, Water, Meat: A History of Sound in the Arts*. Cambridge MA: The MIT Press, 1999.

––. 'Radio was Discovered before it was Invented'. In: *Relating Radio: Communities, Aesthetics, Access*, edited by Golo Fölmer and Sven Thiermann. 24-32. Leipzig: Spector Books, 2006.

Kay, Alan. 'User Interface: A Personal View'. In: *Multimedia from Wagner to Virtual Reality*, edited by Randall Packer and Ken Jordan. 121-131. New York: W.W. Norton, 2001.

Kim, Hyoung-Gook, Moreau, Nicolas and Thomas Sikora. *MPEG-7 Audio and Beyond: Audio Content Indexing and Retrieval*. Chichester: John Wiley, 2005.

Kirschenbaum, Matthew. *Mechanisms: New Media and the Forensic Imagination*. Cambridge, MA: The MIT Press, 2008.

Kittler, Friedrich. *Gramophone, Film, Typewriter*, translated by Geoffrey Winthrop-Young and Michael Wutz. Stanford, CA: Stanford University Press, 1999.

––. 'God of Ears', translated by Paul Feigelfeld and Anthony Moore. In: *Kittler Now: Current Perspectives in Kittler Studies*, edited by Stephen Sale and Laura Salisbury. 3-21. London: Polity, 2015.

Kohl, Jerome. 'The Evolution of Macro- and Micro-Time Relations in Stockhausen's Recent Music'. *Perspectives of New Music* 22, no. 1/2 (Autumn 1983): 147-185.

Kramer, Gregory et al. 'Sonification Report: Status of the field and Research Agenda'. *Faculty Publications, Department of Psychology*. Paper 444. Lincoln: University of Nebraska at Lincoln, 2010.

Kurenniemi, Erkki. 'Oh, Human Fart'. *Framework: The Finnish Art Review* 2 (2004): 34-37.

Lehrdahl, Fred and Ray Jackendorff. *A Generative Theory of Tonal Music*. Cambridge, MA: The MIT Press, 1983.

Lenoir, Timothy. 'Foreword' to Mark B.N. Hansen, *New Philosophy for New Media*. Cambridge MA: The MIT Press, 2004.

Levin, Thomas Y. 'For the Record: Adorno on Music in the Age of its Technological Reproducibility'. *October* 55 (Winter 1990): 23-47.

—. 'Rhetoric of the Temporal Index: Surveillant Narration and the Cinema of "Real Time"'. In: *CTRL[SPACE]: Rhetorics of Surveillance from Bentham to Big Brother*, edited by Thomas Y. Levin, Ursula Frohne and Peter Weibel. 578-292. Cambridge, MA: The MIT Press, 2002.

—. 'Tones from out of Nowhere. Rudolf Pfenninger and the Archaeology of Synthetic Sound'. *Grey Room* 12 (Fall 2003): 32-79.

Licklider, J.C.R. 'Auditory Frequency Analysis'. In: *Information Theory: Papers read at a Symposium on 'Information Theory' held at the Royal Institution, London, 12-16 September 1955*, edited by Colin Cherry. 253-268. London: Butterworths Scientific Publications, 1956.

—. 'The Manner in Which and Extent to Which Speech can be Distorted and Remain Intelligible'. In: *Cybernetics / Kybernetik. The Macy-Conferences 1946-1953, vol. 1: Transactions / Protokolle*, edited by Claus Pias. 203-247. Zürich and Berlin: diaphanes, 2003.

Link, David. 'There Must Be an Angel: On the Beginnings of the Arithmetics of Rays'. In: *On Deep Time Relations of Arts, Sciences and Technologies (Variantology 2)*, edited by Siegfried Zielinski and David Link. 15-42. Cologne: Walther König, 2006.

Lomax, Alan, Bartenieff, Irmgard and Forrestine Paulay. *Choreometrics: A Method for the Study of Cross-Cultural Pattern in Film*. In: *Alan Lomax, Selected Writings 1934-1997*, edited by Ronald D. Cohen. 275-284. New York and London: Routledge, 2005.

London, Barbara et al., eds. *Bill Viola: Installations and Video Tapes*. New York: The Museum of Modern Art, 1987.

Lord, Albert Bates. 'Homer's Originality: Oral Dictated Texts'. *Transactions of the American Philological Association* 84 (1953): 124-134.

Mackenzie, Adrian. 'The Technicity of Time. From 1.00 oscillations/sec. to 9,192,631,770 Hz'. *Time and Society* 10, no. 2/3 (2001): 235-257.

Maconie, Robin. *Stockhausen on Music*. Marion Boyars Publishers: London, 2000.

Maibaum, Johannes. 'Lumped Lines and Bucket Brigades: A Media Archaeology of Dynamic Storage Focusing on Delay Lines'. Bachelor curriculum Musik und Medien, September 2013, Philosophical Faculty III, Humboldt University, Berlin.

Manovich, Lev. 'How to Compare One Million Images?' In: *Understanding Digital Humanities*, edited by David M. Berry. 249-278. Basingstoke: Palgrave Macmillan, 2012.

Marburger, Marcel René. 'Revealing and Concealing. On *Ambiguous Cut into Space of Conjecture*'. In: *Translife – International Triennial of New Media Art, NAMOC – National Art Museum of China Bejing*. Liverpool: Liverpool University Press, 2011.

Marcus, Leah S. 'The Silence of the Archive and the Noise of Cyberspace'. In: *The Renaissance Computer: Knowledge and Technology in the First Age of Print*, edited by Neil Rhodes and Jonathan Sawday. 18-28. London and New York: Routledge, 2000.

McLean, Donald F. *Restoring Baird's Image*. London: The Institution of Electrical Engineers, 2000.

McLuhan, Marshall (with Edmund Carpenter). 'Acoustic Space'. In: *Explorations in Communication: An Anthology*, edited by Marshall McLuhan and Edmund Carpenter. 65-70. Boston: Bacon Press, 1960.

––. *The Gutenberg Galaxy: The Making of Typographic Man*. Toronto: University of Toronto Press, 1962.

––. *Understanding Media: The Extensions of Man*. Toronto: University of Toronto Press, 1964.

––. *Letters of Marshall McLuhan*, selected and edited by Matie Molinaro, Corinne McLuhan and William Toye. Oxford UK: Oxford University Press, 1987.

–– and Bruce R. Powers, *The Global Village: Transformations in World Life and Media in the 21st Century*. Oxford UK: Oxford University Press, 1989.

McMurray, Peter. 'There Are No Oral Media? Aural and Visual Perceptions of South Slavic Epic Poetry'. Presentation given on occasion of the Milman Parry half-centennial conference *Singers and Tales in the 21st Century: The Legacies of Milman Parry and Albert Lord*, Harvard University, 3-5 December 2010.

Mills, Mara. 'Deaf Jam. From Inscription to Reproduction to Information'. *Social Text* 102 28.1 (Spring 2010): 35-58.

––. 'The Audiovisual Telephone: A Brief History'. In: *Handheld? Music Video Aesthetics for Portable Devices*, edited by Henry Keazor, Hans W. Giessen and Thorsten Wübbena. 34-47. Heidelberg: ART-Dok, 2012.

Miyazaki, Shintaro. 'Algorithmics: Understanding Micro-Temporality in Computational Cultures'. *Computational Culture* 2 (2012). http://computationalculture.net.

Moebus, Oliver and Annette Wilke, *Sound and Communication: An Aesthetic Cultural History of Sanskrit Hinduism*. Berlin and New York: de Gruyter, 2011.

Moerchen F., Ultsch, A., Thies, M. and I. Loehken. 'Modelling Timbre Distance with Temporal Statistics from Polyphonic Music'. *IEEE Transactions on Speech and Audio Processing* 14, no. 1 (2006): 81-90.

Montfort, Nick et al. *10 PRINT CHR$(205.5+RND(1));: GOTO 10*. Cambridge, MA: The MIT Press, 2013.

Moring, Kirsikka. 'Conversation Secretly Recorded in Finland Helped German Actor Prepare for Hitler Role'. *Helsingin Sanomat*, 15 September 2004.

Müllensiefen, Daniel and Klaus Frieler. 'Cognitive Adequacy in the Measurement of Melodic Similarity: Algorithmic vs. Human Judgments'. *Computing in Musicology* 13 (2004): 147-176.

Müllensiefen, Daniel, Wiggins, Geraint and David Lewis. 'High-level Feature Descriptors and Corpus-based Musicology: Techniques for Modelling Music Cognition'. In: *Systematic and Comparative Musicology: Concepts, Methods, Findings*, edited by Albrecht Schneider. 133-153. Frankfurt: Peter Lang, 2008.

Müller, Meinard. *Information Retrieval for Music and Motion*. Berlin: Springer, 2007.

Müller, Meinard. *Information Retrieval for Music and Motion*. Berlin: Springer, 2007.

Nijenhuis, W. 'Hörbares Rechnen der PASCAL'. *Philips' Technische Rundschau* 24, no. 4/5 (1962/63): 169-174.

Ong, Walter J. *Orality and Literacy: The Technologizing of the Word*, London and New York: Methuen, 1982.

Oresme, Nicole. *The Medieval Geometry of Qualities and Motions*, edited by Marshall Clagett. Madison: University of Wisconsin Press, 1968.

Palisca, Claude V. 'Was Galileo's Father an Experimental Scientist?' In: *Number to Sound: The Musical Way to the Scientific Revolution,* edited by Paolo Gozza. 191-199. Dordrecht: Kluwer, 2000.

Parikka, Jussi. 'Mapping Noise: Techniques and Tactics of Irregularities, Interception, and Disturbance'. In: *Media Archaeology. Approaches, Applications, and Implications,* edited by Erkki Huhtamo and Jussi Parikka. 256-277. Berkeley, CA: University of California Press, 2011.

−−. *What is Media Archaeology?* Cambridge, UK: Polity Press, 2012.

−−. 'Of Queues and Traffic: Network Microtemporalities'. Lecture at the Glasgow Memory Group symposium *Digital/Social Media and Memory,* 17 April 2013.

Peirce, Charles S. *The New Elements of Mathematics,* edited by Carolyn Eisele. Berlin: Mouton, 1976.

Peters, John Durham. 'Helmholtz, Edison, and Sound History'. In: *Memory Bytes: History, Technology, and Digital Culture,* edited by Lauren Rabinovitz and Abraham Geil. 177-198. Durham: Duke University Press, 2004.

Pias, Claus. 'The Game Player's Duty: The User as the Gestalt of the Ports'. In: *Media Archaeology. Approaches, Applications, and Implications,* edited by Erkki Huhtamo and Jussi Parikka. 164-183. Berkeley, CA: University of California Press, 2011.

Piggott, W.R. 'Ionospheric Research in the Past, Present and Future'. In: *Institut für Ionosphärenphysik im Max-Planck-Institut für Aeronomie 1946-1971.* 29-33. Göttingen: Hubert, 1972.

Pitman, Isaac. *Phonography; or, Writing by Sound; Being a Natural Method of Writing, Applicable to all Languages, and a Complete System of Shorthand.* London: Bagster & Sons, 1840.

Potter, Ralph K., Kopp, George A. and Harriet C. Green. *Visible Speech.* New York: Van Nostrand, 1947.

Powell, Barry. *Homer and the Origin of the Greek Alphabet.* Cambridge, UK: Cambridge University Press, 1991.

−−. *Writing and the Origins of Greek Literature.* Cambridge, UK: Cambridge University Press, 2002.

Price, Peter. *Resonance: Philosophy for Sonic Art.* New York and Dresden: Atropos Press, 2011.

Reynolds, Simon. *Retromania: Pop Culture's Addiction to its own Past.* London: Faber & Faber, 2012.

Riis, Morton. *Machine Music. A Media Archaeological Excavation.* PhD dissertation, Aarhus University, 2012.

Roads, Curtis. *Microsound.* Cambridge, MA: The MIT Press, 2004.

Røssaak, Eivind. *The Archive in Motion.* Oslo: Novus, 2010.

Rushkof, Douglas. *Present Shock: When Everything Happens Now.* New York: Current, 2013.

Saenger, Paul. *Space between Words: The Origins of Silent Reading.* Stanford, CA: Stanford University Press, 1997.

Scarre, Chris and Graeme Lawson, eds. *Archaeoacustics.* Cambridge, UK: McDonald Institute for Archaeological Research, 2006.

Schafer, Murray R. *The Soundscape: Our Sonic Environment and the Tuning of the World.* Rochester, VT: Destiny Books, 1994.

Schwartz, Hillel. *Making Noise: From Babel to the Big Bang and Beyond.* New York: Zone Books, 2011.

Schwartz, Tony. *The Responsive Chord.* New York: Zone, 1974.

Sconce, Jeffrey. 'The Voice from the Void: Wireless, Modernity and the Distant Dead'. *International Journal of Cultural Studies* 1, no. 2 (1998): 211-232.

Shadwick, Keith. *Bill Evans: Everything Jappens to Me. A Musical Biography.* San Francisco, CA: Backbeat Books, 2002.

Shannon, Claude. *Collected Papers.* Piscataway: IEEE Press, 1993.

Sheldrake, Rupert. *The Presence of the Past.* New York: Time Book, 1988.

Shepherd, John and Peter Wicke. *Music and Cultural Theory.* Cambridge, UK: Polity Press, 1977.

Sobchak, Vivian. 'Afterword: Media Archaeology and Re-presencing the Past'. In: *Media Archaeology: Approaches, Applications, and Implications,* edited by Erkkia Huhtamo and Jussi Parikka. 323-33. Berkeley, CA: University of California Press, 2011.

Sokolowski, Kurt. 'Instead of a Prologue: An Epilogue about Julian Jaynes'. *BABEL* 4 (May 2004).

Sorensen, Andrew and Henry Gardner. 'Programming With Time: Cyber-physical Programming with Impromptu'. In: *OOPSLA'10: Proceedings of the ACM international conference on Object oriented Programming sytems,* Reno NV, USA, 2010. 822-834. New York: ACM, 2010.

Smirnov, Andrey. *Sound in Z: Experiments in Sound and Electronic Music in Early 20th Century Russia.* London: Koenig Books, 2013.

Smith, Mark M., ed. *Hearing History: A Reader.* Athens: University of Georgia Press, 2004.

Snyder, Bob. *Music and Memory.* Cambridge, MA: The MIT Press, 2000.

Sterne, Jonathan. *The Audible Past: Cultural Origins of Sound Reproduction.* Durham: Duke University Press, 2003.

––. *MP3: The Meaning of a Format.* Durham: Duke University Press 2012.

Subotnik, Rose Rosengard. *Deconstructive Variations: Music and Reason in Western Society.* Minneapolis: University of Minnesota Press, 1996.

Svec, Henry Adam. 'Folk Media: Alan Lomax's Deep Digitality'. *Canadian Journal of Communication* 38 (2013): 227-244.

Svenbro, Jesper. *Phrasikleia: An Anthropology of Reading in Ancient Greece.* Ithaca: Cornell University Press, 1993.

Thomas, Dave. 'Acoustic Intentionality, Infrasound or No Sound: A Preliminary Acoustic Analysis of Maeshowe (Neolithic) Burial Chambers'. Presentation delivered at *Archaeoacustics. The Archaeology of Sound* conference, Malta, 19-22 February 2014.

Thompson, Emily. Machines, Music, and the Quest for Fidelity: Marketing the Edison Phonograph in America 1877-1925'. *Musical Quarterly* 79 (1995): 132.

The Soundscape of Modernity: Architectural Acoustics and the Culture of Listening in America, 1900-1933. Cambridge MA: The MIT Press, 2002.

––. *The Soundscape of Modernity: Architectural Acoustics and the Culture of Listening in America, 1900-1933.* Cambridge MA: The MIT Press, 2002. 'Machines, Music, and the Quest for Fidelity: Marketing the Edison Phonograph in America 1877-1925'. *Musical Quarterly* 79 (1995): 132.

Trenholme, Russel. 'Analog Simulation'. *Philosophy of Science* 61 (1994): 115-131.

Trippett, David. 'Composing Time: Zeno's Arrow, Hindemith's Erinnerung and Satie's Instantané-ism'. *Journal of Musicology* 24 (2007): 522-580.

––. *Soundscape and Technological Breakthrough. A Dialogue for Late Modernity.* Research project (draft), 2013.

Truax, Barry. *Acoustic Communication.* Norwood, N.J.: Ablex, 1984.

Turing, Alan. 'Lecture to the London Mathematical Society on 20th February 1947'. In: *A.M. Turing's ACE Report of 1946 and other Papers,* edited by B. E. Carpenter and R. W. Doran. Cambridge, MA: The MIT Press, 1986.

Turner, Fred and Ernst Pöppel. 'The Neural Lyre: Poetic Meter, The Brain, and Time'. *Poetry* 142, no. 5 (August 1983): 277-309.

Ulmer, Gregory. *Applied Grammatology.* Baltimore: John Hopkins University Press, 1985.

Uricchio, William. 'Television's First Seventy-Five Years: The Interpretive Flexibility of a Medium in Transition'. In: *The Oxford Handbook of Film and Media Studies,* edited by Robert Kolker. Oxford: Oxford University Press, 2008.

Van Eck, Wim. 'Electromagnetic Radiation from Video Display Units: An Eavesdropping Risk?', *Computers and Security* 4 (1985): 269-286.

Varela, Francisco. 'The Specious Present: A Neurophenomenology of Time Consciousness'. In: *Naturalizing Phenomenology: Issues in Contemporary Phenomenology and Cognitive Science*, edited by Jean Petitot, Francisco J. Varela, Bernard Pachoud and Jean-Michel Roy. 266-329. Stanford, CA: Stanford University Press, 1999.

Viola, Bill. 'The Sound of One Line Scanning'. In: *Sound By Artists*, edited by Dan Lander and Micah Lexier. 39-54. Toronto and Banff: Art Metropole & Walter Phillips Gallery, 1990.

Wicke, Peter. 'The Art of Phonography: Sound, Technology and Music'. In: *The Ashgate Research Companion to Popular Musicology*, edited by Derek B. Scott. 147-170. Surrey: Ashgate, 2009.

Winthrop-Young, Geoffrey. 'Siren Recursions'. In: *Kittler Now: Current Perspectives in Kittler Studies*, edited by Stephen Sale and Laura Salisbury. Cambridge, UK: Polity Press, 2015.

Wyschnegradsky, Ivan. *La Loi de la Pansonorité* [1953]. Geneva: Ed. Contrechamps, 1996.

Zakharine, Dmitri and Nils Meise, eds. *Electrified Voices: Medial, Socio-Historical and Cultural Aspects of Voice Transfer*. Konstanz: Unipress, 2012.

Zakharine, Dimitri. 'Voice – E-Voice-Design – E-Voice-Community. Early Public Debates about the Emotional Quality of Radio and TV Announcers' Voices in Germany, the Soviet Union and the USA (1920-1940)'. In: *Electrified Voices. Medial, Socio-Historical and Cultural Aspects of Voice Transfer,* edited by Dimitri Zakharine and Nils Meise. 201-231. Konstanz: Unipress, 2012.

Zuckerkandl, Victor. *Sound and Symbol: Music and the External World*. New York: Pantheon, 1956.

Works cited (Non-English)

Adorno, Theodor W. 'Die Form der Schallplatte' [1934]. In: *Gesammelte Werke, vol. 19: Musikalische Schriften VI*. 520-523. Frankfurt/M.: Suhrkamp, 1984.

––. *Zu einer Theorie der musikalischen Reproduktion*. Frankfurt/M.: Suhrkamp, 2001.

Alloa, Emmanuel. 'Metaxu: Figures de la médialité chez Aristotle'. Revue de *Métaphysique et de Morale* 62, no. 2 (2009): 247-262.

Angerer, Marie-Luise. *Vom Begehren nach dem Affekt*. Zürich and Berlin: diaphanes, 2007.

Antheil, George. 'Abstraktion und Zeit in der Musik'. *De Stijl* 6, no. 10/11 (1925): 152-156.

Arndt, Olaf. 'Wer nicht hören will muss fühlen' [Voices of the Mind III]. *Babel* 4 (May 2004): 32-41.

Avraamov, Areny. 'Sinteticheskaya Muzika'. *Sovetskoya Muzika* 3 (1929): 67-75.

Barberi, Alessandro. 'Weil das Sein eine Geschichte hat. Ein Gespräch mit Friedrich Kittler'. *Österreichische Zeitschrift für Geschichtswissenschaft* 11, no. 4 (2000): 109-123.

Barthelmes, Barbara. *Raum und Klang. Das musikalische und theoretische Schaffen Ivan Wyschnegradskys*. Hofheim: Wolke, 1995.

Bayreuther, Rainer. 'Heidegger und die Musik' Forthcoming in *Heidegger-Handbuch*, edited by Dieter Thomä. 509-512. Stuttgart: Metzler, 2013.

Berendt, Joachim-Ernst and Nada Brahma. *Die Welt ist Klang*. Reinbek: Rowohlt, 1985.

Bergson, Henri. *Èvolution créatrice* [1907]. Paris: PUF, 1948.

Bolz, Annette. 'Soundpatrouille. Musikklau im Internet zu verhindern ist relativ einfach: Mit Audio-Identifizierungsprogrammen'. *Die Zeit* 18 (26 April 2001).

Bolz, Norbert. 'Die Wiederkehr des Mythos in der Medienwirklichkeit'. In: *First Europeans, frühe kulturen – moderne visionen*. Exhbition catalogue Schloß Charlottenburg, Berlin (October 1993 – February 1994). 88-91. Berlin: Exter & Exter, 1993.

Brandl, Alois. 'Lebendige Sprache: Beobachtungen an Lautplatten englischer Dialektsätze, mit einem Anhang von Wilhelm Doegen, Zur Lautanalyse aus dem Klangbild des englisches Dialektwortes 'man', aus der Lautplatte gewonnen nach dem elektro-oszillographischen Verfahren'. In: *Sitzungsberichte der Königlich Preußischen Akademie der Wissenschaften, Phil.-hist. Klasse* (1928).

Canac, François. *L'acoustique des théâtres antiques*. Paris: Centre national de la recherche scientifique, 1967.

Carlé, Martin. 'Enharmonische Archäologie der griechischen Musiknotation'. In *Die Geburt des Vokalalphabets aus dem Geist der Poesie: Schrift, Zahl und Ton im Medienverbund*, edited by Wolfgang Ernst and Friedrich Kittler. 281-297. Munich: Fink, 2006.

––. 'Geschenke der Musen im Streit ihrer Gehörigkeit. Die antike Musiknotation als Medium und Scheideweg der abendländischen Wissenschaft'. *MusikTheorie. Zeitschrift für Musikwissenschaft* 22, no. 4 (2007): 295-316.

––. 'Enharmonische Archäologie der griechischen Musiknotation'. In: *Die Geburt des Vokalalphabets aus dem Geist der Poesie: Schrift, Zahl und Ton im Medienverbund*, edited by Wolfgang Ernst and Friedrich Kittler. 281-297. Munich: Fink, 2006.

'Das Sonische. Sounds zwischen Akustik und Ästhetik'. *PopScriptum* X (2008), edited by Forschungszentrum Populäre Musik of Humboldt University of Berlin. http://www2.hu-berlin.de/fpm/popscrip/themen/pst10/index.htm.

Deleuze, Gilles. *Schizophrenie und Gesellschaft*, edited by David Lapoujade. Frankfurt/M.: Suhrkamp, 2003.

Diederichsen, Diedrich. 'T.I.M.E. The Inner Mind's Eye'. In: *Die Zeit im Wandel der Zeit,* edited by Bieber et al. 432-446. Kassel: Kassel University Press, 2002.

Dierksen, Sebastian. 'Elektromagnetische Emissionen von Computer-Bildschirmen als Sonifikation'. Paper in Media Studies at Humboldt University, Berlin (September 2013).

Dilthey, Wilhelm. 'Die Abgrenzung der Geisteswissenschaften. Zweite Fassung'. In: *Gesammelte Schriften VII*. Berlin: B.G. Teuber, 1927.

Doegen, Wilhelm. *Fünfzehn Jahre Königliche und Staatsbibliothek 1921*. Berlin: Preußische Staatsbibliothek, 1921.

Ellensohn, Reinhard. *Der andere Anders. Günther Anders als Musikphilosoph*. Frankfurt/M.: Peter Lang, 2008.

Enders, Bernd. *Lexikon Musikelektronik*, 3rd ed. Mainz: Schott, 1997.

Ernst, Wolfgang. 'Medienwissen(schaft), zeitkritisch. Ein Programm aus der Sophienstraße', Inaugural Lecture 21 October 2003. Published in the series *Öffentliche Vorlesungen*, edited by the President of Humboldt-University Berlin Jürgen Mlynek. Berlin (2004). http://edoc.hu-berlin.de.

––. 'Der Appell der Medien. Wissensgeschichte und ihr Anderes'. In: *Rekursionen. Faltungen des Wissens*, edited by Ana Ofak and Philipp von Hilgers. 177-197. Munich: Fink, 2010.

––. *Chronopoetik. Zeitweisen und Zeitgaben technischer Medien*. Berlin: Kulturverlag Kadmos, 2012.

––. *Im Medium erklingt die Zeit*. Berlin: Kulturverlag Kadmos, 2015.

Ernst, Wolfgang and Stefan Heidenreich. 'Digitale Bildarchivierung: der Wölfflin-Kalkül'. In: *Konfigurationen. Zwischen Kunst und Medien*, edited by Sigrid Schade and Christoph Tholen. 306-320. Munich: Fink, 1999.

Ernst, Wolfgang and Friedrich Kittler, eds. *Die Geburt des Vokalalphabets aus dem Geist der Poesie. Schrift, Zahl und Ton im Medienverbund*. Munich: Fink, 2006.

Flusser, Vilém. *Ins Universum der technischen Bilder*. Göttingen: European Photography, 1985.

––. *Gesten – Versuch einer Phänomenologie*. Düsseldorf: Bollmann, 1991.

Foucault, Michel. 'Message ou bruit?' [*1966]. In: *Dits et Écrits vol. 1*. 557-560. Paris: Gallimard, 1994.

Fourier, Jean-Babtiste Joseph. *Théorie Analytique de la Chaleur*. Paris: Firmin Didot, 1822.

Frommolt, Karl-Heinz and Martin Carlé. 'Der Gesang der Sirenen. Homers Dichtung und akustische Realität'. In: *Fortschritte der Akustik. Plenarvorträge und Fachbeiträge der 31.*

Deutschen Jahrestagung für Akustik DAGA 2005 München, edited by Hugo Fastl and Markus Fruhmann. 797. Berlin: DEGA, 2005.

Fülöp-Miller, René. *Geist und Gesicht des Bolschewismus*. Vienna: Amalthea, 1926.

Gottschewski, Hermann. *Die Interpretation als Kunstwerk. Musikalische Zeitgestaltung und ihre Analyse am Beispiel von Welte-Mignon-Klavieraufnahmen aus dem Jahre 1905*. Laaber: Laaber, 1996.

Grieger, Wingolf. *Führer durch die Schausammlung Phonetisches Institut*. Hamburg: Chrstians, 1989.

Großklaus, Götz. *Medien-Zeit, Medien-Raum. Zum Wandel der raumzeitlichen Wahrnhemung in der Moderne*. Frankfurt/M.: Suhrkamp, 1995.

Hagen, Wolfgang. 'Technische Medien und Experimente der Physik. Skizzen zu einer medialen Genealogie der Elektrizität'. In: *Kommunikation, Medien, Macht*, edited by Rudolf Maresch and Niels Werber. 133-173. Frankfurt/M.: Suhrkamp, 1998.

––. *Das Radio*. Munich: Fink, 2005.

Hammerstein, Reinhold. 'Musik als Komposition und Interpretation'. *Deutsche Vierteljahresschrift für Literaturwissenschaft und Geistesgeschichte* 40, no. 1 (1966): 1-23.

Hartmann, Frank. 'Instant awareness. Eine medientheoretische Exploration mit McLuhan'. In: *Soundcultures. Über elektronische und digitale Musik*, edited by Marcus S. Kleiner and Achim Szepanski. 34-51. Frankfurt/M.: Suhrkamp, 2003.

Hausmann, Raoul. *Dada-Wissenschaft. Wissenschaftliche und technische Schriften*, edited by Arndt Niebisch. Hamburg: Philo Fine Arts, 2013.

Hegel, Georg Wilhelm Friedrich. 'Vorlesungen über die Ästhetik III'. In: *Werke vol. 15*, edited by Eva Moldenhauer and Karl Markus Michel. Frankfurt am Main: Suhrkamp, 1970.

––. *Wissenschaft der Logik. Erster Teil. Die objektivbe Logik. Erster Band. Die Lehre vom Sein* [1832], edited by Hans-Jürgen Gawoll. Berlin: Akademie, 1990.

Heidegger, Martin. *Sein und Zeit* [1927], 16th edition. Tübingen: Niemeyer, 1986.

––. *Prolegomena zur Geschichte des Zeitbegriffs*. Frankfurt/M.: Klostermann, 1994.

––. *Beiträge zur Philosophie (Vom Ereignis)*, 3rd edition. Frankfurt/M.: Klostermann, 2003.

––. *Gesamtausgabe*, vol. 70 (Über den Anfang). Frankfurt on the Main: Vittorio Klostermann, 2005.

Hellbrück, Jürgen and Wolfgang Ellermeier. *Hören. Physiologie, Psychologie und Pathologie*. Göttingen: Hogrefe 2. erw. u. aktualisierte Aufl, 2004.

Helmholtz, Hermann von. *Die Lehre von den Tonempfindungen als physiologische Grundlage für die Theorie der Musik* [1863], 6th edition. Braunschweig: Vieweg, 1913.

Höltgen, Stefan. 'All Watched Over by Machines of Loving Grace'. In: *Big Data: Analysen zum digitalen Wandel von Wissen, Macht und Ökonomie,* edited by Ramon Reichert. 385-404. Beilefeld: Transcript, 2014.

Jenny, Hans. *Kymatik. Wellen und Schwingungen mit ihrer Struktur und Dynamik*. Basel: Basilius, 1972.

Kassung, Christian. *Das Pendel. Eine Wissensgeschichte*. Munich: Fink, 2008.

Kittler, Friedrich A. *Diskursanalysen 1: Medien,* edited by Manfred Schneider and Samuel Weber. Opladen: Westdeutscher Verlag, 1987.

––. *Draculas Vermächtnis. Technische Schriften*. Leipzig: Reclam, 1991.

––. 'Musik als Medium'. In: *Wahrnehmung und Geschichte. Markierungen zur aisthesis materialis,* edited by Bernhard J. Dotzler and Ernst Müller. 83-99. Berlin: Akademie, 1995.

––. 'Weil das Sein eine Geschichte hat' [in conversation with Alessandro Barberi]. *Österreichische Zeitschrift für Geschichtswissenschaft* 11, no. 4 (2000): 109-123.

––. 'Das Alphabet der Griechen. Zur Archäologie der Schrift'. In: *Die Aktualität des Archäologischen in Wissenschaft, Medien und Künsten*, edited by Knut Ebeling and Stefan Altekamp. 252-260. Frankfurt/M.: Fischer, 2004.

––. *Musik und Mathematik vol. I: Hellas, book 1 (Aphrodite) and 2 (Eros)*. Munich: Fink, 2006 and 2009.

––. *Und der Sinus wird weiterschwingen. Über Musik und Mathematik*. Köln: Verlag der Kunsthochschule für Medien Köln, 2012.

––. *Musik und Mathematik vol. II: Roma Aeterna, book 1 (Sexus) and 2 (Virginitas)*. Munich: Fink, 2015.

Kolb, Richard. *Das Horoskop des Hörspiels*. Berlin: Max Hesse, 1932.

Lacan, Jacques. *Die vier Grundbegriffe der Psychoanalyse*. Olten: Walter, 1978.

Lamprecht, Karl. *Paralipomena der deutschen Geschichte*. Vienna: H. Heller, 1910.

Lange, Britta. 'Ein Archiv von Stimmen. Kriegsgefangene unter ethnografischer Beobachtung'. In: *Original/Ton. Zur Mediengeschichte des O-Tons*, edited by Nikolaus Wegmann, Harun Maye and Cornelius Reiber. 317-341. Konstanz: Universitätsverlag, 2006.

Lazzarato, Maurizio. *Videophilosophie. Zeitwahrnehmung im Postfordismus*. Berlin: b-books, 2002.

Leibniz, G. W. *Hauptschriften zur Grundlegung der Philosophie,* vol. II: 'Schriften zur Metaphysik III: Die Vernunftprinzipien der Natur und der Gnade', edited by E. Cassirer. Leipzig: Dürr, 1904.

Macho, Thomas. 'Die Kunst der Verwandlung. Notizen zur frühen Musikphilosophie von Günther Anders'. In: *Günther Anders kontrovers*, edited by Konrad Paul Liessmann. 89-102. Munich: Beck, 1992.

Michelet, Jules. *Oeuvres Complètes IV*, edited by Paul Viallaneix. Paris: Flammarion, 1974.

Moles, Abraham A. *Théorie de l'information et perception esthétique*. Paris: Flamariaon, 1958.

Nägele, Rainer. 'Der Einbruch der Geschichtlichkeit in die Struktur der Musik'. *Musica* 49, no. 3 (1995).

Neckenbürger, Ernst. *Elektrische Schallübertragung. Grundlagen elektroakustischer Energie-Wandlung und –Verstärkung*. Braunschweig: Westermann, 1953.

Nietzsche, Friedrich. *Jenseits von Gut und Böse*. Leipzig: Naumann, 1886.

Ohm, G.S. 'Ueber die Definition des Tones, nebst daran geknüpfter Theorie der Sirene und ähnlicher tonbildender Vorrichtungen'. *Annalen der Physik und Chemie* 59 (1843): 513-565.

Ott, Michaela. *Affizierung. Zu einer ästhetisch-epistemischen Figur*. Munich: edition text + kritik, 2010.

Papenburg, Jens Gerrit. 'Stop/Start Making Sense! Ein Ausblick auf Musikanalyse in Popular Music Studies und technischer Medienwissenschaft'. In: *Sound Studies. Traditionen – Methoden – Desiderate*, edited by Holger Schulze. 91-108. Bielefeld: Transcript, 2008.

Pfeiffer, K. Ludwig. 'Operngesang und Medientheorie'. In: *Stimme. Annäherung an ein Phänomen*, edited by Doris Kolesch and Sybille Krämer. 65-87. Frankfurt/M.: Suhrkamp, 2006.

Rademacher, Horst. 'Meeresvulkane schneller zu finden'. *Frankfurter Allgemeine Zeitung* 66, no. 19 (März 1997).

Rehding, Alexander. 'Wie können Untertöne in der Geschichte der Musiktheorie hörbar gemacht werden?' In: *Musiktheorie zwischen Historie und Systematik*, edited by Ludwig Holtmeier, Michael Polth and Felix Diergarten. 373-384. Augsburg: Wißner, 2004.

Rheinberger, Hans-Jörg. *Experiment, Differenz, Schrift. Zur Geschichte epistemischer Dinge*. Marburg: Basilisken, 1991.

Richter, Klaus P. 'Schreck der Pause'. *Frankfurter Allgemeine Zeitung*, 28 October 1995.

Riemann, Hugo. 'Ideen zu einer Lehre von den Tonvorstellungen". *Jahrbuch der Musikbibliothek Peters* 21/22 (1914/15): 1-26.

Roch, Axel. *Claude E. Shannon: Spielzeug, Leben und die geheime Geschichte seiner Theorie.* Berlin: Gegenstalt Verlag, 2009.

Schnebel, Dieter, ed. *Karlheinz Stockhausen. Texte zur elektronischen und instrumentalen Musik,* vol. 1. Cologne: DuMont, 1963.

Schnelle, H. 'Automatische Sprachlauterkennung'. *Kybernetische Maschinen. Prinzip und Anwendugn der automatischen Nachrichtenverarbeitung.* Frankfurt/M: S. Fischer, 1964.

Seitz, Gabriele. *Film als Rezeptionsform von Literatur,* 2nd edition. Munich: tuduv, 1981.

Siegert, Bernhard. 'Das Leben zählt nicht. Natur- und Geisteswissenschaften bei Dilthey aus mediengeschichtlicher Sicht'. In: *Medien. Dreizehn Vorträge zur Medienkultur,* edited by Claus Pias. 161-182. Weimar: WDG, 1999.

——. Passage des Digitalen. Zeichenpraktiken der neuzeitlichen Wissenschaften 1500-1900. Berlin: Brinkmann & Bose, 2003.

Snell, Bruno. *Die Ausdrücke für den Begriff des Wissens in der vorplatonischen Philosophie* (*sophia, gnome, synesis, historia, mathema, episteme*), 2nd edition [1924]. Berlin and Zürich: Weidmann, 1992.

Sprenger, Florian. *Medien des Immediaten. Elektrizität. Telegraphie. McLuhan.* Berlin: Kulturverlag Kadmos, 2012.

Stanke Gerd and Thomas Kessler. 'Verfahren zur Gewinnung von Tonsignalen aus Negativ-Spuren in Kupfernegativen von Edison-Zylindern auf bildanalytischem/sensoriellem Wege'. In: *Das Berliner Phonogramm-Archiv 1900-2000. Sammlungen der Traditionellen Musik der Welt,* edited by Artur Simon. 209-215. Berlin: VWB, 2000.

Stern, Günther. 'Zur Phänomenologie des Zuhörens'. *Zeitschrift für Musikwissenschaft* X (1927/28). Hamburg. 680.

——. 'Philosophische Untersuchungen über musikalische Situationen', typescript, 1930/31. Literary Archive (Literaturarchiv) at the Austrian National Library (Österreichische Nationalbibliothek), fund 237/04, Vienna, Literary estate (Nachlass) Günther Anders.

Stockhausen, Karlheinz. *Die Reihe. Information über serielle Musik* 3. Vienna, Zürich and London: Universal Edition, 1957.

Struck-Schloen, Michael. 'Le voci sottovetro'. In: *Musiktheorie zwischen Historie und Systematik,* edited by Ludwig Holtmeier, Michael Polth and Felix Diergarten. 338-342. Augsburg: Wißner, 2004.

Taschner, Rudolf. *Der Zahlen gigantische Schatten. Mathematik im Zeichen der Zeit.* Wiesbaden: Vieweg, 2005.

Volmar, Axel. 'Gespitzte Ohren. Akroamatische Dispositive und musisches Wissen als Grundlage für eine Geschichte epistemogener Klänge'. *MusikTheorie. Zeitschrift für Musikwissenschaft* 22, no. 4 (2007): 365-376.

——. 'Stethoskop und Telefon – akustemische Technologien'. In: *Das geschulte Ohr. Eine Kulturgeschichte der Sonifikation,* edited by Andi Schoon and Axel Volmar. 71-83. Bielefeld: Transcript, 2012.

Weinzierl, Stefan. *Beethovens Konzerträume. Raumakustik und symphonische Aufführungspraxis an der Schwelle zum modernen Konzertwesen.* Frankfurt/M.: Erwin Bochinsky Verlag, 2002.

Wertheimer, Max. 'Musik der Wedda'. *Sammelbände der Internationalen Musikgesellschaft* XI, no. 2 (Jan-Mar 1910): 300-309.

Zuse, Konrad. *Rechnender Raum.* Braunschweig: Vieweg, 1969.

Index

new media 36, 44, 108, 126
  technical media 12-14, 24, 31, 62-63, 72, 75,
      86, 100, 108, 113-114, 117, 125-126, 137, 143n6
  streaming media 62
mellotron 26
memory 10-12, 15, 27, 35, 37, 40-41, 43, 49-52, 56,
    61-62, 64-67, 71-75, 77-80, 85-87, 90, 96, 107,
    110, 113-115, 119, 122, 124-126, 129-131, 134-135,
    139, 141, 148n63, 154n71, 160n19, 160n20
  sonic memory 27, 35, 49, 85, 96, 98, 108, 116,
      119, 127, 129, 136, 137,
Mendel, Arthur 81
message 23, 25-28, 32-33, 36, 38, 49, 51, 68, 72, 85,
    87, 89, 100, 113-114, 119, 123, 126, 132, 136, 146n14
metaphysics 55, 88
metadata 118, 129-130, 135-137, 141-142
Metropolis 114
Michelet, Jules 62
mnemotechnics 65, 71, 74
modern time 43-44, 90
modernity 10, 15-16, 24-25, 88
modulation 16, 21, 68, 105-106, 110
molecule 23, 109
monochord 10, 14, 26, 89-92, 104
mousiké 43, 117, 120, 134
MPEG-7 131, 136
MP3 137, 162n23, 163n32
mufin 134
Museum of Endangered Sounds 113
music 9-10, 14, 22, 24, 26, 35, 37-39, 43, 51, 54, 59,
    64, 80-81, 85-88, 90-92, 94-102, 107-110, 112, 115,
    119-121, 123, 129-130, 134-138, 140-141, 146n26,
    148n51, 150n15, 157n51, 158n73, 164n55, 164n57
  electronic music 32, 39, 92, 93, 129, 141,
      145n1, 145n6,
  music ethnology 139
  musicIP mixer 134
  musical notation 24, 52, 58, 71, 77, 87, 99, 101,
      109- 110, 115, 133, 147n35
  popular music 35, 80, 136,
mystic writing pad 64

Narcissus (Greek God) 58-59
narrative 10-11, 13, 15, 21, 59-60, 64-66, 87, 94, 118,
    120, 129, 140
negentropy 110, 118
network 34, 44, 143n6
Newton, Isaac 105
noise 9, 24, 39, 41, 49-51, 54-55, 58, 62, 66, 77,
    86-87, 89, 99, 100, 107-110, 112-115, 119-123,
    125-126, 129, 138-139, 146n29, 151n4, 156n5,
    160n29, 163n38,
Nono, Luigi 96
Nintendo 92

Occidental tradition 12, 22, 62
Odyssey, The 10, 12, 49, 52, 65, 68
Ong, Walter J. 33
Ontology 33, 55

operative media 10, 25, 28, 35-36, 43, 90, 94,
    96, 108
operative diagrams 13, 23, 125
optics 7, 24, 28, 31, 52, 54, 58, 67, 100-101, 108, 110,
    112, 121, 124, 127, 130
optophon 29
oral culture 12, 55, 78, 100
oral poetry 12, 52, 65-66, 71-82, 98, 115, 126
Oresme, Nicole 23
oscilloscope 10-11, 22 81, 114, 125, 139

Parikka, Jussi 11, 53, 143n6, 146n10,
Parry, Milman 12, 71-75, 77-79, 98, 111, 155n6
perception 10-15, 21, 24, 26, 28-29, 31, 35, 44, 59,
    62, 65, 79, 85-86, 89, 101, 103-104, 118, 130, 134,
    141, 148n51, 151n8, 160n18, 162n22
performance 14, 22, 39, 72-74, 76, 78-79, 88,
    92-93, 95-96, 98, 100, 111, 133, 135
Phaedrus 71-72
Phenomenology 44, 92, 95, 140
Philology 24, 62, 77, 91
phonograph 12, 21-22, 28, 35, 49, 52-53, 57, 59,
    63-64, 66, 71-79, 81-82, 85-89, 92, 94-95, 98-
    100, 103, 107, 109-111, 113-114, 116-122, 125-127,
    131-133, 136, 138-139, 141, 154n71, 155n6, 157n44
phonautograph 12, 82, 95, 110-111, 121
Phonovision 12, 27-29
photography 61, 107, 120, 140
Physical Modelling 30, 75, 122
Physics 7, 26, 38, 76, 92, 97, 121
piano 38, 43, 75, 86, 97, 145n3, 164n55
Peirce, Charles Sanders 91
pixel 13, 29, 31
Plato 38, 65, 71-72, 74, 97, 101, 134
poetry 9, 12, 52, 63, 65-66, 71-79, 81, 98-99, 115,
    117, 126, 157n45
popular music 35, 80-81, 136
presence 21-22, 24-26, 33-34, 39, 44, 53, 57, 61-62,
    68, 72, 79, 85-89, 94-96, 98, 103-104, 107,
    126-127, 151n6, 152n18
Presence of the Past, The 27
Presley, Elvis 59
printing 24, 62, 102, 104, 122
processing 13, 15, 24, 31, 34-35, 43-44, 49, 53-54,
    66, 69, 74, 78-79, 95, 98, 108-111, 119, 129, 133,
    137-138, 141, 144n18, 148n63, 158n77
Prometeo 96
prosopopeia 58, 60, 62
pulse code modulation 68, 105-106
punctum 59, 124, 161n31
Pythagoras 27, 89, 91-92, 156n25

quadrivium 99
Questioning the Sphinx 61

radar 13, 30-31, 68, 154n79
radio 13, 21, 25, 27-29, 32-33, 37-38, 44, 52, 56,
    68-69, 76, 94-95, 104-106, 111, 123, 141, 141,
    154n79, 159n5